Sociology of "Developing Societies"
The Middle East

Sociology of "Developing Societies"

General Editor: Teodor Shanin

THEMATIC VOLUMES

INTRODUCTION TO THE SOCIOLOGY OF "DEVELOPING
SOCIETIES"
Hamza Alavi and Teodor Shanin

SOCIALIST "DEVELOPING SOCIETIES"?
(in preparation)

THEORIES OF SOCIAL TRANSFORMATION
(in preparation)

REGIONAL VOLUMES

SUB-SAHARAN AFRICA
Chris Allen and Gavin Williams

SOUTH ASIA
Hamza Alavi and Kathleen Gough (forthcoming)

THE MIDDLE EAST
Talal Asad and Roger Owen

SOUTH-EAST ASIA
John Taylor and Andrew Turton (forthcoming)

CENTRAL AMERICA AND THE CARIBBEAN
(in preparation)

LATIN AMERICA
(in preparation)

Sociology of "Developing Societies"
The Middle East

edited by Talal Asad and Roger Owen

Monthly Review Press
New York

Library of Congress Cataloging in Publication Data

Main entry under title:

The Middle East.

(Sociology of "developing societies")
Bibliography: p.
Includes index.
I. Near East — Social conditions — Addresses, essays,
lectures. 2. Near East — Politics and government —
1945—   — Addresses, essays, lectures. I. Asad,
Talal. II. Owen, Edward Roger John. III. Series.
HN656.A8M52 1983   306'.0956   83–42527
ISBN 0–85345–636–4
ISBN 0–85345–637–2 (pbk.)

Monthly Review Press
155 West 23rd Street
New York, N.Y. 10011

Printed in Hong Kong

10 9 8 7 6 5 4 3 2 1

Contents

III. Structures and Processes

Series Preface

The question of the so-called "developing societies" lies at the very heart of the political, the economic and the moral crises of the contemporary global society. It is central to the relations of power, diplomacy and war of the world we live in. It is decisive when the material well-being of humanity is concerned; that is, the ways some people make a living and the ways some people hunger. It presents a fundamental dimension of social inequality and of struggles for social justice. During the last generation it has also become a main challenge to scholarship, a field where the perplexity is deeper, the argument sharper and the potential for new illuminations more profound. That challenge reflects the outstanding social relevance of this problem. It reflects, too, an essential ethnocentrism that weighs heavily on the contemporary social sciences. The very terminology which designates "developing" or "underdeveloping" or "emerging" societies is impregnated with teleology which identifies parts of Europe and the USA as "developed". Images of the world at large as a unilinear rise from barbarity to modernity (or vice versa as a descent to hell) have often substituted for the analysis of actuality, as simplistic metaphors often do. To come to grips with a social reality, which is systematically different from that of one's own, and to explain its specific logic and momentum, is a most difficult conceptual and pedagogic task. It is the more so, for the fundamental questions of the "developing societies" are not of difference only but of relationships past and present with the countries of advanced capitalism and industrialization. It is in that light that we encounter as analysts and teachers not only a challenge to "sociology of development", but also a major challenge to radical scholarship itself.

The Sociology of "Developing Societies" series aims to offer a systematically linked set of texts for use as a major teaching aid at university level. It is being produced by a group of teachers and scholars related by common interest, general outlook and commitment sufficient to provide an overall coherence but by no means a single monolithic view. The object is, on the one hand, to bring relevant questions into focus and, on the other hand, to teach through debate. We think that at the current stage "a textbook" would necessarily gloss over the very diversity, contradictions and inadequacies of our thought. On the other hand, collections of articles are often rather accidental in content. The

vii

format of a conceptually structured set of readers was chosen, sufficiently open to accommodate variability of views within a coherent system of presentation. They bring together works by sociologists, social anthropologists, historians, political scientists, economists, literary critics and novelists in an intended disregard of the formal disciplinary divisions of the academic enterprise.

Three major alternatives of presentation stand out: first, a comparative discussion of the social structures within the "developing societies", focusing on the generic within them; second, the exploration of the distinct character of the main regions of the "developing societies"; third, consideration of context and content of the theories of social transformation and change. Accordingly, our *Introduction* to the series deals with the general issues of comparative study, other books cover different regions, while a final volume is devoted to an examination of basic paradigms of the theories of social transformation. They therefore represent the three main dimensions of the problem area, leaving it to each teacher and student to choose from them and to compose their own course.

The topic is ideologically charged, relating directly to the outlook and the ideals of everyone. The editors and many of the contributors share a broad sense of common commitment, though there is among them a considerable diversity of political viewpoint and theoretical approach. The common ground may be best indicated as three fundamental negations. First, there is an implacable opposition to every social system of oppression of humans by other humans. That entails also the rejection of scholastic apologia of every such system, be it imperialism, class oppression, elitism, sexism or the like. Second, there is the rejection of "preaching down" easy solutions from the comfort of air-conditioned offices and campuses, whether in the "West" or in "developing societies" themselves, and of the tacit assumption of our privileged wisdom that has little to learn from the common people in the "developing societies". Third, there is the rejection of the notion of scholastic detachment from social commitments as a pedagogy and as a way of life. True scholarship is not a propaganda exercise even of the most sacred values. Nor is it without social consequences, however conceived. There are students and teachers alike who think that indifference improves vision. We believe the opposite to be true.

TEODOR SHANIN

Acknowledgements

The authors and publishers wish to thank the following who have kindly given permission for the use of copyright material:

Cambridge University Press for "Urbanization, urbanism and the medina of Tunis" (1978) by Ellen C. Micaud, and "Egyptian state capitalism in crisis" (1979) by Mark Cooper, both articles in *International Journal of Middle East Studies.*

Deutsches Orient-Institut for an extract from "Middle Eastern political cliches: 'Takiti' and 'Sunni' rule in Araq; 'Alawi' rule in Syria; a critical appraisal" by Nikolaos van Dam in *Orient*, XXI, 1, January 1980.

Fontana Paperbacks, London, for material from *Television Technology and Cultural Form* by Professor Raymond Williams.

Humanities Press Inc. for an extract from the article "The Israeli concept of national security" by Professor Dan Horowitz from *Dynamics of a Conflict* edited by G. Sheffer.

Journal of Palestine Studies for the article "And the Fund still lives" by Uri Davis and Walter Lehn from Volume VII, 4, Summer 1978.

Journal of South Asian and Middle Eastern Studies for an extract from the article "Alienation and expatriate labour in Kuwait" by T. Farah, F. al-Salem and M. K. al-Salem, from Volume IV, No. 1, Villanova University, Pennsylvania.

Middle East Research and Information Project for an extract from "Revolutionary Iran and its tribal peoples" by Lois Beck from *MERIP Reports*, 87, May 1980.

North-Holland Publishing Company for material from "Dependent development" by G. A. Amin in *Alternatives*, 11, 1976.

Organization of the Petroleum Exporting Countries for the article "The integration of the oil sector with Arab economies" by Y. A. Sayigh, in *OPEC Review* IV, 4, Winter 1980.

Zed Press Ltd for "The new reality 1948–1965" from *Palestinians, From Peasants to Revolutionaries* by Rosemary Sayigh.

Every effort has been made to trace all the copyright holders, but if any have been inadvertently overlooked the publishers will be pleased to make the necessary arrangement at the first opportunity.

Note on Transliteration and the Citing of References

Given the well-known problems connected with transliterating Arabic and Hebrew words and names into English the authors have thought it best not to try to impose any one general system on all the texts but simply to ensure that the method employed in each text is internally consistent. We have, however, adopted one general principle of simplification through the work and that is to replace the Arabic ayn and hamza and the Hebrew ayin with a single quotation mark: thus '.

General Introduction

There already exist a number of Readers on the Sociology of Middle Eastern development, and the first thing which the editors of a new one must surely do is to set out their own reasons for wanting to produce another.* This is probably best done by outlining their approach to the basic problem of how to analyse complex processes of social transformation together with providing some guide to the type of questions which they think it important to raise. In our case we will do this with only passing reference to the existing literature on Middle Eastern development, most of which, we believe, lacks analytical rigour and consists mainly of the somewhat simplistic employment of concepts taken from the history of modern Europe or from the study of other parts of the non-European world.† This is not to say that the bulk of the work on the Middle East does not contain large quantities of useful information; rather, that the methodology which it employs and the interpretations which it presents are usually very unsatisfactory.

To begin with, we consider that the economies and societies of the Middle East have multiple links with the world capitalist system – political, economic, military and cultural – which influence and affect its structures and processes and act to place strict limits on the way they change over time. We also consider that these links can be seen, very generally, in terms of a relationship of inequality or dependence. The interests of the countries of Europe and North America (whether capitalist or socialist) require varying and variable linkages with the region, and these act

---

* For a list of other Readers, see p.239. Good general bibliographies of such literature can be found in Binder (1976) and Grimwood-Jones (1979). We have set out our own criticisms of much of the existing literature on the Middle East in Asad and Owen (1978). In the same place we also try to show how our own criticisms differ from those of other critics such as Binder (1976), Turner (1978) and Said (1978).

1

to condition the development objectives of the Middle Eastern States.

However, we would also wish to underline the ways in which our formulation of these links differs from the more usual definitions of the concept of dependence.* First, we do not believe that this unequal relationship constitutes a fixed or mechnical set of interactions, but rather that it is generally subject to great change over time. There are many different types of dependency, and their impact may vary enormously from one period or place to another. We would therefore suggest that the relationship be thought of in terms of changing strategic possibilities rather than in terms of fixed roles. This leads on to our second point. We do not support those formulations which tend to present the economic and social systems of the Third World simply as passive recipients of external forces. Rather, we see them as having a dynamic and logic of their own which, at any one moment, provides them with a narrow range of possible paths and choices. Thus it is the pattern of forces to be found within each country which partly determines what strategic options are available – and which are likely to be effective – in relation to outside powers. Finally, in our opinion, the way in which the concept of dependency is usually elaborated depends on the nature of such key words as "linkage" and "level", which are themselves highly problematic. In our view the nature and impact of the forces deriving from the world system have to be specified and demonstrated rather than simply asserted.

By the same token we find ourselves in disagreement with some of the ways in which critics of the concept of "Modernization" have tried to deal with the problem of economic and social transformation. Like them we do not see this transformation as leading eventually in the direction of some idealized modern society. But, equally, we believe that they only side-step the problem rather than solve it by the use of such qualifying notions as the "specificity" of individual societies or the possibility of there being a "multiplicity" of potential paths of transformation. Clearly there are certain regularities and certain constraints, in

* For good statements and critiques of existing theories of dependency see Palma (1978) and the papers in Seers (1981). For a concise description of the world system centre - periphery approach see Hopkins and Wallerstein (1981) and Hopkins *et al.* (1982).

patterns of development, to which all contemporary Middle Eastern societies are subject. In all of them there are attempts, whether eager or hesitant, to change things in the direction of an idealized modernity. But the idealizations are never the same. Politically they range from secure parliamentary freedoms to a genuine representation of mass interests; economically, from unfettered extensions of the market to more efficient centralized planning; culturally, from Islam as a privatized religion of true spirituality to Islam as a movement for confronting all the moral and social problems of the modern world. How these conflicting idealizations come to be realized or altered, in the context of national and international forces, needs to be examined on their own particular terms.

The way in which this Reader has been organized followed closely from these introductory remarks. We begin with a section on the international context as a method of illustrating the huge variety of ways in which forces and currents in the international environment confront and interact with local structures and processes, with consequences which, in many cases, spread throughout the whole society. The second section is concerned with an analysis of problems which arise at the national or state level and involves such topics as the relationship of state structures to classes and groups within the wider society (for example, the nature of the state bureaucracy in Algeria), the impact of rapid change upon certain aspects of the political economy (the Islamic Revolution and the system of pastoral nomadism in Iran) and the relationship between a single-party regime and subnational groupings (the Ba'th in Iraq and Syria). Finally, the third section contains a number of subjects which do not fit into any general model of social transformation: an examination of the different types of socio-economic change to be found among different Turkish villages, the sociology of the Palestinian refugees, changing conceptions of the place of traditional city housing in development and the role of organized urban violence in Beirut. Each section is preceded by a General Introduction in which we discuss the texts and, when relevant, draw attention to useful work by other authors.

As far as our definition of the Middle East is concerned, we have used the widest possible interpretation of its geographical extent: the band of countries running from Iran in the east to Morocco in the west and from Turkey in the north to Sudan and the Arabian peninsula in the South. But we would like strongly to underline our own belief that such a collecton of countries does not constitute a well-bounded area with its own core and periphery or with its own distinctive type of social formation, political behaviour or mode of cultural expression. Rather, we prefer to see the Middle East as a particular part of the Third World in which a variety of forces (political and economic, social and cultural) converge and work themselves out in specific local situations. Thus, when it comes to the choice of texts, we have tried to find those which combine an examination of some of these general processes with an analysis of the way they work themselves out in the context of a group of countries which share some,, but not all, the same socio-economic and political features.

It is also necessary to say something about the choice of the texts themselves. It is our belief that they are all interesting and useful, because they embody good scholarship, or because they contain a valuable argument – or both. That is to say, they raise important questions about the processes and structures under analysis or point to significant problem areas. But in spite of their considerable merits we would like to encourage a critical attitude to these same texts, in the belief that they represent, not closed systems of truth, but sets of ideas which are open for our inspection and further use. In particular we think that each of them could be rewritten, or broken down into component parts and reorganized, or in some other way reconstructed, so as to provide a different perspective or a different set of answers to the original problem.

Finally, in so short a set of texts, a large number of subjects and possible approaches will, inevitably, have to be omitted. One to which we would like to draw particular attention is that of culture. This is certainly not at all well covered in the existing development literature on the Middle East. There are, of course, many excellent individual studies within the wider field of Middle Eastern culture, for example Laroui (1976) and Berque (1978). There is also an enormous mass of usable material on various aspects of contemporary culture, whether 'high culture', folk and popular culture, or the press, education, radio and television, etc. What is lacking, however, are published studies which offer competent analyses of the ways in which Middle Eastern cultural forms are produced, reproduced and transformed within historically determinate social and material conditions. This is not a simple subject, but we would like to stress that it is a very important one, not the least because an adequate understanding of socio-economic and political processes depends in part upon a grasp of the cultural processes connected with them.

Part I

The International Dimension

Introduction

Since the Second World War the international environment of the states and societies of the Middle East has been characterized by three major processes: one, Great Power rivalry and competition for influence over a region of considerable economic and strategic importance; two, further integration into the world economy; and three, as far as the Arab states were concerned, great pressure to unite in the face of threats of domination from without and from a powerful Israeli opponent within. It is these processes which have largely defined the context in which states and regimes have sought to preserve their political independence, in which local structures have been transformed and in which the struggle between local classes has taken place. They have also been responsible for the emergence of new patterns of dependence and interdependence centred largely on the Middle Eastern states' search for economic aid and military assistance and on efforts to win control over the production and pricing policies of the region's main natural resources: oil and natural gas.

Nevertheless, it has to be underlined that the particular path followed by particular states and societies can only be properly understood in terms of an interaction between forces from the international environment and specific local processes and structures with their own specific local logic. One good example of this concerns the different ways in which at different times over the past thirty years different regimes in the region supported by different classes have attempted to reduce or to limit their dependence on foreign assistance and to redefine their place within the international political economy. One such attempt was made by President Nasser's Egyptian regime in the 1960s with its emphasis on planned economic development, control over foreign exchange and the construction of a capital goods industry in close co-operation with the Russians. It is well known that his successor, President Sadat, in alliance with a class of public sector managers and private sector entrepreneurs, inaugurated policies which, under the name of "infitah" or liberalization, aimed at reversing this trend and reintegrating Egypt more securely within the Western or capitalist economic system on the basis of the formula "Arab capital plus Western technology plus Egypt's labour equals economic growth" (quoted in Hirst and Beeson, 1981, p. 216). Other examples of equally comprehensive attempts to redefine economic relations are the policies of the Turkish generals after their coup of September 1980 designed to remove much of the long-lived protective system of tariffs and controls in order to encourage an industrial strategy based on export promotion rather than import substitution; and, in more spectacular fashion, the great reduction in the number of links with the international political economy carried out by Iran's religious leaders since the Revolution of 1979.

As a rule, however, the nature of the relationship and of the links with the international system was influenced not only by purely local factors, but also by movements within the Middle East regional environment as well. The establishment of the state of Israel, the plight of the Palestinian refugees and the competition among the Arab states to create and control a viable movement of Palestinian resistance produced a constant state of tension, five major wars and an arms race in which the need for outside military assistance came to assume a preponderant influence in the relationship between local states and their Great Power suppliers. Again, the enormous increase in oil wealth accruing to thinly populated and militarily weak states on the periphery of the Arab world after the nationalizations and price rises of the early 1970s had a considerable effect on inter-Arab relations, shifting financial power to the more conservative regimes and encouraging a much closer Arab economic integration based on the exchange of migrant workers for remittances and other large flows of funds. But this process also had important implications for the policies pursued by individual Arab states, for intra-Arab co-operation as well as for the intensification of links with the world market.

The texts in Part I have been chosen to illustrate the nature of intra-regional relations and of the links with the international political economy as well as to raise questions about the way in which they have served to alter the relative position of certain local classes and to restructure a variety of important local institutions. The first four are focused primarily on intra-regional concerns, although each of them has important international implications; the next three are concerned with different types of unequal relationships with the outside world – economic, military and cultural – and their effect on local structures.

Owen's text is an effort to provide a description of the special character, and in particular the special intensity, of intra-Arab solidarity, as well as a historical account of the way in which it provided the impetus for schemes designed to mobilize large numbers of people in support of policies designed to curb the influence of the Western powers and their local allies (notably the large landowners) and to encourage greater Arab co-operation. It also shows how it was that the very existence of such a variety of cross-border ties forced individual regimes and their supporters to attempt to manage and contain pan-Arab influence and pan-Arab links lest they provide a challenge to their own vested interests. And he ends by pointing to the paradox or contradiction that the decade of the 1970s was one in which the forces promoting economic integration were at their strongest, while those promoting political co-operation were very weak. In such a short text it is impossible to do more than direct attention to the main areas for analysis. What has had to be left out is any examination of the ways in which the powerful ideology of Arab nationalism has been reproduced over time or of the ways in which it has been contested and altered. Little is also said about the variety of opportunities within the Arab political context for oppositional movements based on support from regimes or parties or groups on the other side of the border or about the presence or absence of classes which have interests which transcend national boundaries.

One central point made in Owen's text is the fundamental importance of Israel and Palestine in both promoting and discouraging the movement for greater Arab unity. Horowitz's text looks at the same point from an Israeli point of view as he examines the development of the doctrine that Arab hostility was unalterable and that Israel had to base its military strategy on constant military preparedness, on instant retaliation against border incursions and on a readiness to meet any perceived threat to its security by pre-emptive or preventive attacks. This at once gave Israel a very special place in the Middle East states system – at least until the Peace Treaty with Egypt in 1979 – with no way of influencing the conduct of its Arab neighbours except by force and threats of force. As Horowitz underlines, there could be no Israel foreign policy towards the Arab states, only a defence policy. And he goes on to spell out some of the implications of this situation: the built-in requirement that Israel maintain superiority over its neighbours even to the extent of obtaining nuclear weapons and the need to base its strategy on the existence of a large reserve army of easy to mobilize soldiers. He might also have added the economic and social instability created in an area like South Lebanon – before 1982 – as a result of Israeli policy of holding any Arab government responsible for attacks against Israel launched from its territory.

The text also raises – but cannot answer - several questions relating to the basic character of Israeli society. One concerns the relationship between the policy of military preparedness and massive retaliation and the interests of particular classes or groups. Were there some groups which derived particular benefit from a policy which, among other things, assured Israel of huge amounts of economic and military assistance, particularly from America? Or is it that class conflicts were only too easily muffled by the constant emphasis on the need to be ready to confront a relentless enemy? Another involves the difficult question of civil-military relations and in particular, the role of the army, the Defence Establishment and the Reserve system in promoting military values and a military point of view throughout the society. In a more recent analysis (Horowitz, 1982) the same author has tried to provide a more systematic examination of the patterns of interaction between what he calls a 'civilianised military' and a 'partially militarised society', with particular reference to the role of the military 'experts in violence' in creating a national consensus which provides the army with a large share of economic resources and (until the invasion of Lebanon in 1982) insulated it from almost all criticism of its conduct of defence policy.

Finally, as far as Israel's neighbours are concerned, there is the effect which the long periods of tension have had on local policies – for example, Jordan's efforts to relocate Palestinian refugees away from their old homes along the common armistice line with Israel (for example, Plascov, 1982, pp. 223-6) or, in larger terms, on the survival or overthrow of or restructuring particular Arab regimes.

Sayigh's text attempts to provide a framework for examining the impact of oil and oil revenues on the economic development of the Arab states of the Middle East. He points to the way in which, during the 1970s, the main producers gained control of production and pricing policy and then began to use the vast increase in revenues which followed as an 'engine' of economic growth. But he also shows how the perceived need to push on with this process as quickly as possible before the oil ran out led to great waste, a vast increase in consumption (mostly of imports) and to an even greater 'dependence' (his phrase) on foreign goods and foreign technology. In terms of his own argument the only answer to these shortcomings is a properly organized system of Arab economic co-operation and planning.

One of the strengths of Sayigh's analysis is that he sees the whole Arab Middle East as an example of a single oil economy, one in which the economies of all the states in the region have become closely interlocked as a result of movements of money and labour and in which they share common structural features which act, among other things, to inhibit agricultural growth and to discourage industrial diversification (Katouzian, 1981). What he does not do, however, is to provide a systematic analysis of the basic characteristics of such an economy and, in particular, of the nature of the relationship between oil-rich and oil-poor states (Owen, 1981 a). Nor does he show how its particular structures are affected either by particular regime and class interests or by its place within the world division of labour. For this reason the types of national development strategies being pursued are a great deal less arbitrary than he seems to suggest and a great deal more difficult to bring under the control of a single Arab plan or a single Arab planning agency. One example of this is the policies of most of the oil-rich states towards taxation and welfare (Owen, 1981b). On the one hand, none of these regimes has either the administrative capacity or the political will to create a progressive system of direct taxation which would bear most heavily on those groups which are their most reliable sup-porters. The result is an inability to control vast differences in income or to ensure that part of the private gains from oil-related activity are guided into productive channels. On the other hand, it is a central feature of the development strategies of all the oil-rich states to create a type of welfare state – on the Kuwaiti model – with free schools and hospitals for all their citizens. And here the result is a huge intra-Arab struggle for access to the scarce resources of trained manpower necessary to run such ambitious programmes.

The question of the oil-rich states' dependence on foreign (Arab or non-Arab) labour and of their reluctance to grant such workers the same economic and political rights as their own citizens is dealt with in the text by Farah, al-Salem and al-Salem. This provides a description of the situation as it existed in Kuwait in the late 1970s. Its special interest lies not only in the details it provides about the status of foreign labour in Kuwait, but also in the fact that the Kuwaiti pattern is being repeated elsewhere in the states of the Lower Gulf as well as in Saudi Arabia, and to some extent in Libya and Iraq as well. Among the important points made are those concerning the huge disparities in income between Kuwaitis and their Asian and oil-poor Arab neighbours, the level of illegal immigration and the regime's policy of allowing non-Kuwaitis access to some of the benefits of the local welfare state and not others. What is lacking is any attempt to examine the implications of what, in world historical terms, is clearly a highly unusual situation for both the social and the political future of Kuwait. Does the fact that non-Kuwaiti workers come from so many different countries and cultures inevitably inhibit them from co-operating together to improve their own conditions? What are the effects on Kuwaiti society itself of its huge reliance on foreign labour? And, more speculatively, what is the effect of providing a Middle Eastern society with government-sponsored free health and education in terms of standards of service and in terms of competition with the private provision of these same services (El Mallakh and Atta, 1981, pp. 106-18; and Khouja and Sadler, 1979, pp. 31-5).

Another question suggested by the text is the effect of labour migration on the economies and societies of the labour-exporting countries. This has been examined in systematic fashion only in the case of Turkey (Payne, 1974; Abadan-Unat, 1976). For the Arab countries, evidence is a great deal more impressionistic and can only hint at the consequences of the loss of large numbers of workers, both trained and untrained (Halliday, 1977; Mustafa, 1980; Birks and Sinclair, 1980). Areas of the subject to be explored include the effect of labour migration on the agricultural sector in terms of shortages, higher wages for those who remain, the increasing economic role of women while their husbands are away and growing inequalities between those districts or villages which export labour – and thus benefit from remittances – and those which do not. Another area is the effect of remittances – sent back in the form of both money and consumer goods – on the domestic economies of large labour exporters like Egypt, Sudan, North Yemen and Algeria. There is some evidence to suggest that very little of it is invested in productive activity (Mustafa, 1980, pp. 86-9). Remittances also alter consumption patterns, help to suck in imports and reduce the market for locally made goods.

The next three texts deal with aspects of the relationship of the Middle Eastern states with the capitalist and socialist states of the First and Second World. In particular they focus on various types of links – economic, military, cultural – the inequalities and dependencies they produce and their role in restructuring a number of important local institutions and practices.

The text by General Hadidi is concerned with a description of Egyptian efforts to break the monopoly of arms supplies from Britain and America in the early 1950s by obtaining weapons from the Soviet Union and the Eastern bloc. But it also demonstrates how quickly this produced a new set of problems, as it proved impossible to re-equip the army and air force with modern weapon systems, and to use them effectively, without a major restructuring of the military organization, including its systems of command, of officer training and of maintenance and logistical support. They also often require quite new sets of tactics and strategic deployment. Hadidi's treatment tends to skate over many of the important implications of this situation and he is clearly quite ambivalent about the nature of the Russian military role in Egypt. Nevertheless, his text raises questions which are only rarely touched upon in a Middle Eastern context, even if they have received a certain amount of general attention in the theoretical literature (Kaldor and Eide, 1979; Luckham, 1976). These include, first, the analysis of the economic and social role of armies in particular societies and, second, the ways in which this role is altered or even transformed as a result of links with outside suppliers of weapons systems – for example, fighter planes, air defence systems and tanks – which require complex organizational structures for their effective use. They thus have implications which go far beyond that of the military itself and directly affect national systems of education and technical training and basic decisions relating to the allocation of national resources. There are also interesting comparisons to be made as between the effect of the acquisition of modern armaments on one Middle East state and another, particularly between Israel and its Arab neighbours (Lutwak and Horowitz, 1975; Vatikiotis, 1967). Finally, there is the whole question of the relationship between major US and European arms manufacturers and those Middle Eastern states which have begun to develop their own arms industries, notably Israel, Turkey and Egypt. In the case of Israel this relationship has gone even further than close co-operation in production and research and development and now includes the repair and, in some cases, the upgrading of American equipment sold to other Third World countries (Klich, 1980).

Williams' text on the creation of an American-dominated world system of communications by television and radio raises another set of important questions about the ways in which people in Middle Eastern states receive particular sets of ideas and images and thus are influenced, directly or indirectly, in the ways in which they live, in which they think about the world and in which they express themselves culturally. As such it is one method of directing attention to a whole variety of related subjects such as the role of foreign-influenced architecture, systems of education or even methods of promoting tourism in altering Middle Eastern belief systems, life-styles and consumption patterns as well as the more difficult to analyse subjects such as the attitudes of particular classes and societies to their own history and their own place in the world. Once again, this subject has only rarely been examined in its Middle Eastern context (see Notes for further reading, pp.248-9). But one area where some work has been done relates directly to Williams' own analysis of the influence of American-dominated systems of broadcasting and concerns the amount of air-time which is devoted to American-made programmes and the American origin of items of news (Rachty, 1978). However, there is still much work to be done on such subjects as the way in which American penetration of the Middle Eastern television market allows US firms to produce cheaper films than their local rivals, or the way in which material made in America is often sold as a single package which Third World stations have no option but to accept in its entirety.

Lastly, Amin's text is an ambitious attempt to illustrate the nature of a combination of forces which are guiding Middle Eastern societies among the path which will ensure their further integration into a world dominated by the capitalist system and its associated structure of values and norms. He stresses the role played by international aid, the multi-national companies and by an ideology of development which emphasizes the need for Third World countries to 'catch-up' with the West. Pressure on the Arab states is further increased by their failure to mobilize sufficient domestic savings and to co-ordinate their economic policies. And he goes on to argue that this has produced a situation characterized by consumption for its own sake, a Western style of life and a system of values which stresses individualism, permissiveness and competition. Variations of this same point are very common in the Middle East and have motivated a number of attempts to reduce local dependence, both of the Nasserite type and of those associated with religious movements like that led by the Ayatollah Khomeini. But what such analyses lack is any well-defined concept of the nature of dependence itself or any sense of the enormous complexity of the links between the Middle East and the world system and thus provide little concrete guidance as to the ways in which the situation could be altered to the advantage of specific societies or social groups.

A number of these points will also be examined in their national or state context in Part II.

Arab Nationalism, Unity and Solidarity

Roger Owen

Academic writing about the phenomenon of Arab nationalism and the movement for Arab unity has been unusually unsatisfactory. Although almost all authors acknowledge their power and importance, little effort is made to understand their development or to explain their role in Arab politics. For some Arab nationalism remains an ultimately "mysterious" force; for others it seems to be seen as so much a self-evident part of Middle Eastern life that it requires no further examination. The problem has been further compounded by the failure to distinguish properly between nationalism as a set of ideas and nationalism as a political movement, and by the interchangeable use of such terms as "unity", "solidarity", and "Pan-Arabism", as though they all had more or less the same meaning.

What I want to argue here is that the subject can only usefully be approached, first, by a careful definition of the concepts involved and, second, by a study of the historical context in which both the ideas and the actions of Arab unifiers and Arab nationalists have developed. By nationalism I mean the theory that the political and ethnic boundaries of those people who constitute a nation should coincide. By national movement I mean the attempt to put such a theory into practice. It is, however, important to note that, in the Arab world, practical attempts to dissolve political boundaries and to create larger political entities have generally been the work of rulers or regimes, many of whom were guided more by dynastic ambition or sheer *realpolitik* than by any strongly held belief in the basic tenets of Arab nationalism. It is also essential to realize that the whole subject cannot possibly be discussed without reference to the lived experience of solidarity and similarity shared by so many Arabs. The multiple links – linguistic, cultural, institutional and, for many, religious – between them, and the intensity of their contacts with one another are the basic context in which the activities of nationalists and unifiers have flourished. Yet it is also true that for large numbers of

---

* For bibliographical support for this paper see Notes for further reading (pp. 239–40).

16

Arabs it has been enough to express this sense of brother-hood or solidarity in a number of mainly symbolic ways – for example, by vocal support for the Palestinians – rather than by working for the immediate creation of a unified or federal state.

To turn to the historical context in which these ideas and activities and experiences have developed, it is necessary to begin with a brief description of the situation in the Syrian, and to some extent the Iraqi and western Arabian, provinces of the Ottoman Empire in the decades just before the First World War. It was there that a cultural revival, based largely on the study of Arabic, combined with an intensification of links between the inhabitants of the different major towns of the region to provide some members of the educated and propertied strata with a sense of a common, shared, Arab identity which transcended more parochial loyalties. This trend was further strengthened by the growing opposition to foreign penetration (both by the major European powers and the Jewish settlers on Palestine) and by the discrimina-tion against Arab officials and merchants practised by the Young Turk governments after 1908. It was in these circumstances that a political vocabulary of Arabism was first developed, mainly in the local press, providing an ideological basis for the activities of small groups of Arab city notables, army officers and others which were beginning to come together to assert their own interests. But, as yet, only a handful of students and intellectuals had gone as far as to call for Arab political independence.

The First World War and the break-up of the Ottoman Empire which followed produced a contradictory effect on the further development of nationalist thought and action. On the one hand, the British-sponsored campaign against the Turks and the brief regime established by Faisal in Damascus in 1919 provided an important focus for a strengthening of Arabist feelings and the first practical attempt to establish a specifically Arab and independent political entity. The fact that the Hashemite Arab army had contained significant numbers of men from the Hijaz and Iraq as well as from the Syrian provinces provided a sig-nificant example of the possibilities of Arab co-operation while the struggle to prevent a French-dominated Syria was the first example of a specifically Arab national response to a foreign challenge. On the other hand, the subsequent division of the Ottoman Empire into a number of successor states controlled by Britain and France meant that nationalist energies were now largely diverted into fighting more specifically local battles against the colonial powers, while the major schemes for unity put forward during the inter-war period were the work not of any Pan-Arab political party or movement, but of a small handful of rulers and their advisors anxious either to reunite the separate parts of Syria or to create an Iraqi-Syrian federation.

Several other features of the political life of this period ought also to be noted. One, given the continued elaboration of schemes for Iraqi-Syrian unity it was more or less inevitable that other, neighbouring states should be drawn into the process, first the Saudis – given their own freedom from direct colonial control and their ruler's fear of a Hashemite-controlled bloc to his north, then the Egyptians. Two, for exactly the same kind of reasons it was also inevitable that one or other ruler or regime would try to take the lead in this process. This, after all, is what happened during the unification of Germany and Italy during the nineteenth century and is probably the only pattern by which independent and sovereign states can be cajoled or coerced into a wider political union. Three, there was an understandable disagreement about the form which any wider Arab union should take, with the Iraqis, the Syrians and latterly the Egyptians anxious for a unitary state and the Saudis pressing for a looser form of federal arrangement. Given the fact that the British also supported the idea of co-operation rather than complete union it is perhaps not surprising that this was the formula which emerged from the meetings at Alexandria in 1944 which led to the formation of the League of Arab States. The presence at Alexandria of a Lebanese delegation speaking for a country containing a sizeable majority of Christians who were either hostile to Arabism or fearful of it acted as another brake on efforts to create a more centralized political system.

Meanwhile, a sense of Arabism and Arab solidarity continued to grow among a widening section of the urban population, fuelled by developments in transport, in mass communications and in the creation of intra-Arab institutions. The first political conferences were held in the inter-war period and the first Arab scientific congresses as well. At the same time the growing practice of co-operation was given a sharper ideological form not only by the struggle against colonialism, but also by a growing response to the particular plight of the Palestinians, the details of which became increasingly obvious to most educated Arabs during the 1930s. Events in Palestine were closely studied. They were also given more resonance by the first appearance of Palestinian school teachers in a number of Arab towns and the first small diaspora of Palestinian land-owners and merchants during and after the Revolt of 1936-9. A few such Palestinians had a small role to play in political events in Kuwait just before the Second World War and their presence there may be taken as a first indication of some of the inbuilt tensions of the growing Arabism. If any Arab could go anywhere in the Middle East and, simply on the basis of his language, obtain a job or engage in political activity this could easily be seen as posing a threat to local power structures or local economic interests. The reaction of the latter was, increasingly, to attempt to monitor intra-Arab movement, to restrict the grant of citizenship and to emphasize their own particular version of Arabism against all others.

The context in which Middle Eastern politics was conducted was transformed once again by the consequences of the Second World War and its aftermath: notably the achievement of national independence in Syria and Lebanon and the Arab regimes' failure to prevent the establishment of a Jewish state in Palestine. This immediately provided the setting for new forms of political activity including, in several states, the attempt by various parties and movements to mobilize an increasingly wide section of the population behind the potent slogans of anti-imperialism, anti-Zionism and Arab solidarity, as well as for and against the radical economic and social programmes put forward by parties like the Syrian Ba'th or military coup-makers like Nasser's Free officers. Indeed it would not be wrong to assert that the appeal to Arabism and to the need to transform and unite Arab society in the interests of intensifying the struggle against a common set of enemies (including the landlord-dominated governments of the immediate post-1945 period) was a central feature of any attempt to obtain wide-spread popular support.

The process of mobilising popular sentiment was taken farthest in Egypt after the Revolution of 1952. This became even more important as Nasser began to augment his appeal to the powerful local Egyptian nationalism with one to the wider Arab world as well. Given the many strengths which his regime seemed to possess, as well as all the prestige which it derived from its challenge to British and American interests and its ability to obtain substantial economic and military support from the Russians it seemed to many Arabs that it was Nasser and his colleagues who were best placed not only to transform Egyptian society and to protect it from its enemies, but to extend this activity to other Arab states as well. The Egyptian example thus produced a powerful effect beyond Egypt's borders and was an important factor behind the creation of the one serious attempt to create a united Arab state: the Syrian-Egyptian union of 1958/61.

As the 1950s progressed the call for Arab unity began to be monopolized more and more by the leaders of Arab regimes rather than the representatives of classes with pan-Arab interests. For obvious reasons the existence of post-independence state structures created particular socio-economic groups with a vested interest in the continuance of those same structures. This at once had a number of important consequences. For one thing it led to a rapid enlargement of the number of Arab states which either contemplated joining some kind of union or, just as important felt it necessary to try to block some other states' plans. By the 1960s North Yemen, Sudan, Libya, Kuwait and to a lesser extent Tunisia and Algeria had begun to be actors in this process; by the 1970s the states of the Lower Gulf as well. The problems thus posed were further exacerbated by the fact that Egypt was so obviously more powerful than any other single state that union with Cairo would inevitably have to take place on Nasser's terms. This is certainly one of the chief lessons drawn by Syrian politicians as a result of their brief experience of such an arrangement.

A second feature of the growth in the number of states jockeying for power and position in the name of Arabism was the increasing tendency to interfere in the internal affairs of neighbouring states in the interests either of building up local sets of supporters who would influence policy decisions or of preventing reciprocal attempts to stir up hostile activity against themselves at home. Nowhere else in the world is the variety and intensity of cross-border interaction between sovereign states so great as in the Arab world, with so many political and religious groups owing allegiance to centres outside their own state boundaries and where it is a perfectly normal and acceptable response of any Arab leader to look for support in neighbouring Arab countries by subsidizing particular newspapers or encouraging particular oppositional groups. Given these conditions the search for unity could easily prove to be enormously divisive inside any one particular Arab state with supporters of union with one external power often engaged in bloody conflict with the advocates of quite a different type of Arab alignment. The development of Lebanon as a battleground between the supporters of rival regimes and rival ideologies was an obvious extension of this same pattern of activity. Perhaps because the Arabs have always tended to regard themselves as brothers there has never been any concerted effort to establish a set of rules or correct practices between the separate states.

The role of the Arab regimes was also a major factor in preventing the growing sense of Arab solidarity from expressing itself in any single ideological programme, let alone in any single political movement. The power of shared experience and of the multiplicity of ties that linked Arabs across state boundaries posed too many threats to the established order to be left alone. By the same token the fact that the feeling of solidarity and the habit of acting in concert with the citizens of other Arab states was so widespread meant that it was too diffused to submit to any one interpretation or to the hegemony of any one class. Even the growing use of the media and of cultural programmes to present a picture of a common Arab historical experience had its own ambiguity in that it encouraged listeners and recipients to make the distinction between the appeal itself and the nature and interests of the persons – whether Egyptian or Syrian or Palestinian – who were making the appeal. In this sense the Cairo radio station, "The Voice of the Arabs", was also the voice of Egypt and thus not the voice of Riyadh or Damascus.

The effects of both these observations can be traced with special clarity in the years after the Israeli victory of 1967. As each regime expanded its administrative structure and, with it, its ability to control and manipulate its people it took good care to ensure that the power of Arabism was harnessed in such a way that it reinforced its own position rather than harmed it. On the one hand, the activities of any group or organization with cross-border loyalties was strictly monitored. On the other, control over the media and over the systems of national education was used to promote a particular brand of Arabism designed to suggest that only the local regime was properly Arab or capable of acting in a truly Arab interest. Little by little the vocabulary of Arabism was altered to accommodate ideas and concepts designed to highlight regional difference and local particularity. Meanwhile, with the simple passage of time, the inhabitants of each separate state were forced to adjust their lives to the permanent reality of separate passports, separate national plans and separate administrative practices.

Nevertheless, for all their efforts to tame or to domesticate Arabism, it is clear that such attempts ran counter to other, powerful, forces which reaffirmed a general sense of Arab similarity and solidarity. One was the emergence after 1967 of a Palestinian Resistance movement which not only acted as a constant stimulus to Arab nationalist sentiment, but also contained small groups with the implicitly revolutionary belief that it was the Arab regimes themselves which stood as the major obstacle in the path towards unity. The sight of Yassar Arafat, constantly in movement from one Arab capital to another, was a constant reminder of a central fact of Arab life that if the Palestinians are nowhere they are everywhere, and thus an inevitable challenge to the existing order. The second force was the intensified economic integration based on the exchange of the labour of the oil-poor, heavily populated countries for the finance from the under-populated oil-rich ones. The result was the creation of a vast pan-Arab institutional network of funds and banks and development agencies staffed by economists and technocrats who moved easily from one country and one institution to another and for whom intra-Arab co-operation has become an important way of life. Meanwhile, at the other end of the social spectrum, the vast army of migrant labourers has been shaken free from their own national economies without being accepted as citizens or even permanent residents anywhere else. In addition they have an obvious interest in the continuation of their unimpeded passage from one Arab country to another and their ability to send money and goods back to their families at home.

To sum up the argument as briefly as possible: first, belief in Arab nationalism and the efforts to create a wider Arab unity have their roots in the existence of a sense of Arab solidarity and a pattern of intra–Arab interaction which has spread over time to include most of the Arab states of the Middle East. Second, Arab solidarity has been manipulated and disrupted both by the separate Arab regimes and by the desire to protect particular local interests against the easy intrusion of Arabs from elsewhere. Third, support for the Palestinians has been eroded by a willingness to deal directly with Israel, or with threats coming from Israel, without reference to its effect on the struggle for Palestine. It is in the interaction of these three tendencies that the future of Arab nationalism and the possibilities for future political unity will depend.

The Israeli Concept of National Security

Dan Horowitz

The Israeli concept of national security is predicated on two interrelated premises: (a) that Israel has no choice but to treat the Arab-Israeli conflict as "given",[1]* and (b) that Israel is bound to take into consideration its narrow margin of security deriving from lack of geographic depth and demographic quantitative inferiority.[2] . . . Foreign policy tended to become an extension of national defence policy; that is, foreign policy was subjected to considerations deriving from involvement in a conflict perceived as a struggle for survival between nation-actors with irreconcilable interests.[3] . . . In this context, some of the components of the Israeli concept of national security are worth mentioning.

A. Self-reliance

In its broader sense the notion of self-reliance is rooted in the fundamental Zionist idea of self-emancipation which has inspired the Jewish colonization in Palestine since the 1880s.[4] In a narrower political sense it has been prescribed by David Ben Gurion and other advocates of "orientation on ourselves" as a guideline for the conduct of Israel's foreign and defence policy.[5] However, partly through the influence of Ben Gurion, who presided over the formation of Israel's defence establishment,[6] and partly under the impact of imposed near isolation in the early 1950s,[7] the notion of self-reliance has been incorporated into the prevailing Israeli doctrine of national security (Peres, 1965, p. 13; Rolbant, 1970; pp. 242–4). . . .

B. Dormant War

The characterization of the "Neither war nor peace" conditions which prevailed in Arab-Israeli relations between 1949 and 1967 (except for the short interval of the 1956 war) as a state of "dormant war" is General Yitzhak Rabin's.[8] In other expositions of the Israeli approach to national security the same idea has been

* End Notes can be found on pages 227–30.

expressed in other terms. Ben Gurion maintained in 1955 that the Arab countries continue to wage war against Israel "by different means".[9] Yigal Allon argued that the Arab claim that the 1949 armistice agreement did not imply a termination of a state of belligerency forces Israel to think in terms of a state of war existing between herself and the neighbouring Arab countries (Allon, 1968, p. 15). Dayan considered what he called "military operations in peacetime" a legitimate instrument of Israel policy making in the particular conditions of the Arab–Israeli conflict,[10] and Shimon Peres, Ben Gurion's closest associate, argued, like Allon, that the rules of the game of the Arab–Israeli conflict are determined by the Arab "belligerency short of war" approach (Peres, 1965, pp. 19–20). Indeed there appeared to be a consensus among Israeli policy-makers about the consequences of the warlike characteristics of the Arab–Israeli conflict even in periods of apparent tranquillity.[11] . . .

Israel's wars were limited wars in more than one sense, since the exercise of violence was invariably subjected to political restrictions deriving not only from the openness of the Arab-Israeli conflict system,[12] but also from Israeli calculations concerning inter-Arab politics.[13] On the other hand, Israel has never experienced a state of formal peace. Periods in which no hostilities took place were invariably associated with less binding legal arrangements such as truce, ceasefire, or, at the most, armistice.

The impact of the nondichotomic perception of war and peace is traceable in aspects of Israeli policy-making. Partial understanding and limited co-operation with potential or actual enemies were pursued and sometimes achieved regardless of the question whether or not hostilities were taking place at the same time. An understanding of this kind with King Abdullah of Jordan accounts for some of the restrictions imposed by the Israeli government on its own field commanders in the later stages of the 1948 war.[14]

The precarious ceasefire conditions after the 1967 war also provided many examples of co-operative activities carried out alongside limited hostilities. Recurrent clashes along the Jordan Valley did not prevent the implementation of the 'open bridges' policy[15] and the production and transportation of oil in the Gulf of Suez by both Israel and Egypt was not interrupted by the 1969-70 War of Attrition.[16] Paradoxically, in fact, the period after the 1967 war was characterized by an increase in both the exercise of violence and the partial co-operation between Israel and her hostile neighbours compared with the prewar period.[17] . . .

C. Controlled Exercise of Violence

The controlled exercise of violence is the essence of the conduct of limited military operations. As a consequence of their experiences in the limited war of 1948–9[18] and the pre-independence struggle of the Jewish military organizations against the British authorities (Slutzki, 1972), the Israeli defence establishment had been predisposed to think in terms of a restricted exercise of force aiming at the attainment of limited and politically conditioned objectives.[19] This predisposition paved the way for the adoption of the policy of reprisals in the early 1950s (Shiff, 1968). Some border incidents in which regular army units were involved on both sides and an increased terrorist infiltration (Ben Gurion, 1969, pp. 482–3) from the neighbouring countries induced the Israeli government and army command to adopt a twofold strategy aiming at responding to two different challenges referred to by the Israelis as "basic security" and "current security" respectively.[20] The problem of "basic security" was that of the threat of a full-scale war which might put Israel's existence in peril. The problem of "current security", on the other hand, was that of limited violent provocation not necessarily carried out by the official military forces of the neighbouring Arab countries.

The Israeli response to the basic security challenge was a defence posture based on the combination of a core of standing army, composed of both professionals and conscripts, and a much larger reserve force, well-trained and available at short notice, based on the concept of a "nation in arms";[21] that is, a nation whose civilians are, as one of the Israel Army Chiefs of Staff once put it, "soldiers on an annual eleven months leave".[22] The answer to the current security problem has been the adoption of a strategy of controlled retaliation involving a restricted application of limited force (Dayan, 1959, pp. 54–60).

But the requirements of basic security and current security competed for the scarce resources of manpower and finance, and the Israeli government and General Staff were resolute in their insistence on an order of priorities which would prevent the army from becoming merely border police. Lacking the necessary reserves to contain infiltration effectively by defensive means, the Israeli defence planners turned to more offensive measures which did not aim at sealing the border, but rather at "putting a high price on our blood", as General Dayan put it (Dayan, 1959, pp. 55–6). This Israeli version of "graduated response" in a non-nuclear environment had been contrived in order to resolve a specific dilemma rooted in the local conditions,[23] but it had much in common with the conceptual framework within which such notions as "escalation", "continuum of violence", and "gradu-ated response" have evolved (Aronson and Horowitz, 1971; Shiff, 1968).

The rationale of Israel's violent response to hostile activities instigated by the Arab countries or carried out from Arab territory was thus rooted in the expectation that the damage inflicted by the reprisals will convey a warning about the cost of similar provocations in the future.[24] The Arab countries were expected to be deterred from initiating provocations or, alternatively, compel-led to restrain other actors such as terrorist groups or guerrilla organizations operating from their territory or crossing through it.[25] The Israeli assumption, at least in the early 1950s, had been that the goal of the reprisals could be achieved without triggering a chain reaction of mutual retaliatory actions (Aronson and Horowitz, 1971). The assumption that military operations are controllable and that escalation can be checked led to attempts by the political level to control military operations to the extent of restricting the number of enemy casualties allowed in particular operations (Teveth, 1971, p. 393). Such attempts were not always successful and some reprisals – such as that made on Kibia on 15 October, 1953 and Kinneret on 13 December, 1955 – exceeded the limits anticipated by the political decision-makers.[26] . . .

D. Deterrence and Compellance

The awareness that military force can be an effective instru-ment of policy-making without being actually exercised is conse-quent upon the non-dichotomic perception of war and peace.[27] This awareness on the part of the exponents of strategic studies led to Herman Kahn's distinction between "force" and "violence" (Kahn, 1965) as well as to the introduction of such terms as "deterrence" and "compellance" to the vocabulary of the study of international relations (Schelling, 1966, pp. 69–91).

In Israel the term "deterrence" is the most commonly used of all the jargon of strategic studies,[28] with the exception, perhaps, of "escalation" since the June 1967 war. It has become an integral part of the vocabulary of public debate since the adoption in the early 1960s of the idea of deterrence as a major component of an Israeli strategy aiming at consolidating the post–1956 *status quo* both in terms of territory and "current security".[29] This adoption of the concept of deterrence by the Israeli defence establishment can be attributed at least in part to the influence of the American strategic studies school.[30] Yet the idea of utilizing military power without actually exercising it had already been familiar to the Israeli political leaders before Israel became an independent state. Indeed, the dominant political élite of the pre-independence Jewish community in Palestine, namely that of the Zionist Labor movement had developed a political strategy that without excluding the possible use of force put an emphasis on the attainment of political objectives by means of accumulation of power rather than by its actual application.[31] . . .

E. Balance of Power

The assumption that the "power to deter" was dependent on the 'power to determine' implied a pursuit of a favourable military balance. The Israeli position has been that, in order to maintain a deterrent stance, Israel needed not only a defensive capability but an offensive one as well.[32] The deterrence strategy has been adopted as an Israeli answer to the challenge created by the lopsidedness of the conflict system, which gave the Arab countries the strategic initiative enabling them to top the balance of power in their favour without actually resorting to force.[33] In this respect it could be (and indeed was) presented as an essentially defensive strategy.[34] But on the operational level its implication was an offensive disposition which required a pursuit of military superiority which would provide not only for containing the enemy, but also for defeating him. . . .

It was claimed that Israel cannot absorb an enemy's attack since she has no territory that can be temporarily sacrificed and not enough men to be spared for territorial defence (Dayan, 1959). In addition, the offensive strategy was in tune with the prospect of a short war which was both anticipated (since the world powers were expected to intervene) (Wallach, 1970, pp. 20–1) and considered desirable (since Israel, whose military capacity was dependent on the reserves system, could hardly endure a long period of mobilization without her economy becoming paralyzed) (Schelling, 1966, p. 246). The adoption of an offensive doctrine on the basic security level coincided with the application of a corresponding offensive doctrine on the current level in the form of reprisals (Dayan, 1959, pp. 52–3). It was also associated with the "de-territorialization" of the Israeli army's infantry reserve brigades, which made them mobile and available for deployment anywhere in the country (Laskov, 1968).

The pursuit of a military balance of power which would enable Israel to conduct offensive military operations preceded the adoption of a doctrine of deterrence which, in the Israeli context, implied a reliance on the deterrent effect of military superiority to secure not only the territorial integrity of the country but also vital interests such as the status quo in Jordan and the freedom of navigation in the Straits of Tiran. The existence of potential triggers of war in the form of manifest casus belli made military equality between Israel and her Arab neighbours seem in Israeli eyes not only militarily insufficient, but also politically dangerous (see Allon, 1968, pp. 66–7). In these conditions the Arab countries and, above all, Egypt needed only a sound defensive capability in order to violate the status quo in one or more of Israel's weak spots and get away with it. The threat to view such a violation as a *casus belli* appeared thus to be meaningful only in conditions of Israeli military superiority. Consequently, in their bid for sophisticated mlitary equipment from the Western powers, Israeli officials repeatedly argued that denial of such equipment in the form of partial qualitative or quantitative embargo might undermine rather than strengthen peace and stability in the Middle East.[35]...

F. Preventive War and Pre-emptive (Interceptive) War

The introduction of the time factor into the Arab–Israel balance-of-power equation might in certain conditions provide a motive for an Israeli-initiated preventive war. The dormant-war assumption and Israel's narrow margin of security imply that the Israeli's could not remain indifferent to a situation in which time was on the Arab countries' side in terms of the military balance of power. Thus, since the signing of the 1949 armistice agreements the probability of war started by Israel has been directly correlated with projected changes in the power ratio between Israel and her neighbours, Egypt in particular.[36]

This implication of the Israeli assessment that militarily time is on the side of the Arabs was demonstrated after the Egyptian–Soviet arms deal in September 1955.[37] The idea of preventive war was openly discussed in Israel during the September 1955–October 1956 period, and Prime Minister David Ben Gurion found it necessary to reject the idea in public speeches.[38] Yet he himself hinted at such a possibility in his secret talks with Robert

Anderson, President Eisenhower's special envoy, which were made public by Ben Gurion himself fifteen years later.[39] Ben Gurion was also aware that the then Chief of Staff, General Dayan, recommended a large-scale Israeli military offensive.[40] However, it was Ben Gurion's eventual conversion to the idea of a preventive military operation against Egypt which paved the way to Israel's participation in the co-ordinated Sinai and Suez ventures.[41] An authoritative Israeli source later described "the main and most salient objective of the Israeli government" in the Sinai campaign as "the defeat of the Egyptian army in Sinai . . . in order to prevent a grim possibility of a war between Israel and Egypt when Israel will be weak and isolated while Egypt is stronger".[42]

The role of the time factor in the context of the Arab–Israel balance of military power was a controversial issue within the Israeli defence establishment after the 1956 war. The prevailing prewar view that time was on the side of Israel's enemies was still held after the war by policy-makers such as the Deputy Minister of Defence, Shimon Peres.[43] But it was increasingly challenged by army officers who claimed that the introduction of modern but non-nuclear was technology tended to increase rather than decrease the role played by the qualitative human factor in warfare.[44] The latter view became the basis for Israel's strategic planning in the 1960s under Levi Eshkol as Prime Minister and Minister of Defence and General Rabin as Chief of Staff.[45] Its adoption had far-reaching consequences for Israel's foreign policy and national defence. In the field of defence planning this view implied a priority for the strengthening of Israel's capability to wage a conventional war over against the development of an Israeli nuclear option. Ben Gurion and Peres placed a stronger emphasis on a nuclear option than did Eshkol and Allon, the expert on strategy in Eshkol's cabinet.[46] Thus, the way was paved also for a new Israeli bid for arms from the United States, which, unlike France, had been committed to a policy of non-proliferation of nuclear weapons and was interested in exercising some control over Israel's advancement toward the attainment of nuclear capability (Peres, 1970, ch. 5; Gilboa, 1969, pp. 63–5).

In the broader sphere of political strategy the assessment that time was on the side of Israel meant that so long as the development of the Israeli Army was not impaired by the embargoes on the sale of sophisticated weapons, aircraft in particular, she could afford to act as a status-quo power without putting her existence in peril.[47] In this context – unlike in those of the allocation of scarce resources and the choice between European and American political orientations[48] – there was a basic agreement between the advocates of an emphasis on the development of nuclear action and the advocates of priority for attainment of conventional military superiority: both aimed at consolidating the territorial and political status quo.[49] Thus Israel's foreign policy between the 1956 and 1967 wars was essentially in tune with the American policy of maintaining stability in the Middle East in conditions of an unresolved Arab–Israel conflict.

The Arab Oil Economy

Y.A. Sayigh

The Oil Sector in the 1970s: Integration with Serious Gaps

The most relevant phase for the present inquiry, and the most intellectually interesting, is the current one. It coincides with the decade of the 1970s, but is likely to stretch several years into the future. This is the phase in which certain progress has been made in the satisfaction of the three basic conditions of integration. These are:

(i) The exercise of decision-making at the national (political), managerial and technical levels;

(ii) The earning of substantial revenues from oil exports, due essentially to a change in the basis on which these revenues are determined, and to a quantitative improvement in the price of oil; and

(iii) The utilization of the bulk of these revenues for the financing of development plans, and more so for a qualitative increase in the long-term developmental capability of the oil countries and the whole Arab region alike. An important component of this capability is the "graduation" of the oil economies from ones merely exporting crude oil to ones active in many downstream activities, particularly in the areas of refining and petrochemicals.

The take-over of decision-making was a crucial development. It consisted in a series of steps taken in the first few years of the decade of the 1970s, mostly in the form of participation arrangements and nationalization measures. Obviously, the national governments took over what had always been their right: the power to decide. That there are still some cases where nationalization has not been carried out qualifies the statement just made only marginally, inasmuch as even in these cases it is no longer the concessionary companies which take the major decisions relating to volume of production, prices, the destination of exports or downstream operations. . . .

As far as the second condition is concerned, the closer integration of the sector during the 1970s with the national economies – and, by projection, with the regional economy – due to the greater contribution of this sector to the financial resources of the exporting countries, can be seen by looking at their national accounts. Thus estimates for 1979 show that oil revenues accruing to the Arab members of OPEC were about $151.2 billion in an aggregate Gross Domestic Product (GDP) for the seven countries of some $234 billion, or 64.6 per cent of GDP. If all the Arab oil-producing countries are taken together the oil revenues amount to $160 billion out of an aggregate GDP of $279.5 billion, or 57.2 per cent. (Aggregate oil revenue for the entire Arab region, including non-oil producers, constitutes 52.3 per cent of aggregate GDP.)[1]

There are serious conceptual and accounting problems involved with respect to the inclusion of the value of oil exports in GDP. These problems apart, however, it is clear from a first general assessment that oil occupies a position of predominance in the GDP of the producing countries and in that of the region viewed as one unit. On the basis of this assessment, therefore, the oil sector has been largely integrated into the financial resource-generation capacity of the oil producers, both OPEC Members and non-Members. With the parallel (but logically preceding) achievement of the sovereign exercise of decision-making in the areas of pricing and volume of production, the sector has gone a considerable distance towards being integrated with the national economies. These economies now have the potential to translate their financial resources into capital goods and significant economic structural change through an energetic and sound development effort. . . .

Oil an an Engine of Development

One significant indicator of the intensity of the drive for development is the growing concern with development at all levels of authority and public opinion. The concern is translated most visibly and prominently into increasingly ambitious development plans and programmes of widening reach and growing sophistication. The investment programmes for the five-year period 1976–80 for all the Arab states except Djibouti reached an aggregate of $326 billion.[2] Although the actual implementation of these programmes has fallen below planned investment by some 35–40 per cent the drive is energetic. Taking private investment into account as well, since most documents show only public investment allocations or projections, total investments *actually* made may well have reached an aggregate of $300 billion for the Arab region. On average this amounts to some 20–21 per cent of GDP, or an annual investment of about $55–60 billion. This had led to an overall average rate of growth of about 6.5–7 per cent per annum.

Nevertheless, the record of growth is less meaningful than appears at first sight. For one thing it is given in terms of current prices with a high built-in inflation factor. In the second place, being an average for twenty countries and for five years, it conceals wide variations from country to country and year to year. Finally, growth is not development. The latter observation is highly relevant to the case in point.

The oil-exporting countries, examined alone, reveal higher rates of investment and growth than the other countries, and wider variation from year to year. This is partly because the main factor in the size of their GDP is oil revenue, which is subject to price and production decisions that are "autonomous". It is also partly because the investment of the less populated among them bears no steady relationship to GDP or oil revenue, in so far as they have a much larger revenue than they can soundly invest and absorb internally, given their human, physical and institutional constraints. . . .

On the positive side, the record in terms of rates of growth is confirmed by concrete achievements and is not merely a paper performance or statistical illusion, although – like all averages – it can and does conceal wide variations in growth among localities and social groups within the same country. The concreteness of the achievement is manifest in the building of physical infrastructure, factories, schools, hospitals, irrigation networks and training centres. Agriculture, however, is a black spot on the record for most countries of the region, with very modest or even negative growth in certain cases. But on the whole the actual standards of living in terms of goods and services available, and educational and health conditions, reflect what the statistics report. To the extent, therefore, that the oil sector has made possible tangible growth in the oil-producing as well as non-producing countries (though to a lesser degree in the latter), it can be said that it has indeed been much more closely integrated with the national and regional economies than in preceding decades, by serving as an engine of development. . . .

Before introducing certain qualifications to the conclusion that oil has served as an engine of development it is necessary to indicate the manner in which this has happened. Obviously, it has provided the financial resources needed for investment: but its basic contribution is what one might call its "finiteness". The realization that oil is a depleting asset, and that its life-expectancy at present rates of production is a few decades on average, has provided the dynamics for development. the oil countries saw with some suddenness in the 1970s the fatal danger of depletion without having new productive capability to replace the oil revenues now flowing in. A pattern has accordingly evolved during the decade which emphasizes education, training and health services; the acquisition of technological capability; diversification of the economy, with special attention paid to industry in general and to the refining and petrochemicals industries in particular; and the building of physical infrastructure. Obviously, the institutional framework necessary for development in these directions has also become a focus of attention, including law and order, a banking system and similar establishments. It is believed that these areas of emphasis constitute the core of the developmental capability required if the oil economies have to prepare for "life after oil". It may sound paradoxical, but it is demonstrable that to integrate an industry based on a fast-depleting asset with the national economy means preparing this economy for the disappearance of the asset that is being so energetically integrated.

Serious Gaps in Integration

How closely and well has the oil sector been integrated in the national and regional economies via the three channels of national decision-making, financial resource availability and development promotion? It will be found here that the three channels interconnect, forming a sort of "network of integration"; but examination will reveal certain wide discontinuities or gaps in this network. The major ones will now be identified. However, the sequence of identification to be adopted will differ from the sequence in which the conditions of integration have so far been examined. Thus decision-making will be left until the end, because analysis shows it to be the determining factor in the gaps in the other channels of integration.

1. The revenue-generating role of the oil sector, which has been seen to have been most beneficial in providing the financial base

for development, has three serious defects. The first is that the volume of revenues it is desired to obtain is associated with the depletion of oil. Consequently, over-eagerness to obtain large revenues well beyond the warranted requirements of the producing country is not sound economics. Financial resources are not an end in themselves, as they seem to be considered in certain instances. . . .

The large volume of financial reserves created by the inflow of oil revenues beyond national and regional requirements and resulting from the legitimate international obligations of the oil-exporting countries, is an issue worth considering in the present context. These reserves are estimated to have reached about $160 billion by the end of 1979, and are expected to reach $470 billion by 1985 on certain conservative assumptions. Inflation and depreciation of the US dollar are expected to reduce the real value of the reserves (in 1979 dollars) by 38.5 per cent by 1985.[3] The Arab countries are already losing heavily on their reserves by producing more oil than it is in their interest to produce. With the exception of two densely populated oil-exporting countries, all the others could be in a much sounder and better position if they produced about 40–50 per cent less oil than their current production volumes. This would mean a cutback of about 7–8.5 million b/d. Arab oil would then last much longer and be available for future generations and for the Arab region's own industrialization needs in the decades to come. The present production policies have serious and costly implications for the Arabs. First, they integrate their economies much more closely with those of the advanced industrialized countries, while the latter continue to pursue policies of exploitative economic hegemony and refuse to meet the Arabs and other Third World nations halfway with respect to the establishment of a New International Economic Order. Second, permissive production policies and the resultant investment of reserves in the money markets of the industrialized countries deprive Arab and other Third World countries of badly needed investment resources.

2. The second observation to make in connection with the volume of production and of oil revenues relates to the utilization of these revenues. The record of the 1970s reveals areas of over-use and misuse of financial resources, whether in the adoption of excessive consumer-oriented patterns of living, or in permissiveness in the design and costing of development works. The unsound utilization of resources is not a phenomenon encountered only in oil-exporting countries, but in almost all the countries of the region. Consumption is advancing fast under the

influence of transnational corporations and their sales promotion campaigns. These campaigns, conducted through the very effective modern mass media, create wants where none existed and transform these wants into imagined needs. They thus reverse the dictum which speaks of the "sovereignty of the consumer" into one of the "sovereignty of the giant producer".

In addition to "high consumption" (in the Rostovian terminology), which threatens to arrive before the stage of "high production" or "high development" and which leads to high importation, owing to the weak and limited productive capacity of the region, there is overspending on development projects; but more significantly the building of projects of a very low degree of urgency. . . . Misallocation, whether for consumption or investment, seriously qualifies the contention that the generation of large oil revenues enhances the process of integration.[4]

The volume of consumption and imports has to be examined further at this point. Total public and private consumption, aggregated for all the Arab countries except Djibouti and Lebanon (for which no up-to-date statistics are at hand), reached $159.7 billion for 1979 out of a GDP of $306 billion, or 52.2 per cent of GDP.[5] Apart from the very high level of consumption, and the fact that it has been rising steeply through the 1970s, three very disturbing features are observable.

The first is that per capita consumption varies sharply between oil-exporting countries and the other 12 countries, standing at $2,128 and $585 for the two groups respectively. But it represented a very high proportion of GDP for the second group, compared with the oil exporters: 89 per cent versus 41 per cent. The fact that the proportion is low for the oil-exporting countries provides only illusory comfort, considering the very high level of GDP in this group of countries. On the other hand, although the high proportion for the non-oil exporters is to be expected, considering their low GDP per capita, its actual level is nevertheless very disturbing. This level is determined by the "imitation effect" of consumerism, coupled with the availability of liquid resources. Some of these resources have been created by the earnings of Arab man power working in the oil-exporting countries and making substantial remittances to their families in the original countries. Another part represents flows from the governments of oil-exporting countries which seep through to the populations of the receiving countries.

The second disturbing feature is the heavy dependence, in satisfying the high levels of consumption, on imports, which causes a serious leakage of purchasing power to foreign economies. Imports per capita are very high in the Arab region – being the highest in the world for a few oil exporters. Furthermore, more than 93 per cent of the imports come from non-Arab countries.[6] Hence the magnitude and seriousness of the leakage. Exports, too, stand at a very high level – the highest per capita level in the Third World, obviously because of oil. Together, imports and exports constituted 88 per cent of Gross National Product (GNP) in 1978, against 60 per cent in 1970.[7]

The combined effect of high consumption and high dependence on imports to satisfy much of the consumption is a legitimate cause for concern. . . . In the present context . . . [it] poses added difficulties for the integration of the oil sector with the producing countries' economies and with the region's economy considered as a unit. The combination leads to the intensification of the region's dependence on, and integration with, the industrial economies from which most of the imports come. The large volumes of consumption and investment could together be a powerful promotive force for the building of productive capacity inside the region. This potential is to a considerable degree wasted, however.

The third disturbing feature is the heavy dependence on oil revenues for the high levels of both consumption and imports. It was stated earlier that consumption represented 52.2 per cent of aggregate GDP for the region. If oil revenues were excluded from GDP consumption would exceed GDP by 9 per cent. Of course this is an absurdity, since consumption would not then be at all near its present high level. But the exercise puts the warning regarding consumption and consumerism into strong relief. Again, to extend the exercise the imports must be considered in relation to oil revenues. Total imports for 1978, which stood at $80.5 billion, represented 26.3 per cent of GDP for 1979. If oil revenues are excluded from GDP, however, imports into the region would amount to 55 per cent of GDP. Much more seriously, imports into the oil-exporting countries by themselves for 1978 amounted to $45.9 billion, while their non-oil exports for the same year amounted to a mere $2.3 billion. Without oil these exports could finance only 5 per cent of the imports. It is as though a large proportion of oil revenue is generated in order to permit vast imports, thus further integrating the sector with the international, not the national, economy. the issue becomes all the more serious once it is remembered that most imports come from the advanced industrialized countries which, judging by their policies, seem to believe that the continued weakness of the productive capacity of the Third World is in their interest. . . .

Table 1 sums up the numerical relationships between GDP, oil, revenue, consumption and imports that have been mentioned so far.[8]

Table 1

	Arab OPEC members	Other Arab countries	Total
Population (millions), 1979	44.92	109.67	154.59
GDP ($ billion), 1979	234	62	306
Oil revenue/GDP (per cent)	64.6	12.5	52.3
Consumption ($ billion), 1979	95.6	64.1	159.7
Consumption/GDP (per cent)	41	89	52.2
Imports ($ billion), 1978	45.9	34.6	80.5

3. The third and final observation to be made in connection with the volume of oil revenues relates to the distribution of private income and wealth. The pattern of distribution reveals very large divergences between social groups, localities and countries. Substantial country differences are understandable up to a point and for a transitional period, before regional financial flows become much more substantial. For this to occur there will have to emerge a much stronger regional identification and a clearer realization that regional well-being and development are of economic value and benefit to individual countries, and not merely of emotional and political value. At the country level, development has to be so redesigned as to permit substantial narrowing of the income and wealth gaps among social groups....

4. So far the discussion has centred around the factors retarding or weakening the integration of the oil sector in the national and regional economies related to the fast increase in the oil revenues during the 1970s. It will be recalled that the generation of such revenues has been used as one criterion for the achievement of integration. Another criterion used has been the role of the sector as an engine of development, and it is to this latter role that attention will now turn.

Examination of the development process, activated and sustained to a considerable extent by the oil sector, betrays several gaps in the network of integration of the sector with the economy. Probably the most serious of these is the insufficient response of manpower in several oil-exporting countries to the challenge of the new work opportunities provided by the intensified development effort. This arises from distortions in the training and incentive systems laid down by government, as well as the weakness of motivation and pressure of certain social taboos on the workforce. Whatever the causes, however, the tolerance level for hard work has dropped in the oil era, and many categories of work are shunned by the national labour force. Consequently, certain categories of skills are not acquired by nationals. Thus, in all but two or three of the oil-exporting countries neither the types of skill required nor the volume of employment of nationals match what is called for by the needs of development. . . .

5. The slow pace of acquisition of technological capability is the second gap to consider in the role of the oil sector as an engine of development, and it is closely related to the problems in education and training. Here lies one of the most serious gaps, where integration has been glaringly defective. The problem is basically the illusion, which financial opulence creates, that the purchase of modern machines and equipment and the hiring of foreign experts and technicians amount to modernization and transfer of technological capability. No doubt there are strong pressures from the industrialized countries to make Third World states import technology rather than acquire it through "learning and doing". However, the importing countries are also to blame, equating importation with modernization and with technological capability, which is fallacious.

In their desire rapidly to modernize their economies the Arab governments have committed the mistake of thinking that there is a short-cut to the acquisition of technological capability, and that this is the importation of capital goods, patents and skills. A seriously and glaringly deficient effort has been put into the building up, at national and regional levels, of those scientific, research and experimentation, and training facilities that alone permit such an acquisition. This involves a lengthy process, but there seems to be no other sure way to the objective. The course of action now pursued leads only to the delay of actual technological transfer, to the continuation – indeed, the intensification – of dependence on the advanced industrialized countries, and to acquiescence in the dictates of the centre-countries in the international economic order and its quasi-monopolistic, giant transnational corporations. In brief, the present course makes integration with the industrialized countries closer than with the national economies. . . .

6. The next weak link in the process of integration is the

pattern of development emerging under the influence of the oil sector and the resources it generates. Four aspects of this pattern will be touched upon briefly.

(i)   The first is the slowness of the process of diversification of oil economies. Understandably, the logic of the arithmetic of sectoral structure tells us that, with the overwhelming preponderance of one sector, the other sectors must appear of minor relative importance. But this is only part of the problem. To begin with, there is the absolute size of the oil sector, whose exports and revenues are disproportionately large compared with the national and regional needs of the exporting countries, added to those international responsibilities which they are rightly called upon to shoulder. The production of oil in volumes greatly beyond the aggregate of these needs, to the point where oil exports now represent 90 per cent of all Arab exports and 99 per cent of the exports of the oil exporters alone,[9] has resulted in the generation of savings much beyond the volume of real investment at home and in the Arab region. . . .

(ii)   The second aspect of the pattern of development is the sluggish expansion of the agricultural sector, and its negative growth in some instances, as a result of the movement of manpower and investments away from it towards service sectors that have been promoted and strengthened by the oil sector and the promise of income and wealth it has generated and/or dramatized. Some of these sectors do not have a strong developmental impact: some are outright parasitic. The implications of the sluggishness of agriculture can best be realized if it is remembered that the Arab region as a whole currently imports a full half of its food requirements, and that every single Arab country is a net importer of wheat.

(iii) The insufficient care in the selection of industries to be developed is the third observation to make with respect to the pattern of development. These are not appropriately related to the assessment of basic needs, which must not be understood in a static manner but in a dynamic one, whereby more and better goods and services will be considered basic as one generation of needs after another is satisfied. Furthermore, many of the industries developed are no more than links in the international chain of industry, which reduces the degree of economic independence as more industrialization takes place, puts the national economies more firmly in the grip of the transnational corporations, and confirms the marginality of the Arab economies.

(iv) The fourth observation to make relates to the emergence of a rentier class of expanding size and influence – a class that flourishes on the fertility of its riches abroad in interest and dividends. The fact that this class also invests at home does not invalidate the point that, in effect, it promotes the integration of a sizeable part of its countries' resources with external economies, not with its national economies.

Arab Labour Migration: Arab Migrants in Kuwait

T. Farah, F. al-Salem, and M.K. al-Salem

Expatriate Labor in Kuwait: A Profile

Most less-developed countries suffer from an abundance of labour and a shortage of capital; the situation in Kuwait is uniquely reversed. Furthermore, the indigenous labour force is concentrated in the finance sector and the government bureaucracy. Approximately 76.2 per cent of Kuwaitis work in the government and 80 per cent of Kuwaitis are white-collar workers.[1]

Al Eassa identifies five factors which account for Kuwait's dependence on foreign labour:

1. The rapid growth of Kuwait's economy opened the door for employment opportunities. Along with this came a high demand for labour which the native Kuwaiti has not been able to fill. This left the majority of jobs to be filled by expatriate labour, who constitute 75 per cent of the total work force in the country. Kuwaiti manpower accounts for only 19.5 per cent of the total population (Al Eassa, 1978, p. 25).
2. The young age of the Kuwaiti population is another contributing factor to the manpower shortage – half of the Kuwaiti population is under fifteen years of age. This makes Kuwait one of the "youngest" countries in the world.
3. The high illiteracy rate among the Kuwaiti labour force is another contributing factor to the manpower shortage. Some 44.6 per cent of the Kuwaiti population is illiterate: 30 per cent of the males and 59 per cent of the females.[2]
4. Kuwaiti women's participation in the labour force is very low; their participation rate was only 3.2 per cent in 1975. Of these women, 94 per cent work in the Ministries of Education and Health.

5. Numerous Kuwaitis refuse to do any manual work because of the lack of prestige. They prefer managerial, professional, and governmental jobs which have more status (Al Eassa, 1978, p. 3).

Further "push" and "pull" factors may be isolated which help explain Kuwait's huge expatriate labour force. The single largest expatriate group in Kuwait are the Palestinians – approximately 260,000, or 20.5 per cent of the population. Their presence in Kuwait can be traced directly to the exodus following the Arab–Israeli wars. Another general factor is the high unemployment in neighbouring countries (Al Eassa, 1978, p. 56). "Pull" factors include the availability of choice consumer goods, the generous system of social benefits, the comparatively high pay scales and Kuwait's political tolerance (Al Eassa, 1978, p. 55). Foreigners have a further incentive in that Kuwait has a tax-free economic structure, which can make Kuwait a very profitable sojourn, despite its high cost of living.

The price of Kuwait's rapid development, brought about by expatriate labour, has been a population explosion which has left the Kuwaitis a minority in their own country (see Table 2).

Table 2 indicates that, after the Kuwaitis (47.5 per cent), the Palestinians and Jordanians account for the largest expatriate bloc (20.5 per cent), with Egyptians following a distant third (6.1 per cent). Between 1957 and 1970 Kuwait's population rose from 206,473 to 738,662. The latest statistical abstracts estimate the population in 1979 at 1.3 million. This figure is low, however; the Arab Organization for Crime Prevention (OACP) points out that the population was already 1.45 million in 1977, 260,000 of which were illegal immigrants whose nationalities are not identified in the report.[3] If the OACP's estimates are accurate the percentage of Kuwaitis in the population would be even less than the present official level of 47.5 per cent of the population. The high number of illegal immigrants – fully 20 per cent of the existing population – demonstrates the attraction Kuwait has for its poorer neighbours. A large number of Indians and Iranians will attempt to enter illegally when normal channels fail. Legal entry to Kuwait is by official entry permit only, with visitors' visas being issued on the invitation of a Kuwaiti. For the Iranian, Egyptian and Indian population, however, the high salaries in Kuwait are worth the risk: a guard in Kuwait may earn more than a university professor in Egypt, and a maid's salary in Kuwait can support a family of ten in India. . . .

Table 2 *Population by Sex and Nationality (1975)*

Nationality	Male	Female	Total	Percentage
				%
Kuwait	236,6000	235,4888	472,0888	47.5
Jordan and Palestine	107,770	96,408	204,178	20.5
Egypt	35,795	24,739	60,534	6.1
Iraq	26,499	18,571	45,070	4.5
Syria	24,641	16,321	40,962	4.1
Lebanon	13,208	11,568	24,776	2.5
Saudi Arabia	6,620	5,907	12,527	1.3
South Yemen	10,311	2,021	12,332	1.2
North Yemen	3,755	1.076	4,831	0.5
Oman	5,117	2,196	7,313	0.7
Other Arabs	3,709	2,955	6,664	0.7
Total Arabs	474,025	417,150	891,275	89.6
Iran	33,359	7,483	40,842	4.1
India	16,779	15,326	32,105	3.2
Pakistan	14,996	8,020	23,016	2.3
England	1,293	1,130	2,423	0.2
United States	351	343	694	0.1
Other Nationalities	2,713	1,451	4,164	0.5
Total Non-Arab	69,743	33,819	103,562	10.4
Grand Total	543,768	451,069	994,834	100.0

Source: State of Kuwait, Ministry of Planning, Central Statistical Office, *Annual Statistical Abstract, 1976*, table 17.

Government projections indicate that the dependence on expatriate labour will continue into the 1980s: Kuwaitis will number only 29.1 per cent of the labour force then (see Table 3).

Although the government characterizes foreign labour in Kuwait as transient (Moubarak, 1979, p. 135) the average stay is 5.8 years for Arabs and 5.3 years for non-Arabs (see Table 4). In the government civil service the ranks differ, with Lebanese staying for the longest period of time (12.3 years) and the Egyptians the shortest time (4.4 years).[4]

Table 3 *Population and Labour Force in 1980-1 (in thousands)*

	Kuwaiti			Non-Kuwaiti			Total	
	Male	Female	Total	Male	Female	Total	Male	Female
Population	32.1	323.7	648.8	408.0	364.5	773.4	733.1	689.1
Labour force	109.5	10.1	119.6	244.7	47.9	292.6	354.2	58.0

Source: State of Kuwait, Ministry of Planning, *The Five Year Plan 1977-81.*

In general, government civil servants stay longer than the average for the total labour force.

Expatriates in the Administration of Kuwait

Kuwait is vulnerable in its dependence on expatriate labour. Whereas on the highest managerial levels, 93 per cent of the labor force is Kuwaiti (as required by law), the remaining managerial levels are staffed by non-Kuwaitis. In 1972, 72 per cent of professional and technical workers in the civil service were non-Kuwaitis; in 1976, 68 per cent were non-Kuwaiti. Even with a stated policy of Kuwaitization of the labour force the decline in foreign manpower was only 4 per cent. Interestingly, Kuwaitis are outnumbered by foreigners (approximately 1:2, respectively) in almost all categories of labour, which reflects to some degree their relative population proportions. However in the "clerical and related fields" category, Kuwaitis outnumber expatriates, 14,181 to 7,074, roughly double, which bears no relation at all to the relative population proportions. These statistics reveal that Kuwaitis have come to expect jobs in the bureaucracy (Moubarak, 1979, p. 130). Thus, since the government guarantees Kuwaitis jobs, posts of a bureaucratic nature are created to absorb the Kuwaiti labour force. Unfortunately the posts created are often staffed by unqualified people; it has been estimated that 55 per cent of the civil servants do not have the educational qualifications for their jobs.[5]. . .

Vital services are manned almost exclusively by expatriates. Kuwaitis are barely represented in blue-collar occupations: out of 317 painters listed in 1976 only 13 were Kuwaiti, and out of 2,188 construction workers (bricklayers, carpenters, etc.) only 384 were

Table 4   *Foreign Labour Force and Median Stay by Nationality*

Rank	Nationality	Median stay by years
1	Gulf emigrants	7.9
2	Saudi Arabia	7.4
3	Lebanon	6.9
4	Iraq	6.6
5	Pakistan	6.5
6	Oman	6.3
7	Yemen Arab Republic	5.7
8	Jordan and Palestine	5.7
9	India	5.4
10	United Kingdom	5.2
11	Syria	5.0
12	Iran	4.8
13	South Yemen	4.7
14	Egypt	3.6
15	Western European countries	2.6
	Total Arab countries	5.8
	Total Non-Arab countries	5.3
	Grand Total	5.7

Source: M. S. Al Akhrass, *The Study of Labour Force Residency* (Kuwait: The Arab Planning Institute, 1976).

Kuwaiti. Kuwaitis prefer to work for the government; benefits are better than in the private sector, even though the salaries may be higher there. Promotion in the civil service is almost guaranteed, as are social security benefits upon retirement. Furthermore, the private sector works longer hours and can dismiss incompetent employees.

Expatriates dominate the labour force in the private sector to an even greater degree than in the government, because the private sector demands profit and performance. While the actual number of employees in the private sector is slightly higher than in the government sector (169,397 to 129,018), these figures are misleading. It is common practice for a government employee to hold another job in the private sector, either self-employed or in a business concern, in the afternoon, since all government agencies close around 2.00 p.m. Thus, the private sector figure may represent the same employee counted twice. This practice is widespread in spite of the fact that legally a government employee may not hold an outside job.

Excluding the self-employed Kuwaitis, there are few who are willing to work their way up in a company. As an expatriate banker remarked: "Most expect immediate promotion for minimal performance." Furthermore, Kuwaitis traditionally dislike working for another Kuwaiti, in the sense of being "bossed" by a peer.

In the private sector, companies may be run almost exclusively by expatriate staff. The percentage of expatriates in six selected companies varies between 98.2 per cent to 83.2 per cent, with an average of 93.6 per cent expatriate staff. Family-owned business concerns are estimated to have an even larger proportion of expatriate labour – approximately 95 per cent. In the banking sector there are five Kuwaiti general managers among the twelve banks in Kuwait. In the Commercial Bank, 91 per cent of the employees are expatriates; top management, outside of the Kuwaiti board, is American.

Table 5 *Employment at Government and Private Level by Nationality Census 1975*

Nationality	Percent distribution			Government%	No. of employees		
	Total	Private	Government		Total	Private	Government
Kuwait	29.2	12.1	51.4	76.2	86,971	20,736	66,235
Iraq	6.0	7.7	3.8	27.5	17,999	13,053	4,946
Saudi Arabia	0.9	0.9	0.9	43.6	2,644	1,490	1,154
Jordan and Palestine	16.0	16.1	15.8	42.8	47,653	27,261	20,392
Egypt and	12.6	11.7	13.8	47.3	37,558	19,800	17,758
Syria	5.5	7.7	2.7	21.2	16,548	13,044	3,504
Lebanon and	2.4	3.4	1.1	19.6	7,232	5,814	1,418
Yemen (N. and S.)	3.8	4.4	3.1	35.3	11,415	7,390	4,025
Arab Gulf	1.5	1.2	1.8	52.6	4,444	2,108	2,336
Other Arabs	0.4	0.6	0.2	19.8	1,225	983	242
Iran	9.7	16.0	1.4	6.4	28,933	27,094	1,839
India	7.2	11.1	2.0	12.1	21,475	18,873	2,602
Pakistan	3.7	5.7	1.1	12.9	11,038	9,609	1,429
Others	1.1	1.3	0.9	34.7	3,280	2,142	1,138
Total	100.0	100.0	100.0	43.2	298,415	169,397	129,018

Source: State of Kuwait, Ministry of Planning, Central Statistical Office, *Annual Statistical Abstract, 1978* p. 124.

Whereas 76 per cent of the Kuwaitis work for the government (see Table 5) even some of the ministries are dominated by expatriates. An examination of the government sector reveals the following:[6]

Ministry of Foreign Affairs	76.4% Kuwaiti	23.6% expatriate
Ministry of Housing	66.0% Kuwaiti	34.0% expatriate
Ministry of Information	52.4% Kuwaiti	47.6% expatriate
Ministry of Interior	50.0% Kuwaiti	50.0% expatriate
Ministry of Justice	46.2% Kuwaiti	53.8% expatriate
Ministry of Education	41.2% Kuwaiti	58.8% expatriate
Ministry of Religious Affairs	35.3% Kuwaiti	64.7% expatriate
Ministry of Defence	33.9% Kuwaiti	66.1% expatriate
Ministry of Health	29.1% Kuwaiti	70.9% expatriate
Ministry of Oil (as of 1976, prior to nationalization)	3.0% Kuwaiti	97.0% expatriate

From these statistics one can observe that Kuwait depends on expatriates for its judges, doctors, teachers, journalists and soldiers, as well as its business managers and bankers. Clearly the role of the expatriates in Kuwait's administration is formidable. Even the most vital aspect of Kuwait's economy, oil, was virtually controlled by expatriates prior to nationalization. Today, Kuwaitis are still a minority in the ministry, although they account for 22.6 per cent of the labour force in the actual oil industry. Al Eassa suggests that the low percentage of Kuwaitis in the oil industry was the deliberate result of the oil companies' policies. It was against their interest to train Kuwaitis because the Kuwaitis would then want to take over (Al Eassa, 1978, p. 32) . . .

The Problem of Citizenship

Because foreign labour plays such an important and potentially disruptive role in the administration of the country, Kuwait has laid down stringent rules regarding residency in Kuwait. Since 1967, when state security started determining immigration policy rather than supply and demand factors, good conduct certificates have been required for entry to Kuwait (Moubarak, 1979, p. 139). Good conduct certificates are also required by Kuwait prior to assuming a job. . . .

There is no principle of equal pay for equal work and there is a policy of granting benefits according to citizenship rather than merit. Citizenship itself is very difficult to obtain.

To begin with, the Kuwaiti government, in the interests of security and the good will of its citizens, has the stated goals of promoting an equitable distribution of income among the Kuwaiti population and of Kuwaitizing the labour force wherever possible (Al Eassa, 1978, p. 30). The latter objective does not seem to be succeeding, even though in most cases, Kuwaitis have priority in employment and promotions. Since there are so few Kuwaitis in the labour force, there is competition for them (in the form of high salaries and rapid advancement) among the various economic sectors trying to Kuwaitize.

These policies have created strong support for the government among the Kuwaitis and achieved a remarkable level of political stability in the country. That Kuwait is good to her citizens is without a doubt. By contrast, expatriates, in general,

1. do not receive retirement benefits, but rather a severance payment equal to one month's salary for each year employed;
2. are not entitled to own land or houses, but must rent from Kuwaitis;
3. cannot own businesses without a Kuwaiti partner;
4. do not have job security and can be fired with one month's notice;
5. do not enjoy subsidized housing; and
6. may not practise certain professions (law) or run for public office.

All residents of Kuwait enjoy free medical care; free education, subsidized food, water, and electricity; and tax-free earnings. The problem with this largesse, however, is that is such a demand for medical care and education that the supply threatens to run out and the quality has deteriorated. And while these welfare benefits are extremely favourable to the expatriates, the expatriates compare themselves to the Kuwaitis and realize that they are in a less-privileged position.

In most cases a Kuwaiti is paid more than an expatriate for doing the same kind of work. In some cases a Kuwaiti will earn more even if he is less qualified than the expatriate. Al Eassa cites the following example:

A Kuwaiti school guard will often have a monthly salary three times higher than an Arab high school teacher who teaches 48 hours per week (KD 285 ($696) as opposed to KD 91 ($309) respectively). Further, the Kuwaiti guards usually are illiterate, while the foreign teacher must have a B.A. or B.S. degree to teach in Kuwait (Al Eassa, 1978, p. 75)

On the other hand, it is also true that the top expatriate managers (qualified Kuwaitis being relatively few) enjoy significant benefits in addition to their tax-free salaries. Top-level Western expatriates and highly qualified Arab professionals can command perks such as housing, the cost of which can equal the salary itself; cars; entertainment allowances; paid rest and recreation leaves abroad; and air freight privileges.

Kuwait University is another prominent exception to the rule of Kuwaitis first. Foreign faculty members are granted higher rank and salaries upon acceptance at the university, in addition to housing and airline tickets for the families every summer.

Because Kuwaitis are outnumbered, the government protects them legally with what expatriates feel are unfair advantages, such as the exclusive Kuwaiti right to own businesses.

Expatriates cannot legally engage in business without a Kuwaiti partner or sponsor, called a *kafeel*. The *al kafala* system was cre. ted to minimize competition of foreign entrepreneurs with the Kuwaiti merchant class. Surprisingly, among the businessmen interviewed, none appeared to object to this system of *al kafala*.

But the expatriate businessmen are not the only ones exploited by this system. It is the people on the lower end of the economic and social ladder. In many cases it is the Indian or Pakistani drivers, cooks or housemaids. Al Eassa explains:

The *Kafeel* system is frequently abused by the merchant or employer. For example, if a Kuwaiti national is interested in an Indian or Pakistani cook or driver, he initially contacts the Indian/Pakistani community and correspondence is then established to find such a person. After agreement of a salary, the Kuwaiti employer agrees to pay for the travel allowance. When the prospective employee arrives in Kuwait, he or she is *obliged* to remain in the service of that person up to the time agreed upon his or her contract, which is normally two years. In certain ways, this system is similar to 'indentured servitude', since the employed person is forced by law to remain with his employer, regardless of the particular working conditions he is confronted with. In other words, the employee is prevented legally from seeking other employment (Al Eassa, 1978, pp. 76–7).

A new regultion recently issued by the Ministry of the Interior states the following in Article 3 concerning the private servant: "If the servant leaves his employer before the expiration of the contract, the residency permit will not be given to him unless his employer agrees to it . . .[7] Therefore, if foreigners do not have a residency permit or a job, they are subject to immediate deportation.

Expatriate labour cannot form trade unions. However, the law allows expatriates to join Kuwaiti trade unions after working for five years in one job. But expatriates are not allowed to vote or to run for office in the union.[8] This in itself is not as discriminatory as it seems, for trade unionism in this part of the world is still unimportant or else used as an instrument of the state (Beling, 1960, p. 5). Yet, even though the expatriates are not unionized, occasionally they go on strike.

Certain jobs in Kuwait are limited to Kuwaitis only. For example, a non-Kuwaiti lawyer cannot defend a client in court without special permission from the Minister of Justice. If the permission is granted, the non-Kuwaiti lawyer needs to be accompanied by a Kuwaiti lawyer who is a member of the Kuwaiti Lawyers' Association.[9]

While co-operative markets are open to everyone, expatriates cannot buy shares in these co-operatives or in the Kuwaiti stockmarkets. As a result the profits are divided among the Kuwaiti shareholders only, despite the fact that the majority of customers are non-Kuwaitis (Al Eassa, 1978, p. 96).

In the housing sector a clear distinction exists between the Kuwaitis and the expatriates. Expatriates cannot own real estate. As the *Financial Times* describes it:

> Foreigners cannot own land or speculate. Arab nationals may, by law, own their own homes and a surrounding plot no bigger than 1,000 square metres but may not rent them or speculate with them. However, in practice, they find their way through red tape to do so. If successful, they probably could not afford the incredible land prices. Foreigners are therefore forced on to the local market for housing where rents are of astronomical degree. Kuwaitis on the other hand can buy Government-built houses for as little as $27 a month.[10]

In education, more distinctions are evident between Kuwaitis and non-Kuwaitis. Education in Kuwait used to be free for every child. However, during the last decade the public educational system has become overloaded. As a result the government admits the children of Kuwaiti citizens to public schools on a priority basis. The demand is so great that classes operate in three shifts, with Palestinian children attending afternoon sessions. Children of expatriates who are not admitted to public schools attend private ones, which can be very costly.[11]

In other words there is discrimination against non-Kuwaitis. Yet Kuwaiti citizenship is particularly hard to obtain. First-category citizenship includes the theoretical right to vote for literate males if their ancestors were residents of Kuwait by 1920. As Article 1 of Nationality Laws states: "The Kuwaitis are basically those people who inhabited Kuwait before 1920 and have continued to reside there until the date of publication of this law."[12]

Naturalization requirements have changed several times. Much has been made over Kuwait's "second-class" citizenship, which is an unfortunate translation of the Arabic. The more accurate translation is "second category". The only distinction between first- and second-category citizenship is the right to run for public office: however, there being no parliament to run for [in 1980], the distinction is purely academic. It should be noted that suffrage does *not* extend to women of either category (Al Eassa, 1978, p. 27).

In 1960 the Naturalization Law was amended to include Arabs of ten years' residence and non-Arabs of fifteen years' continuance residence. In 1966 the law was amended to grant citizenship to Arabs residing in Kuwait since 1945 and to non-Arabs residing since 1930. The power to confer citizenship lies with the minister of the interior. It is *not* granted merely for fulfilling residency requirements; one must have entered the country legally and prove good conduct.

Article 4 of the law presents many problem, in stating that only fifty people may be naturalized each year. This issue is neatly sidestepped in Article 5, which grants the minister the authority to naturalize any person who has served Kuwait well.[13]

Citizenship is further granted to women married to Kuwaitis, after one to five years of marriage. However, Kuwaiti women married to foreign men, a rare occurrence, cannot convey their citizenship to them. Only 13,570 non-Kuwaitis were naturalized between 1961 and 1973. Yet in the period 1965–70 48,000 Bedouins immigranted to Kuwait, mainly from Saudia Arabia; "contrary to the recommendations of the Planning Board, 81% of them were granted citizenship" (Moubarak, 1979, p. 145). Thus, Bedouins were naturalized at a rate approximately three times higher than other groups. One unexpected result of the government's actions was that the literacy rate actually declined for 1965 due to the number of illiterate Bedouins naturalized. After 1965 mostly women were naturalized, probably wives of Kuwaitis; the largest group were Iraqi, followed by Persians and "other nationalities".

Economic and Cultural Dependence

G. A. Amin

I. Social Welfare and the Westernization of the Third World

So far, I have been trying to argue that: (1) a heavy reliance of a poor country on foreign aid and foreign investment must inevitably lead to an accentuation of economic and social dualism in its society; (2) the adoption of "the elimination of the gap between developed and underdeveloped countries" as a goal for poor societies merely helps to bring about the same result; and (3) the real function of such interaction between the poor and rich countries of the world is to integrate the former countries into the Western economic and value systems.

I would now argue that it is highly questionable that such interaction can bring to the countries of the Third World a significant increase in welfare, even to those who are most able to afford Western consumption levels. Indeed, it may be argued that the more late a poor society is in embarking on westernization the greater is the danger of dualism within it, the more insignificant is the gain in welfare realized even by its higher-income groups, and the greater is the danger of its losing its cultural identity in the process.

As developed countries further increase their productive capacity they tend to produce goods and services which get progressively more trivial, but not less costly, even to the consumer of the developed countries themselves. Some eighty years ago, Thorstein Veblen wrote:

> As increased industrial efficiency makes it possible to procure the means of livelihood with less labour, the energies of the industrious members of the community are bent to the compassing of a higher result in conspicuous expenditure, rather than slackened to a more comfortable pace. The strain is not lightened as industrial efficiency increases and makes a higher strain possible, but the increment of output is turned to use to meet this want, which is indefinitely expansible, after the manner commonly imputed in economic theory to higher or spiritual wants. It is owing chiefly to the presence of this element in the standard of living that J. S. Mill

was able to say: "hitherto it is questionable if all the mechanical inventions yet made have lightened the day's toil of any human being" (Veblen, 1959).

This tendency towards the production of increasingly trivial or, in the words of Mishan (1974), 'demerit' goods may not be as harmful in its impact on distribution and social welfare within a developed country as it is in a poor society. Because these goods originate in the developed countries themselves, their prices are usually more compatible with the average per capita incomes in these countries. With the help of a little persuasion and sales-promotion campaign (though with great risk of further accentuating income inequality) a sufficiently wide market within these countries can be found for these goods, however trivial they may be. In a poor society, however, where the prices of such goods are out of proportion with the country's average income, and where the cultural milieu conducive to their consumption is largely absent, the successful marketing of such goods inevitably causes both greater income inequality and greater cultural dualism. Again, however trivial such goods may be, a consumer who belongs to the same culture where they originate can probably derive a greater satisfaction from them than an "under-developed" consumer (except perhaps the satisfaction due to their use as status symbols). If, in an affluent society, the production of such goods and services as electric shavers and electric toothbrushes, water-proof and shock-proof watches, instant cameras, instant coffee or birthday cards, midday papers or late-night news bulletins may seem no more than a waste of resources (which could have been directed to more useful goods and services) the introduction of such items into a poor society, before essential needs are met, may be regarded as comic or tragic according to one's inclination.

There are other goods which may fulfil useful functions in the countries of their origin, but which in a poor society fulfil no useful function whatever. Obvious examples are computers introduced into a society where there is neither sufficiently reliable data to process, nor even a need for a high degree of precise information; feasibility studies to evaluate projects which simple common sense is sufficient to judge whether they are obviously necessary or utterly useless; and a modern army, expensively equipped, when there is no war to fight.

There are still other goods which, although usually regarded as items of final consumption, are really part of the cost of living in an affluent society. High-speed motor-cars may be so regarded if the car-owning employee is obliged daily to travel long distances to and from work, and so may some household labour-saving devices which are often a condition for allowing the housewife to have a job outside the home. Such goods make little sense in a poor society where the distances one is obliged to travel are often short, and where most housewives have no outside jobs.

A good part of the output of an affluent society consists of goods that are neither consumer goods nor producer goods, but simply a means of consumption. With increasing affluence, not only production but also consumption becomes more and more "roundabout", and a large part of advertising and sales-promotion effort consists of attempts to convince the consumer that such articles are really necessary for consumption. Electric peelers and kitchen gadgets of all sorts, lighters, food-catering outside the house, TV dinner trays, etc., are all examples of goods and services that do not satisfy new needs, but are simply new ways of satisfying old ones, unless we follow the modern economist in equating the desire for any good with genuine human satisfaction. Little wonder that the pleasure of acquiring such items often vanishes as soon as they are acquired.

Much of what appears to be an increase in output, and is therefore regarded as an increase in welfare, is really an exchange of one basket of goods and services for another. Much of modern sport, for instance, which often requires costly equipment, is merely a substitute for normal physical activity which is naturally done at no cost in a less sedentary way of life. Television programmes are a substitute (and many may regard them as a poor one) for direct human contact.[1] If, in an affluent society, such exchange of baskets may be regarded by some as harmless (although others may regret the passing of old ways), in a westernizing society the exchange, worthless as it is, involves no less than cultural suicide.

So many of Western novelties can become sources of satisfaction only in a society which has become as highly individualistic, permissive and competitive as modern Western society. If a society attaches much value, for instance, to strong family ties, to the presevation of the relationship between grandparents, their children and their grandchildren, there would be little need for all kinds of goods and services that supply the young with separate homes, or alleviate their feelings of loneliness. Similarly, a non-permissive society, with little pressure from its members to satisfy every whim and desire, which does not accept the tenet that "a thing is good if you like it", will neither need nor desire the multiplicity of goods that cater for every possible caprice. Nor does every society attach a high value to rapidity of change or to speedy movement. Stability and continuity and a slow tempo of life may be given a high rank in a society's scale of values. Continuous changes of fashion and the introduction of high-speed means of transport may therefore fail to have any positive impact on social welfare and may even reduce it, unless the society's value system is itself changed accordingly. To be able to "enjoy" such goods the society has to give up its established values and traditions; to introduce these goods before these values are abandoned helps to accelerate the process of disintegration.

The same could be said of the welfare effect of a large number of goods and services on two societies having different values and outlooks with regard to material possessions, sources of security and social status, attitude of man to god and nature, "proper" way of bringing up children, or with regard to the relative importance of immediate as compared to delayed gratification and to reducing the burden of physical labour as compared to the reduction of psychological tensions of a mechanical civilization.

So much biting criticism has been made of the way of life of modern Western society, of its "mistaken" assumption that there is no limit to what man could, in his own interest, consume, of its virtually equating "more" with "better", and of the tendency to regard what is possible as necessarily desirable. What I am trying to argue, however, is not that these criticisms are justified (although I do believe they are), but merely that the adoption of such values, assumptions and mental attitudes, though of doubtful worth and validity, is a precondition for the "enjoyment" of much of Western material output. But if this is true, there can be no way of telling whether there is a net gain in the welfare of a westernizing society as a result of its accepting the Western basket of both material output and value system. And if we cannot be sure of this, it seems highly "uneconomic" exercise to put so much effort in trying to bring this transaction into effect.

It is ironic that Western economists, while regarding as illegitimate the interpersonal comparison of welfare, and thus denying the possibility of judging whether the loss of welfare to one person is more or less than the gain to another resulting from income redistribution, are nevertheless ready to advise a so-called underdeveloped country to bring a Western basket of commodities that tears apart the whole pattern of their way of life, taking for granted that its welfare is thereby increased. The error lies, of course, in ignoring the fact that a westernizing society is changing its "taste" in the process, and once a change in taste is allowed, there is no way of ascertaining if the "new" society is better off. . . .

II. Economic Co-operation or Economic Isolation?

Some 150 years ago the German economist Freidrich List, protesting against the English Classical economists who were preaching free trade, taught Germany that economic interaction between two unequal parties must benefit one of them at the expense of the other. Such "co-operation" may indeed be in the interest of an abstract entity called "the world economy", but not in the interest of the weaker partner in the relationship.

Now the UN Declaration is again singing praises of economic co-operation among all countries, irrespective of their economic and social conditions:

> The interests of the developed countries and those of developing countries can no longer be isolated from each other . . . there is close interrelationship between the prosperity of the developed coun-tries and the growth and development of the developing countries, and . . . the prosperity of the international community as a whole depends upon the prosperity of its constituent parts. International cooperation for development is the shared goal and common duty of all countries.[2]

Here, we believe, is a new example of how the poorer countries are being continuously taught lessons which are irrelevant and premature. Just as they have been taught the value of capital-intensive technology before their labour has become scarce, taught how to reduce mortality rates long before their birth rates could be reduced, they are now being taught the value of internationalism before they achieve national economic and social integration.

Rather than sing praises of co-operation and interdependence Third World Countries would be better advised to follow a policy of isolation, however shocking this may sound to those who have become too accustomed to the language of internationalism with which we are being continuously bombarded. "All the great nations have been prepared in privacy and in secret", wrote Walter Bagehot, "They have been composed away from all distraction".[3]

The three examples of Japan, Russia and present-day China indicate most clearly how a prolonged period of self-imposed isolation is a favourable factor, not a hindrance, not only in achieving balanced economic development but, more important, in allowing a nation to make a distinct contribution to civilization. . . . But even among today's less-developed countries, many have passed through periods of successful industrialization, which coincided, not with the adoption of liberal policies, but with involuntary isolation. This is as true of the experience of many Latin American countries – such as Argentina, Brazil, Mexico and Chile during the two World Wars and the interwar period – as it is of such Arab countries as Egypt, Syria and Iraq. The beginning of successful industrialization in these countries occurred, not when they depended upon foreign imports or foreign aid, but, on the contrary, when both were virtually impossible to come by. These, it may be noted, were periods, not of "prosperity in the developed countries", but of economic difficulties in the West and of the Great Depression.

The main point is, not that in all these examples it was the domestic market rather than foreign trade which constituted the main engine of growth, although this was also true, but that development was more balanced and less lop-sided than when rapid growth relied heavily on foreign trade, foreign investment and foreign aid.

But if this is true of the past, it is likely to be even more true of the present and the future. In other words the later in point of time is a country's commencement of the attempt to achieve a balanced and equitable development along with cultural revival the more necessary it is for it to pass through a period of economic isolation. This is so, not merely because savings and investment become more difficult to mobilize as a result of the "demonstration effect", but because the greater the gap in the levels of income and ways of life between different societies, the greater the pressure on the poorer of these societies to develop a dualistic pattern of growth. Mere growth of output may be easier to engineer for a country that starts raising its average income rather late. This has been proved by the experience of the Third World over the last two decades. A lop-sided growth, inegalitarian distribution, and cultural disintegraton become very difficult to avoid with time, unless the country is insulated from foreign pressure.

By economic isolation we certainly do not mean permanent isolation but a temporary, even if prolonged, period of isolation which would last until the country could compete economically and culturally with more integrated societies. The infant-industry argument should indeed be extended not only to cover the whole economy, but also the cultural as much as economic life. Nor does this policy imply a complete boycott of foreign trade and development strategy, just as we have suggested with regard to foreign aid, so that we can have our development goals determine, instead of being determined by, the pattern of foreign trade. As Mahbub Ul Haq (1973) puts it:

> Trade should not be regarded as a pace setter in any relevant strategy for the developing world, but merely as a derivative. Developing countries should first define a viable strategy for attacking their problems of unemployment and mass poverty. Trade possibilities should be geared to the objectives of such a strategy.

What the UN Declaration states about the need to establish "just and equitable relationship" between the prices of developing countries" exports and the prices of their imports "with the aim of bringing about sustained improvement in their unsatisfactory terms of trade and the expansion of world economy" is, of course, welcome, but only in so far as our goal is modest enough to make us satisfied with a small improvement in the terms of a transaction the very establishment of which is objectionable.

The real difference between the Old International Economic Order and the New can therefore be seen as little more than the difference between selling cheap and selling dear. To those who reject the whole transaction of buying and selling, not merely as unjust but as dehabilitating, it matters little what price is being offered. An alternative analogy is that of the difference between a race in which two competing but unequal parties are unjustly required to start from the same point, and another race in which the weaker party is given the advantage of starting a few steps ahead. We are inclined to reject the whole race as wasting the energies of the weaker party in an unworthy pursuit.

The International Communications System

R. Williams

In the whole non-communist world the determining factor in broadcasting development, since the 1950s, has been the expansion of the American communications system. This has to be understood in two related stages: the formation, in the United States, of a complex military, political and industrial communications system; and then, in direct relation to this, the operation of this system to penetrate the broadcasting systems of all other available states.[*]

There has been a close relation in the United States, since the Second World War, between military and political communications research and development, and what is still thought of in a separate way as general broadcasting. There has been continual interaction between governmental investment in new communications and electronic techniques and the general development of broadcasting facilities: the case of television satellite broadcasting . . . is only the most spectacular. During the 1950s and 1960s the institutional framework of broadcasting became very complicated, with an uncertain frontier between military and political and general institutions. Thus the Interdepartment Radio Advisory Committee, concerned with the allocation of frequencies, moved from civilian to military control, and this emphasis was extended into international negotiations. In the early 1960s a National Communications System, with a directorate of telecommunications, was established for direct governmental purposes, but had some effect on the development of general broadcasting. The overlap of procurement between state and network agencies, and the ties between general electronic and broadcasting corporations (e.g. the Radio Corporation of America, which is an electronics manufacturer as well as the owner of one of the three main networks, the National Broadcasting Corporation), led to a situation in which it was not possible to separate, into distinct categories, military electronics, government agencies concerned

* I am especially indebted . . . to Herbert I. Schiller, *Mass Communications and American Empire* (New York: Kelley, 1969).

with information and propaganda, and the most visible institutions of general "commercial" broadcasting. From this it was only a short but deliberate step to the operation of this network on an international scale, over a range from space communications and communication satellites to the planned export of propaganda, information and entertainment broadcasting. Thus the Department of Defence has a world-wide network of thirty-eight television and over two hundred radio transmitters, and the great majority of its audience is non-American. The United States Information Agency has transmitters and prepares programmes for use in foreign countries: many of these programmes are not identified, when shown on foreign American-controlled or American-sponsored stations, as USIA-originated. In quantity this direct governmental intervention beyond its frontiers is overshadowed by the dynamic export policies of the broadcasting corporations, over a range from equipment and management to programme sales. In more than ninety foreign countries, the three leading corporations have subsidiaries, stations and networking contracts; they are particularly strong in Latin America, the Caribbean, Africa, Asia, and the Middle East. From this base there is continual pressure, some of it already successful, to penetrate societies with developed broadcasting systems, in which various forms of local governmental control have prevented ordinary expansion. This pressure has included arrangements with local groups seeking commercial broadcasting, often requiring a change of national law. In a number of cases, including some planned "pirate" broadcasting – often represented in local terms as a few small independent operators against the local state monopoly – the planning and finance have come from the United States. Much of this penetration is seen only in terms of the sale of programmes, which is indeed important, representing the difference between profit and loss for all US telefilm production, and already, in some countries, accounting for a significant and in some cases a major part of all television programming. But the expansion has to be seen also as serving the international advertiser, for in a trading world dominated by para-national companies and US subsidiaries the provision of programmes and types of service which open the way to international commercial advertising has this inevitable perspective. The "commercial" character of television has then to be seen at several levels: as the making of programmes for profit in a known market; as a channel for advertising; and as a cultural and political form directly shaped by and dependent on the norms of a capitalist society, selling both consumer goods and a "way of life" based on them, in an ethos that is at once locally generated, by domestic capitalist interests and authorities, and internationally organised, as a political project, by the dominant capitalist power. It is then not too much to say that the general transition, in the last twenty years, from what was normally a national and state-controlled sound broadcasting to what are now, in world terms, predominantly commercial television institutions, is a consequence of this planned operation from the United States. What surfaces in one country after another is a local argument, and is quickly and persuasively described as a choice between "state monopoly" and "independent broadcasting", is in the overwhelming majority of cases a put-up job by these American interests, their local associates and the powerful international advertising companies.

The terms of the older argument about broadcasting institutions are then not only inadequate but sometimes positively misleading. In the developing world old films and television programmes are in effect dumped, at prices which make any local production seem ludicrously expensive by comparison. A market is then created in which available entertainment, advertising and general political and cultural influence come in a single "cheap" package. In developed countries, including those in which primary television production is at a higher level than in the United States itself, the graded export price is still favourable competitive with primary national production, and the degree of dependence on advertising revenue, within a broadcasting institution, tends to settle how far the door will be opened to this kind of commercial penetration. Where any particular nation holds out there are internal campaigns for a change of policy, in which local branches of the international advertising agencies are heavily involved, and, as has been noted, there are planned frontier stations and pirate transmitters, aiming to "capture" domestic audiences. Even in Britain, where another tradition was strong, the campaigns to commercialize both television and radio have eventually succeeded, at least in part. In many other countries and especially in small and medium-scale societies which find a primary-producing television service expensive, the effective penetration is now virtually complete.

It is then in this precise context that new and very powerful technical means are being introduced: especially satellite television transmission. It is clear that in some societies, with established national traditions and institutions in modern broadcasting, certain controls against the global commercialization of television have some chance of success. But throughout the monopoly-capitalist period of communications institutions it has been evident that the level of viability, the scale-mark of independent survival, rises continuously, and at times dramatically, as the general market is extended. Just as a nineteenth-century popular newspaper, in Britain, could survive and flourish with a circulation of 100,000 but is now in danger with anything less than 2,000,000 so a television service, in conditions of uncontrolled and therefore unequal competition, may pass very quickly from healthy viability to chronic financial crisis. It may then, if nothing else is done, either surrender to the general trend or, more subtly, change itself internally to survive within the trend: a change which will have its clear origins in the general pressures but which will usually be rationalised as some form of independent "modernization".

Military Dependency: The Egyptian Case

Salah al-Din Hadidi

The Egyptian armed forces' association with the Eastern bloc began in the second half of 1955 when the first batch of weapons coming from Czechoslovakia reached the harbour of Alexandria amidst great secrecy and [stringent] security measures. This was followed by further shipments of weapons which were immediately distributed among the various units of the Egyptian armed forces in replacement of the British weapons with which the armed forces had until then been equipped: thus did Egypt sever a connection with British armament which went back to the 1882 occupation. There is no doubt that the first batch of weapons from Czechoslovakia came as a result of the Bandung Conference which was attended by an Egyptian delegation headed by the late President Nasser, who met with many world leaders, and among them most of the leaders of the socialist countries.

Military equipment was indispensable to the modern state to which the 23 July Revolution had given birth; and, following Egypt's unsuccessful attempts at buying weapons from the USA, the only way left was to bypass all traditional sources of supply. And this is precisely what happened in 1955 – a political, military and mental turning-point in Egyptian history as time was to prove. The arrival of the first shipment of arms from Czechoslovakia met with great joy from the military circles, who applauded the political leadership's successful breaking of [the West's] monopoly on arm supplies, irrespective of the nature and identity of the new source of supply.

The Egyptian armed forces began taking delivery of the new equipment and reorganizing themselves on the basis of the weapons that had already reached Egypt, as well as on the basis of the weapons which were expected to arrive in the near future. No effort was spared to integrate the new equipment and to train the units in its use. The reorganization had to be effected rapidly because of the prevailing circumstances and of the armed forces' need to remain on constant alert in view of the Israeli threat.

It was natural that Israel should feel increasingly apprehensive as regards the equipment of the Egyptian armed forces with new and modern weapons, and as regards Egypt's successful breaking of the West's monopoly on arms supplies. Israel realized that the

65

time factor would be determining, for the longer Israel refrained from striking at Egypt and destroying its armed forces the better would these forces' chances be of integrating the new military equipment and digesting it in view of its successful use. Having reached this logical conclusion Israel then awaited the political opportunity and the international situation propitious for dealing a lethal blow to the Egyptian armed forces. This golden opportunity came in the aftermath of the nationalization of the Suez Canal on 26 July 1956. Israel jumped on the Franco-British bandwagon, as General Dayan put it in his memoirs on the Sinai War, and the aggression on Egypt became a tripartite one.

The first shipment of modern military equipment – a shipment which included T34 tanks and MIG fighter-bombers – arrived in Egypt unaccompanied by experts from the Eastern bloc who would help the Egyptian armed forces to comprehend the new weapons and become familiar with them. The first batch arrived with booklets and instruction manuals translated into English, yet it should be added that a limited number of Czechoslovakian navy and air force experts did come to Egypt. The various military academies spared no effort in trying to come to terms with the new equipment in its most intricate details (engineering, maintenance, etc.) since a proper knowledge of the weapons was necessary to ensure optimum usage.

I should add, here, that the idea of integrating Soviet experts and using them on a large scale in the Egyptian armed forces, and the adherence to what we used to call the Eastern military tactics and organization, only came to the mind of the leadership in the aftermath of the (1956) tripartite aggression. In view of the tremendous losses in military equipment incurred by Egypt as a result of the intervention of the French and British air force, and in view of the unambiguous enmity towards Egypt which was expressed in the West – and by West I also mean the USA, whose political aims, in the final analysis, were the same as those of France and Britain – the Egyptian leaders realized that it would be useless to try and conciliate yesterday's foes, or even to request military equipment from the USA, who had just refused to finance the Dam and has pressurized the World Bank (which it controlled) into depriving Egypt of financial assistance. All this at a time when Czechoslovakia was willing to satisfy all our needs for military hardware, and at a time when the USSR – and all the socialist camp – was siding with Egypt during and after the aggression. Public opinion in Egypt had been favourably impressed by the historic warning which Bulganin had issued to both France and England – irrespective of the seriousness of the said warning. It was therefore with great political acumen and courage that the Egyptian leaders took the decision of sending a selected number of superior officers to the Frunze Academy in the Soviet Union; and, indeed, this first Egyptian military mission began its training early in 1957, i.e. a few months after the withdrawal of the forces of aggression and before the Israeli withdrawal from Gaza. This first mission was followed by a second, which left Egypt at the beginning of 1958; and at the same time Egyptian navy and air force officers were sent to the appropriate Soviet academies.

The return, from the Soviet Union, of these military missions, is a milestone in the modern history of the Egyptian armed forces. The officers returned home and were given the command of various fighting units as well as some major positions on the General Staff. They expended tremendous efforts in reorganizing the forces, in arming them and in training them along the Soviet lines with which they had become familiar. At that time the need was felt for a certain number of experts in minor tactics and tactical use of the new weapons, as well as for experts in the servicing and maintenance of the said weapons: menial tasks which were not included in the curricula of the Egyptian superior officers who attended the Soviet academies. As a result, a number of Soviet experts arrived in Egypt at the end of 1957, and they immediately started working with the armed forces. Their numbers grew to meet the requirements of the existing units, as well as the needs of the new units being set up in accordance with the policy of expansion of the armed forces supported by the Egyptian leaders.

The Egyptian leaders were not being rash in allowing Soviet experts to join the armed forces, nor was there any fear that military secrets might be leaked to an enemy country. The Suez war had thrown unambiguous light on the attitude of the Western powers towards us and towards our cause; and as for the US position, the declarations of Secretary of State Dulles were casting doubt on President Eisenhower's admirable stand during the tripartite aggression – an aggression he condemned for reasons which had to do with America's bid for the leadership of the Western world. Whereas, on the other hand, the stand and conduct of the Soviet experts, up till the June 1967 defeat, were irreproachable, and in no way could they be accused of interference in Egyptian affairs. They were only concerned with their work and with furthering, in all earnestness, their military skills and achievements – similar, in that, to the Soviet peoples who sanctify and worship their work. Never did these experts attempt to extend their power and influence, and in no way did they antagonize the Egyptian officers. Rather, they were placed under the command of Egyptian officers, they fulfilled all the missions to which their superiors assigned them, and they were always willing to give their opinion in all loyalty when they were requested to. They were skilled and serious in their work and extremely correct and well-behaved with the Egyptian officers.

Such behaviour was not individual but collective: a conscious policy to which all Soviet experts abided, which goes to prove that directives to this effect had been issued by the Soviet hierarchy laying down rules for behaviour and forbidding all excursions into matters unrelated to the immediate task assigned to each individual, so that nobody could level at them the accusation of being communist agents groping for power in Egypt. . .

As regards war strategies and participation in the elaboration of battle plans – be it in Yemen or in the Sinai – the Soviet experts did not interfere, they were not asked to participate, nor did they request to do so. At no point was any strategy put to them for comments or advice. The experts went about their task honourably, they did not interfere in any political or personal matter, and the Soviet general who first commanded the experts for a period of more than four years was the epitome of correctness, discretion and professionalism.

The experts were of great assistance in training the troops and preparing them for battle. They contributed to the widening of the Egyptian officers' military thinking and taught them to go beyond the purely tactical subjects pertaining to specific battles – that being the highest level of military thinking which we had been taught by the British – and to come to terms with overall strategic moves in which the army is supported by the navy, the air force, and the air defence force. Furthermore, the experts laid down sound bases for the proper training of the Egyptian superior officers.

The Soviet experts never volunteered any information: they simply answered the questions put to them by the Egyptians. The reason being that they were most eager to avoid being accused of interfering in internal Egyptian affairs . . . Yet one cannot forgive the Soviet experts their approval of and support for the establishment of a General Army Command despite the fact that the experience of the Soviet armed forces had taught them the triviality and frivolity inherent to the creation of such a command. Despite this, the Soviet experts seconded to the Egyptian armed forces backed the idea in 1964, and this was to have most unfortunate consequences.

Part II

The State Dimension

Introduction

A major theme in the previous section was the way in which international processes and relations have made some kinds of development in the Middle East more difficult while facilitating other kinds. But it cannot be stressed too often that the course of development in particular countries is not a simple function of the international system, however sophisticated our understanding of the economic, political and cultural dimensions of such a system might be. In this Part, therefore, the texts focus on various aspects of the state in the Middle East, and especially on some of its internal tendencies and contradictions. These texts introduce a number of important questions about "internal" conditions of development. But we must try in each case to see these conditions not merely as forms of "inadequate development" (where this is measured against some ideal type of "modernity"), but as forms of politics and economics which have their own social logic.

Like many Middle Eastern regimes, but earlier than most, Egypt's government under Nasser (1952-70) was officially dedicated to achieving greater "social justice" (the elimination of poverty, and a more equal distribution of income), and to developing a fully "modern" economy (a vigorous, broad-based industrial sector, and significant GNP growth). It is well-known that, in spite of massive state intervention, the achievement of Nasser's regime was not very impressive in either respect.

Cooper's article begins from a statement of this relative failure, which was signalled by the economic crises of the mid-sixties and dramatized by Egypt's military defeat in 1967. Cooper argues that the failure was due to a contradiction between "the investment demands of developmentalism" and "the consumption demands of populism", (2) that this contradiction was resolved by the regime's decision to opt for "pure developmentalism" (in the last years of Nasser, and more openly since his death), and (3) that such a decision has meant in effect opting for the interests of the army, the technocrats and the middle classes.

Cooper's article focuses generally on the relations between a regime's economic policies and its political options. It raises two important problems: (1) the connections between a state which directly undertakes or presides over projects of social and economic development, on the one hand, and, on the other, the classes which support or constrain such a state; and (2) the connections between policies of redistribution and those of growth.

With reference to problem (1), we may ask ourselves, for instance, whether it is entirely satisfactory to see such a state as being an expression of the class interests of its main supporters. Was the Nasserite state a petty-bourgeois state, as many commentators have suggested, defending above all the interests of the petty bourgeoisie? Or was it an abnormal (and hence inefficient) regime, attempting to respond to the incompatible interests of its many constituencies? But perhaps it might be useful in this context to conceptualize the state not as an agent with a single political will (ideally coherent but sometimes confused), but as an arena within which a variety of shifting struggles were waged at several levels of the state's institutions. In such struggles class is always important because and to the extent that the productive property which different groups control forms a crucial part of the conditions and of the objectives of struggle over policy. So although policies concerning growth and redistribution directly affected questions of property, it should not be assumed that growth performance and actual income distribution were simply the direct effects of government policies. There were always other factors involved.

Regarding problem (2) we might consider whether GNP growth and redistribution of income are necessarily incompatible, or whether they merely appeared to be so because of the particular form that political struggles took in Nasser's Egypt. Development economists are by no means agreed that increased productive investment can only be secured at the expense of greater social inequality. After all, if a substantial rise in productive employment among the impoverished population in Egypt had been attempted (through small-scale, labour-intensive production, etc.) its success would have meant at the same time an additional contribution to GNP, and a shift in the pattern of income distribution. But of course an economic equation like this one is not a political solution. The relative success of such attempts depends both on international conditions being favourable (terms of trade, etc.) and also on the efficiency of various institutions (credit banks, co-operatives, government offices etc.) and the latter depends, in part at least, on an appropriate mobilization of class forces – as we shall see below.

Countries in which the state itself undertakes the task of industrialization and "modernization", such as Algeria, are heavily dependent on their bureaucracy. But Middle Eastern state bureaucracies are notoriously inefficient, and corruption at all levels is by no means uncommon. In Algeria the paradox seems to be that the main instrument of modernization (the bureaucracy) is itself very unmodern.

The analysis by Roberts focuses on this paradox. He argues that although massive state intervention is essential for social and economic development, the inevitable expansion of the bureaucracy also reinforces traditional loyalties – the family, the village, the tribe, the religious brotherhood, etc., because there is no developed sense of disinterested public service. The result is not merely that patron-client networks pervade the administrative network, but more importantly that crucial decisions at the top are taken in virtue of factional struggles rather than with regard to the objective requirements of government policy. The bureaucracy does not function primarily in accordance with a rational-legal code, observes Roberts. Such a code exists, of course, but is subject to extensive manipulation when it is not straight-forwardly honoured in the breach. The bureaucracy is not autonomous enough, for autonomy from private interests is one of the hall-marks of a modern state. This is one of the main reasons why the Algerian state may be described as "modernist" although not yet a "modern state".

The problem of the relation between public and private interests is a complex one. To begin with it may help if we distinguish (a) cases in which state regulations are broken by requiring officials to perform special favours in return for a consideration (whether this is misplaced personal loyalty or a bribe), from (b) those in which administrative functions of the state are manipulated in a competitive situation to realize particular interests, without the law being broken. Policemen who are paid to turn a blind eye to criminal entrepreneurs is an example of the first; armaments manufacturers who succeed in persuading the government to increase military spending at the cost of building more schools and hospitals is an example of the second. In both cases private interests prevail over public ones – and in the second they do this by defining what the public interests are. However, it may be argued that it is only in the first case that the bureaucracy's autonomy is undermined, because its general regulations are broken in order to favour particular interests.

Why are corruption, clientalism, etc., so common in the Algerian administration? Is it primarily because a modern notion of disinterested public service is lacking - or is this answer merely a rewording of our question? Perhaps one way of arriving at some sort of answer may be to ask ourselves about the historical conditions which have led to a greater autonomy of the state's bureaucracy in the industrialized countries of the West. More specifically one might ask: What are the conditions in which it is crucially in the interests of a dominant class alliance to ensure an autonomous bureaucracy (as in Britain) – or alternatively to subject the state bureaucracy to the politics of patronage (as in many of the states of the US)? The essay by Roberts should encourage the reader to ask comparable questions with regard to the various Middle Eastern countries.

The question of the autonomy of the state apparatus has often been seen in terms of a conflict between objectively necessary and politically motivated decisions. This distinction is, of course, central to a technocratic conception of politics. Yet to the extent that the state and its constituent institutions can be conceptualized as so many arenas of political struggle, it may not be easy always to distinguish between the two kinds of decision. Decisions by government office-holders may well be perfectly legal, and they may be directed at the fulfilment of public interests, but the precise way in which such interests are realized usually benefits different classes rather differently. A consequence of this truism is that various interest groups are concerned to influence the formation of public policy, as well as the manner of its implementation, in their own favour. Should we not ask ourselves, therefore, whether what most sharply distinguishes the Algerian state bureaucracy from its counterpart in a "fully modern" state is not so much the predominance of "private" interests as against "public", but the different ways in which private interests come to realize and define public interests?

A famous "traditional" feature of most Middle Eastern countries has been something called the tribe, a socio-political entity which is usually thought of as being only loosely integrated within the central state, because it has its own leaders, its own customs, etc. The typical tribe in the Middle East is also thought of as being nomadic – or at least as having been nomadic in the recent past – and so too as economically based on animal husbandry. A major development problem for countries such as Iran in which there are large tribal populations is often described as the problem of "integrating" the tribe politically, economically and culturally into the modern nation-state. This is because the existence of tribes is conceived of by modernizing governments as a threat to its integrity and a symptom of non-modernity within its domain.

Beck's article describes briefly some aspects of the relationship between Iran's tribes (and also, those larger population units labelled "national minorities") on the one hand, and the central government in Tehran on the other, before and after the 1979 revolution. She explains in what ways the revolution has reversed certain trends in the life of Iran's pastoral nomads, making them often economically better off and politically less subject to centralized control than before. "The resurgence of tribalism," she observes, "rather than being the 'survival' of an archaic form of organization, is instead a very contemporary response to current conditions of central weakness and to the centre's attempts to establish political domination." Similarly, although the demands by "national minorities" for regional autonomy are vigorously opposed by the Tehran authorities, revolutionary conditions make it difficult for the centre to consolidate its control over every part of the country as effectively as before.

Beck's account raises several interesting questions which are worth thinking about: To what extent are "tribes" always (a) the same kind of unit, and (b) internally homogeneous units? In what conditions can tribal leaders who are separated by their property and status concerns from their fellow tribesmen still come to represent the interests of the latter? Are tribal notables who are settled in towns, whose incomes derive from different kinds of financial investment, who intermarry with rich and powerful urban families, who perform local administrative functions, a part of "the state" or of "the tribes"? Should "tribes" be thought of as counterposed to "the state" or as an aspect of it? If the latter, then what aspect? Is it not a question of degrees of political and cultural decentralization? Perhaps we can also approach this from another angle: Why are "tribes" usually thought of as being formerly traditional (whether a "surviving" or a "resurgent" tradition) whereas "national minorities" are thought of as being at least potentially modern?

Finally, a more general question: In what ways does the "modernizing" state necessarily involve itself in the homogenization and control of all its political subjects? For whatever else "modernization" means, it involves the state's trying to transform, or at least to facilitate the transformation of, a total population along "rational" lines. Disease, poverty and superstition must be eliminated, and the organizational conditions for the modern conception of "the good life" must be created. People must be *made* to form new desires, and to respond to a new order of truth. All of this requires the manipulation of populations, and the efficient manipulation of populations in turn depends on the removal or containment of anomalies ("irrationalities") - in which, so it may be said, Middle Eastern states abound.

Most Middle Eastern states are very recent creations, established by the European Great Powers after the First World War with primary regard to considerations of imperial strategy. They all include varying populations of what are increasingly described in social science literature as "ethnic groupings" (based on religious, linguistic or other criteria), whose geographical distribution does not coincide neatly with international borders. An ethnic group may inhabit two or more sovereign territories, and also share the same territory with other groups. Foreign commentators as well as local dissidents have sometimes pointed to cultural differences between such groups in order to infer forms of political confrontation which are not always easy to substantiate. Equally, governments in power have usually been inclined to dismiss or minimize the political importance of ethnic distrust and opposition. In this context single-party organizations directed by the regime, such as the Ba'th Party in Iraq and in Syria, have been seen both as a means of transcending divisive loyalties and wasteful conflicts in the drive towards modernity, and also as an instrument of authoritarian control wielded by unscrupulous cliques which prevents the growth of a modern politics.

Van Dam's comparative essay is concerned to argue that in Iraq what appears to be nothing more than sectarian control of state and party apparatuses is really not so; and that the conspiratorial politics and frequent purges among the leadership, as well as the socio-economic interests of the mass base, help to explain the convergence between sectarian affiliation and dominant power positions. In Syria, on the other hand, the sectarian character of the regime is more real, and it is ensured by rampant corruption and nepotism which is without parallel in contemporary Iraq. A consequence of this, van Dam maintains, is the more open sectarian distrust, not to say violent conflict, characteristic of recent Syrian politics.

Van Dam's precise assessment of the difference between the Syrian and Iraqi regimes may be subject to argument. But it raises nicely two general questions: (1) Is it useful to describe ethnic conflicts and sectarian politics in the Middle East as signs of "non-modernity"? Think of French- and Flemish-speakers in Belgium, of Blacks and Whites in the United States, of Catholics and Protestants in Holland. This does not mean of course that politics in these Western countries is essentially no different from politics in the Middle East, but only that the difference cannot be expressed in terms of glib formulae such as "sectarian politics =

the politics of backwardness". (2) How much effective control do the modernizing one-party states of the Middle East really exercise over their citizens? Is their frequent and often brutal use of force a sign of the *traditional* political attitude of Middle Eastern rulers towards their subjects? Or is it more appropriately seen as a sign of the *modern* political desire to organize and manipulate entire populations, but a desire that cannot yet be efficiently realized? It is worth remembering that the effective range of operations of the legal, administrative and financial institutions of Western post-liberal states is far greater than anything to be seen in the Middle East (except in Israel), and that therefore in a sense power in Western states is more pervasive and more effective than it is in the Middle East. Middle Eastern regimes today also have this will to power, but they rarely possess more than the means of violence.

Like many Middle Eastern states, Israel too is a recent creation (1948), but unlike any of them it is a state whose citizens are overwhelmingly immigrant settlers. Unlike any other state also, it has continuously received massive and indispensable support, at once material and moral, from Western countries. But the uniqueness of the Israeli state lies most clearly in the privileged constitutional status it accords to a (Jewish) population, the majority of whom are neither its citizens nor within its territorial borders – at the expense of a minority of its own citizens (Christian and Muslim Arabs) who have always lived in the area today known as Israel. This is done by the legal device of distinguishing between "Nationality" (Jewish, Arab, etc.) and "citizenship" (Israeli/non-Israeli), and by according special legal rights to Zionist institutions – i.e. those devoted exclusively to organizing the settlement of Jews in Israel and to promoting the Jewish character of the state. The importance of this distinction emerges more clearly when it is understood that Zionist institutions in Israel dominate the social, political and economic life of the country. In a sense the Zionist institutions constitute a "private" domain which is closed off to the citizen *as citizen*, and the citizen as such has access only to a very restricted "public" domain. It is precisely because Israel is a modern state, committed to the liberal democratic principle of one-man-one-vote, that the problem of ensuring unequal treatment for different parts of its population becomes acute. In an archaic state discrimination against one part of its population poses no problem; in a modern state it does. One way of solving this problem is to define the distinction between "private" and "public" interests in such a way that discrimination becomes a function of legitimate "private" institutions, and not of the state. In Israel this is a viable solution because the crucial definition between "private" and "public" is itself democratically ensured by the existence of an appropriate "demographic balance" between Jews and non-Jews in the country.

Davis and Lehn describe in some detail the legal agreements between the Israeli state and the largest and most influential Zionist institution, the Jewish National Fund, which belongs to the World Zionist Organization. These agreements, they argue, virtually make the WZO and its various institutions into "a state within the State of Israel", thus enabling a legally privileged position to be given to Israeli Jews, not directly by virtue of their citizenship, but indirectly by virtue of their nationality. In this way, Davis and Lehn suggest, the state appears to be upholding the principle of equality for all its citizens, but in practice it supports a form of separate but unequal "national development".

Egyptian State Capitalism in Crisis: Economic Policies and Political Interests

Mark Cooper

Introduction

Most analyses of Egypt in the 1970s, whether political or economic, have a central concern, the liberalization policies of the Sadat regime. The reason for this focus is clear; rather striking and deep-seated changes took place in Egypt under the heading of that policy. Most analyses, however, suffer two major drawbacks: they fail to integrate the political and the economic and they take an approach with a very short historical vision. In doing so, they run the risk of critical misinterpretations of the nature of the policy, the regime and the changes in Egypt.

This paper seeks to rectify both these drawbacks by analyzing the political basis and economic impact of policies made in the period between, roughly, the June War of 1967 and the death of Nasser in September 1970. It is argued that there is a fundamental continuity between the Nasser and Sadat regimes and that an understanding of this continuity is vital to an understanding of the Egyptian political economy in the 1970s.

The Egyptian Political Economy: Pre-1967

The economic history of the Nasser regime up until the June War has three salient features from the point of view of this analysis. First, by 1964-5 the economy had run into some fairly serious bottlenecks. It represents a good example of two-gap stagnation – a savings consumption gap and a foreign exchange gap which grinds economic growth to a halt. The two gaps are transmission mechanism by which more basic problems in the structure of the political economy are translated into stagnation.

Second, the Egyptian revolution made significant populist socioeconomic gains. By any definition of the distribution of welfare in Egyptian society, and in comparison with other nations at similar levels of development, the "masses" made some real gains. Third, there was, none the less, a clear bias in the distribution of these gains. In agriculture there was a mixture of distribution of land and services to peasants, reinforcement of the position of middle farmers and generation of revenues for the state. In industry there were gains for certain workers, and an even more rapid expansion of lower and upper level bureaucrats.

These three features of the Egyptian economic regime in the early 1960s, admittedly summarized in the briefest fashion, highlight the basic nature of that regime. It was a form of semipopulist, state capitalist, developmental nationalism. It was an economic halfway house, aiming to distribute gains to all groups, save a handful of 'exploitative' capitalists. Investment policy was aggressively developmental, aiming at a rapid and broad-based industrialization. Consumption policy was aggressively populist, guaranteeing rapidly expanding living standards all around. All this was channelled through the state, with the state becoming not only the super capitalist, but the provider of first resort.

The regime, coming to power in a thorough political vacuum, and without a political organization, had used the state to create a political base. It used the repressive apparatus, to be sure, but above all it used the state's absorptive capacity to create a political constituency by constantly increasing distributive rewards, thus co-opting groups that would otherwise have been in opposition. The ease with which it seized the economic structure (less than 2,000 feudalists and 1,000 capitalists had to be expropriated, and with very little bloodshed) reflects weakness in the system rather than power in the regime.

Because of the political weakness the state claimed an extremely broad constituency, and because of the constant co-optation of contradictory interests and demands the regime never built a basis of independent political power that could break its dependence on the distributive/consumptive economic policy. Occasionally it could lash out at strong economic interests on the periphery of the state, but it could never reorganize economic interests within the state. In fact, the most striking thing about economic policy in the pre-June 1967 period is, perhaps, its repeated about-facing. The suggestion here is that such behaviour balances the contradictory interests the state is claiming to represent.

This populist developmental nationalism showed its limits rather quickly, as the investment demands of developmentalism clashed with the consumption demands of populism. Even in the face of the severe bottlenecks that arose out of the resulting resource squeeze, the commitment to expanding consumption could not be abandoned. The solution was always in greater rates of expansion. For such a regime the concept of contraction, even stabilization at some point, was inadmissible because that would force a hard political choice between the constituencies of the regime. There was, in 1965, a brief interlude (with the Zakariya Mohiedein government) in which the criticalness of the economic situation was recognised but the moment was brief and the political consequences of rectifying the situation too dear.

With the defeat in 1967, however, there was no longer any possibility of avoiding difficult decisions. The structure had been forcibly deflated and the impact of contraction had to be distributed. A debate will probably rage on, *ad infinitum,* as to the impact of the war on the economy – whether the economic structure was generating the collapse that the war brought on. While this may be an important theoretical point, it is not terribly relevant empirically. The point to be underlined here is that the war forced the reorganization of interests within the economy for political reasons. The debate that existed at that time, and persisted throughout the 1970s, between a radicalization and a liberalization of the economy was never economic. The resolution of the debate was on the side of the liberalizers, and the basic change took place in 1968 when the regime finally made a choice between the interests that had been sustaining it. That choice went under the heading of economic reform, and, while in absolute economic terms it may have been "timid", in political terms it was anything but timid. Having opened to certain economic interests for political reasons, those interests began propelling political and economic change. Economic reform in 1968 was the jumping off point for economic liberalization in 1973.

The Politics and Ideology of Economic Reform

While it cannot be said that the 30 March [1968] Program, which was raised to the highest level of political documents through a plebiscite, has anything more than general economic prescriptions, it has a clear ideological intent, and audience. These intentions were almost immediately translated into policy.

It is not suprising that the statement calls for repair of the economy, nor that this is tied to "conservative" Arab states, via the Rabat Summit conference (September 1969). What is significant is the specific path chosen. The path is one of high modernization.

> I want to make clear before you now some of the primary missions in the coming stage of our struggle . . . Support for the operation of building a modern nation in Egypt, and a modern nation is not created, in addition to democracy, except on the basis of science and technology . . . Giving complete development the great push in industry and agriculture to realize a rise in the level of production and total work, with stress on the importance of administration of public projects – on economic and scientific administration.

Scientific and economic management are one means for the creation of a modern nation. Three others are also specifically stated:

> Focusing a centralized effort toward the operation of the search for petroleum since . . . petroleum can give to the effort of complete development bountiful possibilities . . .
>   Distributing individual incentives, honouring the value of work on the one hand, and maintaining for the nation its human potential and expanding the desired opportunities before it . . .
> Realizing the placing of the right man in the right position.

The statement ties the economic reconstruction to the rebuilding of the armed forces, "for we will not be able to do it without a sound economy". It also maintains the definitions of economic sectors from the National Charter: "Specified in the constitution [should be] guarantees of the protection of public property, cooperative property, and private property, and the limits of each, and its social role."

Before examining the translation of this general statement into concrete measures, it is worthy of a moment's reflection. The political questions are, for which constituency is such a policy intended, and why? The masters and consumers of science and technology, the advocates of efficiency through science, incentives, and promotion by merit, are a small group in the society. The policy raises the expert to a dominant political position. He is to be free to practise his role and benefit from that practice by promotion (implicitly) and incentives (explicitly). It can be argued that the political prescriptions in the document are aimed at precisely the same educated middle class. Why is this class singled out? There are clear historical reasons in the political economy of the regime. The officer class was centred there, and they had been severely demoralized by the defeat and by the negative social reaction to them. As members of this class they are targeted by the policy; by tying the armed forces to the modernization of the economy they are doubly targeted. The technocracy is also clearly singled out. Part of it had been borrowed – co-opted from the pre-socialist day – and the scientific tone of the document, the depoliticization of the economy, certainly was for their ears. It can also safely be said that that part of the technocracy created by the socialization [of the economy] was severely under-ideologized. The technical-efficiency implications of the statement, as well as the opening of opportunities it promised, was welcome to them as well. Practically the revolution had also reinforced the agrarian middle class and tied it with expanding education into this same educated middle class.

Why this constituency? Without fully accepting the idea of a charismatic situation, or a catastrophic equilibrium, it seems clear that the regime had gathered together very disparate interest in a fragmented social structure. The expansion of the state was an effort to routinize the amorphous popular support it had enjoyed (embodied in the dominant personality). Nevertheless it had rested squarely on these groups. In the wake of the defeat, policy was aimed, and not the least economic policy, at shoring up the core of its support. The army had splintered (in August), and students and workers had got out of control (in February 1968). In seeking a routinized, dependable basis of support, the regime fell back on its core. Claims to generalized populism were subjugated to the interest of the core groups. The regime became dominated by a single set of interests, the about-facing of policy was a thing of the past.

This is not to suggest that there was not opposition, within the core, to these policies; it suggests, rather, that the regime aimed to reorganize its support on what it conceived as the most dependable part of these groups. The 30 March Program initiates what might be conceived of as a reorientation of the regime and a narrowing of its constituency. It consisted of shedding constituencies on the left and gaining them on the right. One may wish to speak of a qualitative shift in this movement, after the accession of Sadat, but it should become clear in the following analysis that the process had begun long before. Though most of the authors of the 1968 policy had been driven out of the regime's core constituency by 1975, it was they who had begun the process and set the basic conditions for its execution.

The clearest indication of the bias in the policy is revealed in the effort to recapture hard currencies held abroad by Egyptians. The types of people likely to hold such currencies, and therefore able to benefit from the policy, is strikingly clear. The Minister of Economy and Foreign Trade, in a speech of 4 July 1968, is explicit in referring to a decision made the month before (apparently Decision 364/1 June 1968).

> First, foreign residents in the country, and UAR subjects who have emigrated, as well as those who have been working abroad for more than 5 years have been allowed to open accounts in foreign currencies with local banks, where they may deposit their earnings. They have the right to draw on these accounts either wholly or in part, and dispose of them in any way, without permission from foreign currency authorities and without any controls or restrictions.
> The free currency deposits will thus enjoy complete freedom in transfer into and out of the country . . .
> Second, those working abroad for periods [of] less than 5 years, and those rendering services abroad, such as *physicians, lawyers, artists, engineers, publishers, agents of foreign firms, and investment offices, and the like*, have been allowed to open foreign currency accounts, thus realizing the following advantages:
> > a. to benefit by sales in foreign currencies (of flats, engineering and consumer goods),
> > b. to finance import transactions in favour of both the public and private sectors.
> Whoever has a foreign currency account may obtain on debit to such an account imports of consumer or capital goods in the interest of the two sectors . . .
> > c. To use such deposits in travel, for himself or family, when going abroad for study, or visit, or medical treatment . . .
> Third, an agreement was reached between the ministry and the sector concerned for opening of a trade store where foreign and quality local goods will be offered for sale against convertible currencies.[1]

Coupled with the foreign exchange policy is an import policy that expanded and freed the right of individuals to bring in items for personal consumption. This includes, apparently, the expansion, if not the origin, of the much heralded "own exchange imports" policy of the 1970s. A series of decisions follows which implement this policy; these are analyzed in the next section.

The minister gave a rather tortured defence of this policy to the Arab Socialist Union in September 1968. This policy of expanding consumption for the upper middle classes came at the time when the ASU was calling for a redoubling of the war effort and a consequent alteration of consumption patterns.

> I heard a recommendation for non-import of luxury goods. The UAR does not, actually, import such goods in the ordinary sense, for the price of these goods is part of the price of advertisements by foreign exporters. For example, the exporters of watches place their advertisements in local papers. They pay for their advertisements in foreign currency in part, and the balance in watches.
>
> Extravagance in consumption affects in great part education services, services in hospitals and social services in their efforts to realize socialism, sufficiency, and justice.
>
> Deviations stem from individual behaviour. Such deviations immediately become public because it is the people that possess the public sector.[2]

The significance of this defence lies in two directions. First, it is clear that the ASU was putting forward criticism of the policy. The war of words being carried on in the press betweeen the "centrists" at *al-Ahram*, and the "radicals" at *al-Goumhouriya*, was clearly not limited to that sphere. Second, the issue of private consumption is avoided, while problems of social consumption are raised. This is a basic element of the reformist policy, which sought to reform the social, or public, side, while liberating the private side.

The heart of that reformism was the reform of the public sector. This was carried in the Hegazi scheme for financial and administrative reform. Administrative rationalization has the centre stage, but ultimately the scheme had to come to grips with the core of the problem, productivity and efficiency in production. It would ultimately imply the imposition of "economic" criteria on the sector, which, at the extreme, meant its contraction.

> It is important in this field that agreement should be reached in principle on the objectives, the realization of which by these units is required, together with the definition of their relations with [the] state . . .
> 1. The realization of a surplus . . .
> 2. Balancing between current revenues and current expenses . . .
> 3. Excess of current expenditures over current revenues on account of one or two factors:
>   a. State intervention in fixing prices at a level below costs for social considerations.
>   b. Wish of the state to preserve economic activity for national or strategic objects.

The balancing here is realized by charging the state with the difference in shape of consolidation subsidies. This necessitates however, that efforts should be exerted for reduction of all costs.

Non-fulfillment, by the unit, of its activities on an economic basis, and consequent losses:

It is imperative that such units be eliminated, or at least shrunk, in case of need, after it is proved that their maintenance is no longer possible from an economic point of view, and a decision should be taken for their liquidation.[3]

It is safe to say that the document is permeated by the ideology of efficiency, the scientific administration approach of the 30 March Program. This policy, when it impinged on the public sector and meant change in the distribution of resources – either between the public and private sectors, or among units within the public sector – immediately raised political temperatures. The first sparks were struck in the summer of 1968 when some relatively minor denationalizations took place. The steps occasioned an open debate in the press. By September 1968 the regime was already defending the socialist character of the reform of the public sector and its intention to preserve it.

I personally feel that we should know the real position of the public sector. Figures show that this sector can stand firm and develop and help in the battle for economic development.

This is the responsibility of the public workers, the administrators and the executives, each in his own sphere. We are all responsible for the public sector. Any economic development is bound to be accompanied by errors . . .

In speaking today about financial and economic reform in the public sector, we must reaffirm the principles of efficiency and justice; efficiency in production and performance, and justice in distribution. We are not going back on our socialist line. We affirm that socialism is efficiency and justice.

Restraint and caution should be observed in criticism of the public sector which is the prop of socialism in our country. By this, I do not mean that constructive criticism should not be practiced, but only that we should not be tempted to follow the attack on the public sector.[4]

Again, the forum is the ASU, and the regime is defending its socialist nature. This was the basic rhetoric that would run throughout the 1970s. Hegazi would repeat the speech time and again (Feb 1969, June 1969), but one gets the impression that it ran into serious and consistent political troubles. Insight into these political troubles can be gained from a debate which took place in the National Assembly in February 1971. This is before the purges of May, but political struggle had already become intense.

The incident involves the creation of a specialized company for hard currency foreign transactions. Workers in the already extant trading company had complained to the ASU secretary general, who had, in turn, taken the issue up with the concerned minister. Unsatisfied with the response, the issue had apparently been routed to a member of the National Assembly, one of those who would later be expelled from the assembly and the party. The issue arose in the form of a question to the minister. He defended the creation of the new company, arguing that the old company had gone into a severe deficit situation when it tried to assume free currency operations:

> The creation of a specialized independent company for the practice of free market activity and the business of selling foreign currency to citizens and commercial activity carried out in the import market accords with the plan of financial and administrative reform which the government assumed in the period following the aggression, acknowledging the fact that the new company has all the necessary facilities to be a successful company and the power to permit it to obtain a more appropriate price from the places of production as well as providing a greater opportunity for research and follow up and better evaulation.[5]

Underlying the issue is the relationship of the workers and the ASU to the company.

> It [the original question] was based on the objection of the workers in one of the units, who said that the decision to create an independent company for free markets – which was in process of being issued at the time – would affect the profits and production of their company. This was what we asked the opinion of the minister [sic] and he did not cooperate in his answer, and we in the ASU felt that the answer did not supply anything new to enable us to respond to the popular workers in this unit. And the minister put forth three considerations in his answer:
> 1. This decision protected the public wealth.
> 2. This decision dealt with a point of the internal operation of the company, and the ASU had no right to enter into the internal organization operation of the company.
> 3. The company was completely successful before the expansion [into free market activities] and the minister would study the means to support the company if there was a need for that.[6]

In this debate and others, right from the start, the rationalization of the public sector was defined as an assault on the socialist gains of the revolution. Certain groups saw their rights, privileges, power diminished by the policy. Within Egyptian Arab socialism, with its expansiveness and socialist rhetoric, the conclusion was easy to reach. Tying income to "work and productivity", imposing economic criteria, would indeed damage their interests in the structure.

One of the central problems in the reform of the public sector was dealing with the input of these groups, for these groups represented a "noneconomic" input into the economic process. The philosophy of a response to these groups, and a strategy, was put forward by the Minister of Economy at a conference of administrative leadership held in September 1968. . . .

There is a true feeling among the workers that they are the possessors of the true interests in the production units and they are responsible for them and they feel they must carry out their share in participating in this work, and the administrator must not narrow this. Also, the political organizations feel, themselves, the responsibility, and there appears in the laws of the ASU in a clear form the role of this apparatus in the control of the productive apparatus.

Therefore, the political organization has a responsibility to ask for the support from it, and therefore we must permit it this opportunity. But how to organize these relations?

There is no doubt that the fundamental responsibility lies with the administration, but in order to guarantee that this administrative responsibility leads to a correct path, the workers and the political organization must participate to know that what happens is correct.

Therefore, as far as the participation of the workers and the political organization in administrative and productive affairs, I saw the experiment (Kafr ad Dawar) in which what was a production committee was created; represented in it the Administrative Council, the Union Council, the ASU Council; and the president of the Administration Council did not head it, the president of the factory did. The Council debated everything in the company and the Council reached all announcements, and its opinion was advisory, not obligatory, and [decisions] went to the Administrative Council to see if they were possible to implement or not. When the specialized technical apparatus advised the Administrative Council of the nonexecutability in the opinion of the Council, they would be informed of the reasons which led to that.[7]

This policy, which would place political and noneconomic input below technical expertise, was institutionalised in Presidential Decree 280/3 March 1969.

If there are clear indications of a degree of resistance to the reform of the public sector from the popular and political sides, there are also indications of resistance from the bureaucracy itself. An example can be taken from the same conference. Hegazi had mentioned, almost in passing, the surplus of labour in the public sector. This drew an immediate response.

> In relation to the manpower surplus, and I have been on the council of distribution of workers for many years, it does not happen that one surplus graduate is forced on the public sector, as a public sector, but the distribution of graduates is left to the public sector as a whole and the internal distribution is left to the whole sector.
>
> If errors in application have occurred in putting a person outside his speciality this is not the error of the state, as a state, but the error of the organizational units within the sectors. This operation can be rectified in stages. There may be a surplus in the public sector as a result of the shortage of investment. For example, a contracting company has a number of individuals; because of a shortage of investment it uses only 70 per cent of its capacity and 30 per cent are considered surplus. It falls to the heads of the production units to look for other work.[8]

The statement reflects a very common phenomenon, bureaucratic buck-passing. This plagued the reform throughout. It also reflects something more basic. The attitude toward the state drives the location of the problem to the level of the individual. At stake here are very basic questions of the relationship of that state to productive units, and the role of individuals, or enterprises, within that relationship. In the pre-1967 ideology the state was supreme, with the substate level absorbing all problems as deviations.

> Certain public sector enterprises under the socialist system might imagine that their success is to be measured by the yardstick of profit, regardless of the method by which these profits are made . . . In so doing, such enterprises would be deviating from the course of socialism and from the principles of sufficiency and justice . . .
>
> Bureaucratic and administrative complications can cause much damage in the production process. If they be of a general nature they will wipe out all positive activity in this sector.
>
> But, the deviation of the leaders, who think themselves a new class, and the result [of] such deviations . . . all this means they detach themselves from the alliance of the working powers of the

people to make themselves an exploiting class, not at all different from feudalists and exploiting capitalists.

However, as we exercise self-criticism, we realize that our revolutionary experiment, which made workers represented on the boards of establishments [sic] has produced the best results and enabled our socialist society, as a result of the democratic system it adopted,to protect itself against the deviations of leadership in the public sector.[9]

We have seen that the reformers make the claim to sufficiency and justice. We have seen the reformers willing to mobilize the level of deviation, albeit in defence of their consumption. This speech, by Prime Minister Ali Sabri in April 1964, raises the question whether there is a basic difference between the ideologies. One point of difference has already become clear, the role of the workers. We shift from the aggressive, ideological affirmation of the worker input, to the administrative scheme to remove it. A second point of indisputable difference is the attitude toward the state. Hegazi/Sidqi are diametrically opposed to the pre-1967 role of the state.

> The basic responsibility of the state is the application of laws and the promotion of its application in a basic way in the various sectors. But, when it became the owner of the production units and entered in a major way into a new operation, i.e. the production operation, here, in my opinion, is the beginning of the problem . . . The means of operation in production units differed from the means of operation in the government . . . but the production units became part of the state apparatus and its responsibility [and] every person has come to believe that he has the right to debate the work of the public sector.[10]

> Such a sector cannot be ruled by the restrictions which rule government departments and the system of work in it cannot be developed in a manner which brings it within the scope of government control and thus loses its basic element of success. Consequently, this sector has to be managed on scientific and practical principles.[11]

In the argument of the reformers, the reduction of the intervention of the state does not imply the reduction of the public sector; rather it implies the liberation of the technocrat.

> The largest part of the administrators believe faithfully that if they obtained more power or freedom in work they could achieve the ideal means in work. This issue is, in my opinion, the base of the subject . . . My opinion as the minister responsible for some of the units of the public sector, or a large part of them, is that we practised an excessive control and an excessive intervention, for

the results which we expected did not occur as a result of increased intervention, which led to an increase in difficulties rather than goals. Also, it did not lead to an increase in the delimitation of responsibility, but the opposite, it led to an increase in avoiding responsibility.[12]

It seems clear enough that the scientific management reform ideology represents a significant ideological break with the past. When the general prescriptions were given a more concrete form, it became immediately apparent whose interests were being damaged.

At the side of the policy of reforming the public sector stood the policy of encouraging the private sector, which worked in the same direction. In the 4 July speech at which the Minister of Economy had heralded the foreign currency decisions, he also announced the private sector decisions.

> In order to open wider scope for expanding exports to various markets and to raise our exports, especially of nontraditional goods through narrow scale operations in which the private sector is interested and to achieve the flexibility which characterizes this sector, the old system of confining some markets to certain companies of the public sector was abolished.[13]

The policy was reaffirmed several times, and a host of individual decisions were made (see below), generally freeing the private sector in acquiring inputs and disposing of output.

At the same time, two other debates were engaged which tended to encourage the private sector. The new law regulating landlord-tenant relations was specifically aimed at "encouraging the private sector to play its proper role". While not giving free play to private interests, it did return certain rights to the landlord. The debate over desequestration falls in the same line. Here was a clear signal that things had changed.

The tendency to open up opportunities to specific classes of individuals is also present in agriculture. The statements in February 1968 to the National Assembly, if carefully evaluated, show the direction:

> There is a point which I would like to stress, namely that of competition. Competition may arise through amelioration for excellence of quality, which enables the producer to realize the best price without local marketing troubles.
> I esteem that the cultivator should receive his due price in

ready money on delivery of his cotton. We should admit a repetition of sorting of the cotton so that he may be quite satisfied; cultivators may also have the facility of collecting their cotton in private stores providing that the quantities be not less than 50 kantars.[14]

With an average yield of five kantars per feddan, those eligible for the benefit of keeping private stores would have to own a minimum of ten feddans. The significance of this right was made clear in the speech of the Minister of Agriculture:

> After a general debate it was agreed in the assembly on the following points on cotton marketing.
> 1. Cotton should be collected in stores of limited capacity and cotton purchases should be made from these stores.
> 2. The producer should receive at least 20% in cash of the value of his cotton supplies immediately upon delivery, irrespective of the value of his debt.
> 3. A system should be laid down whereby the producer may sell his cotton in more than one course [sic] so that he may be satisfied as regards the price offered for his cotton.[15]

Whatever leeway there was in the system was given to the large holders by these decisions. A similar tendency is reflected in the decision to permit the sale of orchards by the Agrarian Reform Authority in plots of up to twenty feddans, an increase of ten feddans per plot. Even Law 50/1969, lowering the size limit of holdings, permitted a delay for sale and had several mitigating clauses. Very little land passed out of the middle and upper classes as a result of this law. In fact, it may well have served only to reinvigorate the agrarian middle class which the regime had so strongly favoured.

This is also the impact of the policy encouraging the production of fruits and vegetables. The exportation of these crops, which were capital intensive and very middle class, was made almost a national duty.

> In spite of satisfactory results we must increase the exportation of oranges in a fashion to compete with Israel.
> Israel has depended for its export of oranges on the Arab effort. It was not she who introduced cultivation of this crop into that country, but it was seized among the Arab riches which she has looted. . . .
> Now, in order for our citrus crops to compete with Israel on the international market, we must export 500,000 tons annually [total production in 1969 was 100,000 tons].[16]

As for meat production, another middle-class speciality, the minister's statement speaks to the operation of that market.

> One often hears repeated that it is the meat organization under the ministry of agriculture that is responsible for the rise in the price of meat. In my opinion that is an unfounded accusation, for the provider of meat is not the organization, but the peasant. . . .
> The organization is placed in a dilemma; if it buys at a high price and sells at a low price, it loses, and there is a demand to liquidate it, if it buys at a high price and sells at a high price, it is accused of exploitation.[17]

It is demonstrated below that the rising price of these "grocery" crops, with which the government had little to do, since they did not control them, was part of a general pricing policy which turned the terms of trade in favour of the middle-class farmer.

Perhaps most obvious in the agrarian sector was the reform of agrarian co-operatives. Here, a literacy requirement was placed on membership in the administrative councils, and the mandatory proportion of small-holders was reduced, thus reducing whatever peasant input there had been.

The Impact of Policy

Analyzing ideology and politics in policy credits policy with a certain efficacity. The policy decisions are seen to have some meaning and impact. This is always dangerous, especially with heavily ideologized policy; it is doubly true in Egypt, where form and content tend to diverge drastically. The nature of decisions and the responses they provoked seem to indicate that they had some impact and meaning. Here one should separate the intention of policy from its impact, or its executability. Certainly, the class bias in the policy was never acknowledged by its authors. If policy is class based, its stated intentions will always diverge from its structural impact.

While all the policies have been seen to have had a political rationale, expressed in its class bias, not all can be said to have an economic rationale. Most of the policies that have been referred to can be said to have an economic rationale. Even the consumption/currency policy could be rationalized economically, if it had led to the attraction of currency for investment purposes.

Here the question becomes whether the policies were executable, and what the classes were likely to do with their new "privileges". The anomaly of the Egyptian case, at this critical juncture, is that the policy that was most likely to achieve the basic economic goals of the reform – if executed – was also the least executable. The rectification of the public sector was indispensable to the rectification of the economy because of its size, and the particular goals chosen (high-technology modernization). That rectification cut across too many political interests to permit a thorough and effective execution. A thorough radicalization of the regime – as was, and occasionally still is, suggested – could have cut through those interests, but the regime had always lacked the necessary power and in the shaky days after the June defeat it took the opposite direction.

On the other hand, the most executable policies were also the least likely to achieve the economic goals. The expansion of private and individual economic activity, the encouragement of capital crops, were easily achieved. The interests were there, ready to seize the opportunities once restraints were lifted. The pursuit of those interests did not necessarily drive toward the economic goals. The private sector was small. The forms of profit available, in all parts of the private sector, were not necessarily productive. The consumption policy was marginal and easily led away from productive ends.

What emerges from this matrix of political and economic factors is a public sector bogged down in a morass of conflicting political and economic interests, and a private sector that became a centre – a pole – not necessarily of economic development, but of economic activity. The public sector became a treadmill dominating the economy, the private sector an escalator driving into the polity. Ultimately, one should separate the individual actors from the structural interests involved. While it may be naïve to suggest that there were genuine reformers behind the policies, it is overly cynical to suggest that the whole thing was a blatantly class action. The fact that the "genuine" reformers withdrew from the regime when the implications of the policy became clear indicates the reality lies somewhere between the two. That reality is defined by the matrix of the political and economic interests operating and the impact of policy is in terms of that matrix.

The optimum in the assessment of policy would be to reveal the process of decision-making in individual policies, and to measure the impact of each decision individually. Unfortunately, neither is possible with the policies discussed here. It is not certain, however, that such a strategy would reveal the nature and structural impact of policy, as described above. Here, a different strategy is carried out. The mass of policies are examined, first from a qualitative point of view, and then from a quantitative point of view. It is shown that the basic parameters of the economy changed direction in the 1967-71 period. It is argued that these changes are a result of the policies, and that the change in direction of the economy projects, fairly directly, into the Sadat liberalization era. . . .

Conclusion: State Capitalism in Crisis

Perhaps, one of the most remarkable features of the Nasser regime was its ability to survive June 1967. It was a bitter and crushing defeat, the kind few regimes do survive. That survival may have been more a function of the continuing fragmentation of the social structure than the strength of the regime. Having survived, it appears that the regime seriously misjudged its basic weakness. The 30 March Program and the cabinet shake-ups earlier that month are direct reactions to the severe rioting in February 1968. The absorptive, expansive etatist policies had failed to create a sound political base, and there could no longer be any doubt about that. Immediate steps were necessary to shore up the supports of the regime. Those steps were a strongly class-biased set of political and economic rforms. The economic reforms have been studied in this paper. A proper understanding of these reforms is crucial to a proper understanding of the postwar political economy. Indeed, since they mark so clear a turning-point, they may be vital to an understanding of the entire revolutionary period. In particular, they throw an important light on the nature of Egyptian state capitalism, and, perhaps, Third World state capitalisms in general.

As has been argued, the revolutionary economic structure was always a mixture of four elements – capitalism, etatism, populism and developmentalism. The 'new' élite secured its position at the top by pandering to the consumption demands of broader masses at the bottom. The new class promised, and delivered, in stages, expanding consumption payoffs. What is genuinely etatist about the structure is not that the new élite is located in the state, but that the new lower middle and upper working classes, in addition to the subproletariat, are dependent on that state. Etatism and populism become intertwined via an indispensable consumptive/

distributive policy. In this process the state becomes as dependent on development as the new lower classes are upon the state, for development is indispensable to the constant expansion of consumption demands. . . .

At that point the fundamental conflict lies between developmentalists and populists. The scientific administration argument was seen and labelled as anti-populist from the outset. For populist interests it was the principle, if not the form, of "exploitative" capitalism returned to dominance. The other policies, necessary to cement the developmentalist alliance, were not only blatantly antipopulist, but also a clear return to private capitalism. There was never a question of banishing the state, for neither the populists nor the developmentalists, nor the private capitalists for that matter, can survive with it significantly reduced. The question was always along which principles it would be organized, whether it would subsidize populism or developmentalism, which economic activities it would specialize in, and how much activity it would leave undisturbed?

The basic direction in Egypt, after the 1967 War, is from an internally contradictory populist developmentalism to a pure developmentalism. This is the direction in which Sadat's liberalization moved. It insisted on taking scientific management, economic rationality and encouragement of the private sector to their logical conclusions, all in the name of developmentalism. It was a direction that was set in the immediate postwar period and one that grew naturally and directly out of the configuration of interests, political pressures and resulting policy choices in that period.

The Algerian Bureaucracy

Hugh Roberts

1 Introduction

The term "bureaucracy" is used by contemporary social scientists in two distinct ways. It is used to refer to a form of organization and administration specified by the combination of characteristics such as strict hierarchy, meritocratic recruitment and promotion and the impartial and impersonal application of clearly defined rules and procedures. As such, "bureaucracy" has no necessarily pejorative connotations and has indeed been viewed positively, as conducive to the rational management of large-scale undertakings. More recently, a negative evaluation of bureaucracy has gained ground, not so much on the basis of its tendencies to inertia and "red tape" – the basis of public impatience with the thing – as on the basis of an ethical preoccupation with the individual, the quality of human relations and the general question of "alienation".

The term is also used, however, to refer, not to a form of administration (rule by officialdom), but to a social category (the officials) who are often credited with the defining characteristic of any social group, namely a collective material interest. Several Marxist authors have used the term in this way, from Trotsky in his writings on the Soviet Union in the 1930s to more recent authors such as Milovan Djilas, Ernest Mandel, Tony Cliff and Charles Bettelheim. (References are inserted in the 'Works cited in the Text', pp. 251ff.) In this perspective, usually concerned with the analysis of avowedly socialist states, the term continues to be used with uniquely negative associations, but the problem is not "bureaucracy" so much as "*the* bureaucracy", variously conceived as a kind of "caste" or "stratum" or even, by Djilas for example, as a "new class".

Leaving aside for the moment the question of whether it is appropriate to regard the bureaucracy as a social group rather than merely a social category, we may note three important features of most contemporary Marxist discussion of this phenomenon. First, there is frequently a crucial lack of precision regarding the boundaries of this category: the term is used to refer to not only the functionaries of the administrative apparatus of the state, but also full-time members of the party and other organizations (trade unions, youth movements, women's organizations, etc.) and even the military. Second, discussion of the bureaucracy is invariably negative in its evaluation of its role. There is no recognition of the possibility that the bureaucracy performs historically necessary functions and thus plays a progressive role in the process of social development. Third, this negative evaluation is consistent with, and expressed in, two quite distinct interpretations of the significance of the bureaucracy in the context of socialist or post-revolutionary states. The first interpretation is that the bureaucracy is a negative feature of an otherwise sound (i.e. socialist) system: thus orthodox Trotskyist analyses, such as Mandel's, hold the Soviet Union to be a "degenerate workers' state", that is, socialist but subject to "bureaucratic deformation"; the possibility that the bureaucracy has been a necessary feature of the construction and administration of the socialist system in the Soviet Union and elsewhere is not entertained. The second interpretation, put forward by Cliff for example, is that the bureaucracy, taken to constitute a "new class", is proof that the revolution has failed to realize its socialist potential and that a bureaucratic counter-revolution of sorts has taken place and given rise to the rule of a new kind of exploiting class. These two interpretations, evidently, have very different political implications.

2 Bureaucracy and State Capitalism in Algeria

Both of these views have been put forward in Marxist discussion of Algeria. The first, acknowledging "the problem of bureaucracy" while denying the existence of a new exploitative class based on the public sector, is held by the most influential Marxist formation active in Algeria, the Parti de l'Avant-Garde Socialiste (PAGS – the Algerian Communist Party under a new name). The PAGS supported Boumedienne and the left wing of his regime from 1971 onwards but has been increasingly critical of the Chadli government and accordingly subject to growing harassment over the last two years (1982). Its political stance is based on the view that Algeria is, if not actually socialist, at least in transition towards socialism, a view in turn derived from the fundamental theoretical assumption that state ownership of the means of production is sufficient to guarantee the intrinsically socialist character of the public sector. It thus implicitly if not explicitly rejects the concept of state capitalism as having any application to the Algerian case and accordingly abstracts "the problem of bureaucracy" from the wider question of the relations between classes in Algerian society.

The second view denies that there is any question of socialism in contemporary Algeria and affirms that the Algerian economy is capitalist and the Algerian state bourgeois in class character. First propounded somewhat tentatively by Gerard Chaliand and Juliette Minces and more uninhibitedly by Ian Clegg, this thesis has subsequently been restated by Kader Ammour, Christian Leucate and Jean-Jacques Moulin and, more recently, by Marc Raffinot and Pierre Jacquemot. It has thus been the prevailing view of Marxist academics and journalists not engaged in practical political activity in Algeria. It is also the view of the small Parti de la Révolution Socialiste (PRS), an opposition group mounted from exile by one of the founders of the wartime FLN, Mohammed Boudiaf. All variants of this view agree that the Algerian public sector is state-capitalist, not socialist in character (although their grounds for doing so differ.) All, moreover, assert that this implies the existence of a new capitalist class, variously referred to as the "bureaucratic bourgeoisie" or the "state bourgeoisie". The error inherent in this view of things is thus the complement of that inherent in the first position. The first holds the problem of bureaucracy to be separate from that of class relations, the second reduces it to a mere instance of these relations, as being essentially no more than the phenomenal form of bourgeois rule. Ironically, therefore, the second position also fails to come to terms with the fact of state capitalism. For all its insistence on the state-capitalist character of the Algerian public sector, its conclusion that a new exploiting class exists, based on the public sector, rests on the failure to acknowledge any difference *of substance* between state capitalism based upon public property and free enterprise capitalism based upon private property. Just as the bureaucracy is reduced to a matter of phenomenal form, state ownership of the means of production is reduced to a matter of juridical form. The denial of the relative autonomy of the bureaucracy thus corresponds to the denial of the specificity of *state*-capitalism, namely its profoundly contradictory nature which may be summed up in the formulation: capitalism *without* capitalists.

In short, to assert that the Algerian public sector is state-capitalist, far from implying the existence of a "state bourgeoisie", implies the very opposite. For, whereas in the absence of working-class control over production exercised through an effective system of imperative planning, commodity relations continue to exist within the state sector such that the managers of public enterprises perform the entrepreneurial functions of the capitalist, state ownership of the means of production ensures that appropriation of the product and thus of surplus labour time is social. To assert that a "state bourgeoisie" exists is to presuppose that appropriation is private. It is therefore to deny the fact of public ownership, to dismiss it as a "fiction", in which case it ceases to be meaningful or accurate to speak of *state* capitalism as such.

Two variants of the assertion that the surplus labour time of the workers continues to be privately appropriated on capitalist lines have been put forward with regard to the Algerian case. The first is the thesis that the new economic bureaucracy collectively appropriates the surplus through its control of the levers of economic decision-making in the administrative apparatus of the state. There is a fundamental theoretical problem with this conception of things. A bureaucracy does not function collectively as a matter of course. It does so only in so far as its various activities are co-ordinated and orchestrated by a central directing body, such as a government. As Bruno Etienne has pointed out, however, one of the main characteristics of the Algerian bureaucracy is precisely the relative absence of co-ordination between its various branches and levels, and the extent to which the latter have been autonomous in relation to the government and have acted independently of one another. The second variant abandons the notion that the bureaucracy collectively appropri-ates the surplus for its own ends and by virtue of this assumes the character of an exploitative class and suggests instead that individual managers, possessing "real control" over the means of production, are able, in consequence, to appropriate the surplus. The problem with this view lies in the dichotomy it posits between the juridical form of state ownership and the real relation of private control. The implication of this dichotomy is that in order for the manager of a state enterprise to engage in capital accumulation for his own account he must engage in criminal activity, namely embezzlement or similar practices. Thus the class character of the Algerian state becomes a function of the ability of its ruling class to indulge in law-breaking on a large scale. Of course such practices exist in Algeria. However, the fact that abuse of public property is a crime and is punished with severity – the death sentence exists for certain categories of "economic crime" and has already been applied – is enough to refute the notion that those who engage in such behaviour constitute the new ruling class in virtue of it.

Both variants of the "private appropriation" thesis receive superficial support from certain, but by no means systematic, observations concerning the higher salaries, the "European" living standards, superior accommodation and other material privileges enjoyed by the managers and other senior administrative personnel in the public sector. But this is by no means proof of the existence of private appropriation or of capitalist exploitation. It is entirely explicable in terms of the differential remuneration of mental as opposed to manual labour which, as Marx and Lenin were careful to note, was to be regarded as regrettably inevitable in the initial phase of socialist development.

I must now make clear my own view of the matter, since it will underlie my subsequent analysis. First, by "the bureaucracy" I mean a social category consisting of all persons employed in administrative posts within the administrative apparatus of the state, including the state sector of the economy. This excludes the armed services and the police force, which merit separate consideration, and all non-administrative personnel employed by the state; it also excludes officials of the party and other "mass organizations" such as the national trade union, peasants' union, women's movement, youth movement and so forth. (Whether these organizations are to be regarded as an integral part of the administrative apparatus of the state is a question of considerable political significance, but a matter for empirical analysis, not *a priori* classification.) The members of this social category do not constitute a social group although they may, and in fact usually do, belong to different social groups, as we shall see.

Second, analysis of the relation of senior administrators and managers within the public sector of the economy to the means of production does not establish their class character as capitalist. In order to establish their class character, it is necessary to take other factors into account. Class character is not only a matter of class situation (relation to the means of production), it is also a matter of class allegiance, and it is the latter which is of primary importance for the purposes of political analysis. Moreover, class allegiance may be an unpredictable and highly fluid affair for certain categories of the population, particularly in the context of rapid social and political change. The most constant of these factors have been two in number and diametrically opposed: on the one hand, the commitment of the political leadership to the construction of a socialist economy, on the other hand, the existence of a substantial private sector capable of exerting a measure of influence on both the conception and, more important, the application of government policy. The former has at no stage been an unequivocal affair, for the political leadership has been characterized by a high degree of ideological heterogeneity and even incoherence throughout; only the left wing of the regime can be regarded as having a consistent socialist economic policy, although it is to be noted that the left was in the ascendant from 1971 until Boumedienne's death in 1978 and that Boumedienne himself was increasingly identified with its perspectives. The relationship between the public sector and private capital has also varied over time and from one branch of economic activity to another, ranging from complementarity verging on symbiosis to competition or indeed, as in the case of agriculture, outright antagonism. In these circumstances, a substantial number of senior public servants in Algeria may be characterized as bourgeois, not in virtue of their relation to the means of production in the state sector, but in virtue of their relationship to *private* capital. That is, the Algerian bourgeoisie properly so-called, based on its ownership of the means of production in the private sector of the economy, undoubtedly possesses important allies in the bureaucracy who may be regarded as part of the bourgeoisie in virtue of this relationship and the social and political outlook which goes with it.

Such a state of affairs is highly likely to obtain in the early phases of socialist development, especially in a relatively backward country. It clearly constitutes a major obstacle to the consummation of this development. The particular problem of the bourgeois character of elements of the bureaucracy is, however, reinforced and often overshadowed by a more general feature of the Algerian bureaucracy, namely the absence, except in rare individual cases, of a developed and effective sense of disinterested public service. Put another way, the general problem of the Algerian bureaucracy is that it is not yet a proper bureaucracy: rather than excessively bureaucratic, it is insufficiently so. Unlike its counterparts in, for example, Western Europe, its failure to conform to the Weberian ideal type is not a matter of marginal shortcomings, it is systematic. This state of affairs is a corollary of the backwardness of the Algerian state.

The Algerian state is modernist, but Algeria is not a modern state. The state, in the sense of state machine, is, under the direction of its political leadership, engaged in promoting the transformation of Algerian society through an ambitious prog- ramme of economic development. At the same time, the Algerian state, in the sense of sovereign political community, is not yet a modern state. It will not be so until the transformation in question has been completed. In Marx's view, two crucial features of the modern state, by which it is distinguished from its predecessors, are the separation of politics from religion and the radical dichotomy between the private and public domains.

3 Religion and Politics in Algeria

In Algeria the separation of politics from religion is far from complete. The constitution enshrines the role of Islam as the state religion and the Head of State must be a Muslim. Only one non-Muslim has held a ministerial portfolio since Independence. The official status of Islam, established by the Constituent Assembly in 1963, although not without opposition from the left, was confirmed in the National Charter adopted by referendum in 1976.

Moreover, Islam's position as the state religion is by no means a matter of form, but is taken seriously by the authorities. *Ramadan*, the month of fasting, is officially enforced, inasmuch as cafés and restaurants are obliged to close and bank, office, factory and school timetables are uniformly altered for the duration, and religious feast days *(Aid el Fitr, Aid el Adha, Mawlid*, etc.) are public holidays. The Ministry of Traditional Education and Religious Affairs runs its own network of seminaries and Islamic Institutes to train the officers of the cult. Each week it decides the content of the *khotba* – the sermon to be delivered in the mosques on Friday, and every year it organizes the pilgrimage to Mecca, the Minister himself going to the airport to see the *hajjis* off. More generally, much government policy is justified by official spokesmen in religious terms: thus the "Agrarian Revolution", launched in 1971–2, was presented as an act of national solidarity and hence as a duty which the community *(umma)* was obliged to undertake in order to maintain its own cohesion and health. We may note, moreover, the frequent identification made in official pronouncements of the *umma* (community of believers) and the *watan* (the nation): the latter is effectively defined as the former, that is, in religious terms.

Thus religion plays a substantial role in the affairs of state. It is very important not to exaggerate or misconceive the significance of this, however. Algeria is not a religious state, even if we cannot describe it as a secular one. As Marx pointed out in his polemic against the editor of the *Kölnische Zeitung:*

the truly religious state is the theocratic state; the prince of such
states must either be the God of religion, Jehovah himself, as in the
Jewish state, God's representative, the Dalai Lama, as in Tibet, or
finally, . . . they must all submit to a church which is an "infallible
church". For if, as in Protestantism, there is no supreme head of
the church, the domination of religion is nothing but the religion of
domination, the cult of the will of the government. (Marx and
Engels, *On Religion*, pp. 32-3)

There is no church in Algeria, still less an 'infallible" one with a
supreme head. It is not the case that Islam, or any more or less
organized tendency within it, exercises the kind of conscious and
coherent hegemony over state and society that the Catholic
hierarchy has exercised over Southern Irish society since the
middle of the nineteenth-century and over the state of Eire since
1921. It was, perhaps, conceivable that the Association of the
Ulama (doctors of religious law) might aspire to the exercise of
such hegemony in the independent state, as the Ayatollahs have
done in Iran. Unlike their Iranian counterparts, however, the
Algerian *Ulama*, despite playing a substantial role in the genesis of
Algerian nationalism, at no stage succeeded in constituting the
political leadership of the national revolution and since Independence they have been obliged to accept a subordinate and
dependent position *vis-à-vis* the political leadership in the Algerian
state. As Fanny Colonna has pointed out, the significance of the
Ministry of Traditional Education and Religious Affairs in
Algeria is that it is the institutional expression and organizational
instrument of the hegemony of the state over the religious field, not
of religion over the political field. In Southern Ireland the
Catholic hierarchy has never brooked the slightest interference in
its affairs on the part of the political leadership and this autonomy
has been a precondition of its hegemony over the politicians. In
Algeria the religious leaders collectively have little practical
autonomy of the political leadership; in so far as they constitute an
organized force, this is principally in virtue of their orchestration
by the state which pays their salaries and supervises their
activities in accordance with *its* "reasons".

The corollary of this domination of the religious by the political
is that the two spheres, although analytically distinct, are
empirically confused, at least to the extent to which they overlap.
Theoretical distinctions which the sociological observer is capable
of making do not necessarily correspond to the experience of
Algerian Muslims. In addition, the state's supervision of the
religious sphere undoubtedly represents a strategic decision by
the Boumedienne regime (to which its successor has so far

adhered) to make a virtue out of necessity. The conditions do not yet exist for a secular, let alone anti-religious, stance on the part of an otherwise effectively modernist regime. For the regime to forsake Islam in the name of modernity would be to break the single most important ideological and cultural link between it and the mass of the population. It would also, of course, deprive the regime of much of its historical legitimacy as the heir to a revolution which was popularly conceived of as a *jihad* (Holy War) fought by *moujahidin* (warriors of the Faith). For the social and political mobilization of this population to be effective it must be conducted in terms intelligible to it, i.e. *inter alia*, in religious terms.

The brand of Islam which constitutes the state religion in Algeria is substantially appropriate to the performance of this political service. Official Islam is the puritan, scripturalist, nationalist and modernist Islam of the Reform movement (*islāh*) led by the Association of the *Ulama*, whose founder, Abdelhamid Ben Badis (died 1940), is one of the principal national heroes of the independent state. The modernism and nationalism of the regime's policies therefore find ready legitimation in religious terms. In so far as socialist policies appear necessary to the realization of the programme of modernization, they too can claim this religious legitimacy. In so far as such policies involve egalitarianism and "social justice" and so require measures of expropriation and redistribution, they can seek legitimation in religious terms as being necessary for the preservation of the cohesion and unity of the *umma*. Official Islam in Algeria is thus precisely "the cult of the will of the government", which is why popular resistance to that will is frequently expressed through "unorthodox" or dissident versions of the faith, as has been seen in the revival of the Sufi brotherhoods during the 1970s, and, more recently, the growth of the Muslim Brethren. At the same time this overlap between religion and politics testifies to the lack of modernity of the Algerian state in that it directly reflects the degree of confusion which exists between private and public domains.

4 Private Domain and Public Domain

By private domain I mean the domain of private (or particular) interests, be they those of an individual, a family, a firm, an association or whatnot. By public domain I mean the domain of the public (or general) interest. In Hegel's political theory, Civil

Society was the arena for the play of private interests, the State was the arena for the determination and realization of the public interest. The distinction between private and public domains is not yet fully established in the social consciousness in Algeria. There is, however, a radical difference between the two main sectors of the economy in this respect.

In the capitalist private sector (which accounted for 37 per cent of industrial production and 47 per cent of industrial employment in 1975) the distinction is clear. The conflict between rival private interests is recognised and allowed for, for example the conflict between labour and capital and between competing capitals. The private domain has a clear material basis in private property, including the property of workers in their own labour power and the corresponding right to withdraw it.

In the public sector the distinction is obscured. Private interests and the public interest are systematically confused. The bureaucracy does not predominantly, let alone exclusively, represent the general interest over against particular interests, it is pervaded by particular interests. The reason for this is linked to the fact that the emergence of the state sector of the economy has not been, for the most part, the economic corollary of the growth of the power of the state at the expense of domestic private interests, as it has been elsewhere, whether in revolutionary fashion, as in the Soviet Union, or through an evolutionary mode of development, as in the United Kingdom. Undefeated and largely unscathed in Algeria, but denied the opportunity for unlimited development by the expansion of the state sector, these private interests have taken their revenge by systematically infiltrating the administrative apparatus and thereby impeding the coherent collective management of the public sector of the economy. Decisions at every level of the administration are taken in the name of the People, but determined to a considerable extent by the play of private interests. Bruno Etienne, who has provided a most penetrating analysis of this phenomenon, suggests that the influence of private interests decreases in intensity the higher up the bureaucratic hierarchy one goes, and it is very likely that this is the case. In general, however, with the exception of a small number of conscientious or merely prudent (because highly remunerated) senior functionaries at the apex of the administrative pyramid and a scattering of idealists at other levels, there is little practical recognition of or respect for the concept of disinterested public service. The bureaucracy does not function primarily in accordance with a rational-legal code; such a code exists, of course, but is subject to extensive manipulation when it is not straightforwardly honoured in the breach. On the contrary, administrative action is determined in large measure by personal ties and obligations and is characterized by the preferential treatment of friends and relations. If bureaucrats in Algeria appear much less inert than their counterparts in many other countries, this is only partly to the credit of the government. To a substantial extent it is in virtue of their need to "render service" (*ma'ouna*) in order to honour a debt to, or contract a debt from, kinsmen and allies whose pressure is all the more intense for the fact that Algerian society is undergoing an extremely disorienting process of unusually rapid economic and social development. In such times those without allies are not simply left behind, they are liable to lose what they have.

In the private sector the explicit recognition of the existence of competing and conflicting private interests simultaneously permits both the continued development of these interests and the social forces which embody them *and* the intervention of the state as the public power guaranteeing the general interest of the community as a whole by subjecting the interplay of these interests to the rule of law. Recognition of the private domain and of the public domain, and of both the distinction and the relationship between the two, is thus free to develop and attain a good deal of clarity in the social consciousness. Thus in the private sector the distinction between Civil Society and the State is clear.

In the public sector, on the other hand, the existence of private interests is clandestine. The private domain has no clearly demarcated material basis in private property and its rights, for these are, of course, non-existent in the state sector, even in regard to an individual's labour-power (strikes are illegal). At the same time public property rights are not sufficiently backed up by a public power capable of enforcing them fully; they thus tend to fall prey to particular private interests. Because private interests are illegitimate, the only recognition officially accorded them is that implied by the intermittent presidential denunciations of nepotism and corruption, notably in the series of extremely forceful speeches which Boumedienne delivered in the summer of 1974. The existence and importance of these interests is thus the open secret of Algerian politics, the scandal of Algerian public life.

In these circumstances, the illegitimacy of these interests means that their development and that of the social forces and individuals which embody them have been continuously impeded, headed off by irregular clampdowns on corruption and generally discouraged and frustrated. But, because they have not been allowed to achieve an explicit existence, their development has not simultaneously permitted the general interest to be clearly distinguished from them and acquire public recognition as such, as has been possible within the confines of the private sector of the economy. The resulting confusion not only impedes the rational management of state property, it also engenders massive popular cynicism, since every Algerian is in turn accomplice and victim of this confusion, obliged to profit from such "contacts" (*ma'arifa*) and "pull' (*piston*) as he possesses within the bureaucracy when he can do so, denied the treatment to which he is, in principle, entitled when such privileged access is lacking.

Since the state sector as a whole (in agriculture and services as well as in industry) is hugely dominant in terms of the proportion of GNP it accounts for and, although less decisively as yet, the workforce it employs, the social relations and the corresponding forms of consciousness which obtain within it determine the general character of the state as a whole. Thus the Algerian state is not yet a modern state, for the distinction between State and Civil Society is not yet generally established in the social consciousness. This situation finds its ideological reflection in the survival of highly charged vestiges of the Arab–Muslim political order in which, of old, state power had its origin in "a people formed by a community" instead of, as in modern Western states, "a people composed of citizens" (*Flory*, 1962, p. 19). The order itself has not survived, for the colonial disruption of Algerian society destroyed its material basis. And its vestiges are being shrewdly enlisted, as we have seen, to perform a last historical service, that of legitimizing policies which are consummating the transformation initiated by the French.

In the meantime, however, confusion reigns. And it is here that we can see in its fullness the profound ambiguity of the dominant role of the state in Algerian society at the current stage of its development. On the one hand, only the state could impel the rapid economic development which is creating the material basis for a modern political order. On the other hand, the massive expansion of the state apparatus and the fact that the state is the principle allocator of the society's resources have given a new lease of life to the traditional solidarities based on family, clan, village, tribe and religious brotherhood to the variable but often substantial extent that these have survived the colonial impact, since it is only by invoking these solidarities (and more recent ones, for example those born of service in one or other branches or regions of the wartime liberation front) that the majority of Algerians can obtain access to the administration and it is, to a great extent, on the possession of such a clientele that the ambitious bureaucrat is obliged to build his career. These circumstances, by no means peculiar to Algeria, have given rise to a number of studies on the theme of 'patron–client' relations, among which, for the Algerian case, that of Bruno Etienne holds pride of place. As he remarks, "today, the system of patron–client relations can either gangrene the state apparatus or serve to diffuse the new rationality of Algiers" (Etienne, 1977, p. 92). In fact, however, it does both at once, for, "as a mechanism through which to integrate a marginal and peripheral population which possesses its own system of values, the system of patron–client relations is used by the elite which dominates the Nation-State in order to impose its own system of values and reinforce its power" (Etienne, ibid.).

As in the case of Reformist Islam, a virtue has been made of necessity, *faute de mieux*. But while the political use of Islam for modernist purposes has required no justification, since to most Algerians it appears as its own justification, the use of patron–client relations in this way has been surreptitious and the object of a good deal of double-think. It has also been much more of an objective process than the product of a conscious strategic choice. But at the same time it has meant that the importance of the private interests involved in the system of patron–client relations within the public sector has been systematically underestimated in the official discourse of the regime. The government simply has not possessed, at any rate until very recently, the political resources to police, let alone purge, the administrative apparatus. Official regulation of the interplay of private interests within the state sector has been out of the question since these interests have no official existence, yet political suppression of the interplay of these interests has also been impossible.

5 "Clannishness" and the Political Development of the Bourgeoisie

Before examining the reasons for this and also whether the assertion of systematic political control over the administrative apparatus is now becoming possible, we need to consider the relationship between these general features of the Algerian bureaucracy and its mode of operation on the one hand and the development of the Algerian bourgeoisie on the other. The connection between the two is an intimate one.

There exists a plethora of patron–client networks, but also a definite tendency for them to cohere into factions or "clans". Many clans, naturally, are rather short-lived affairs, but equally many may well possess a certain corporate stability, although their membership will usually include a "floating" element. This phenomenon, usually referred to as "clannishness" in the Algerian case, has been widely noted. As Etienne has remarked, if the bureaucracy has varying relations with its environment,

> at the level of the capital, Algiers, it is more a question of clans within the administration and the power structure, which confront one another over questions of patrons, that is, questions of personality and recent history rather than over doctrinal debates. . . . [O]ften one has the impression that certain administrative services constitute veritable segments opposed one to another, the ties of blood being interwoven with the legitimacy of the various coteries of the war period. . . . (Etienne, 1977, p. 105).

Accordingly, the specific and principal problem of the bureaucracy in Algeria is not so much that patron–client relationships, articulating private interests, pervade the apparatus as that crucial decisions, particularly at higher levels, are taken in virtue of factional struggles and so determined as much by the state of play between opposed clans as by the requirements and priorities of government policy.

Problem number one of the Algerian bureaucracy, then, the phenomenon of clannishness is also the link between the general system of patron–client relations on the one hand and the bourgeois leanings of important elements of the bureaucracy on the other, for it is precisely through these factional struggles that the Algerian bourgeoisie is developing itself as a national class. To understand why this is so, it is necessary to bear in mind not only the extent to which this bourgeoisie has come to depend upon its relationship with the state sector of the economy – a dependence accentuated by the loss of major areas of economic activity in agriculture (since the launching of the "Agrarian Revolution" in 1971/2) and the wholesaling of agricultural produce (since 1974) – but also its general political immaturity and its substantial incoherence as a "class for itself".

The notion of a class weakened by internal divisions arising from conflicting material interests within it is a familiar feature of Marxist theory since Marx's own analysis of Bonapartism in mid-nineteenth century France. In Algeria, however, the incoherence of the bourgeoisie has not been a matter of the competing and, at least temporarily, irreconcilable interests of agrarian, merchant, industrial and finance capital. In a mature capitalist society where the bourgeoisie is the ruling class, political factions within it may well predominantly represent different fractions of capital. In a country where the bourgeoisie is not yet the ruling class, where it is still, in fact, engaged in simultaneously acquiring power *and* becoming a class for itself, the divisions within it are likely to reflect rather the competition for political power and for membership of this rising class, for the two are indissociable inasmuch as participation in or access to political power is a prerequisite for obtaining, consolidating or simply preserving economic power, and those engaged in this competition are likely to invest, for reasons of political rather than economic prudence, in a wide range of activities, agrarian, commercial, financial and so on. Such competition is, by definition, between social groups in transition, groups which have emerged from the previous social order and which are defined at least partially in terms of this order. They use the mechanisms of social solidarity and political mobilization offered by this order to gain a position in the emerging class structure, in which they will finally become independent of these old ties.

In Algeria the transitional social groups engaged in this competition for membership of the emerging bourgeoisie are constituted on the basis of three types of social origin: first, the remnants of the old, essentially mercantile, bourgeoisie of pre-colonial Algeria, which has survived principally in the two inland cities of Constantine in the east and Tlemcen in the west and, to a lesser extent, in smaller towns such as Mila, Bejaia and Jijel in the east and Mascara, Nedroma and Mostaganem in the west; second, the descendants of the old tribal nobility, both military (*jouad*) and religious (*chorfa*) and, third, the more vigorous and dynamic elements of the detribalized peasantry which, through access to French education during the colonial period, acquired the cultural prerequisites for subsequent upward social mobility.

It is largely out of these three elements that the modern Algerian bourgeoisie has been forging itself, but it appears that the integration of formerly noble or peasant families into the bourgeoisie has been accompanied by the reinforcement of the regional fragmentation of the class as a whole. The reason for this is that the principal arbiters of this process of integration have been the great bourgeois families of Constantine and Tlemcen, notably through the orchestration of marriage alliances, but also through a multitude of less visible procedures. The multifaceted process of absorption of new elements into the bourgeoisies of Constantine and Tlemcen has entailed the extension of the hegemony of these bourgeoisies over their respective hinterlands (eastern and western Algeria) and, at the same time, has tended to accentuate the political divisions within the bourgeoisie as a whole.

In the past, there has been very little connection between the bourgeoisies of Constantine and Tlemcen. Prior to the colonial period, eastern Algeria had possessed much stronger economic and cultural links with Tunisia than with western Algeria, while the latter had been primarily oriented towards Morocco. Before the advent of Turkish rule in the sixteenth century, these two regions had been the more or less autonomous peripheries of the Tunisian and Moroccan states. The Turks formally unified Algeria in administrative terms, but did very little to integrate its various regions into a national economic community. French colonialism laid the foundations for the subsequent integration of the Algerian economy, but in the short run the customs union with the metropolis largely undermined the traditional artisanate of the towns and the old commercial networks upon which the prosperity of the Muslim bourgeoisie had been based, and the new commercial networks which replaced them were dominated by European capital. Thus, before 1962, the changes which had occurred had done little to unify the Algerian bourgeoisie. It was for this reason that the Algerian bourgeoisie never developed a coherent and united attitude towards the colonial regime and, although elements of it played an important part in the genesis of Algerian nationalism, notably through the Association of the *Ulama,* this did not represent the collective outlook of the bourgeoisie as a whole. On political questions there was no collective outlook. It was this lack of coherence which prevented the bourgeoisie from assuming the political leadership of the nationalist movement and through it acquiring hegemony over the Muslim population. The failure of bourgeois leadership permitted the emergence of autonomous and more radical forces, which have retained political power in Algeria ever since.

If the structure of the national economy prior to Independence was not conducive to the integration of the Algerian bourgeoisie into a national class, we might, none the less, expect subsequent economic changes to have favoured such a development. It is certainly possible, even likely, that this will be the long-run effect of the changes which have occurred since 1962. In the short run, however, it would appear rather that these changes have led the old relationship between the regional components of the bourgeoisie, characterized by the looseness of the links between them, to be superseded, generally speaking, by intense rivalries. Because the state rapidly assumed a dominant role in the economy after 1962 and the private sector accordingly became increasingly dependent upon the public sector, and since the personnel of the administrative apparatus was, initially, drawn very largely from precisely those sections of the population with access to French education out of which the modern Algerian bourgeoisie has been constituting itself, competition for social and economic advancement within this developing class, or for entry into it, has been inevitably accompanied by political competition for influence and representation within the bureaucracy. In so far as this depends upon personal ties of kinship and alliance and to the extent that such ties are, for the most part, geographically circumscribed, the resulting factions within the administrative apparatus have tended to assume distinct regional complexions. While clans of a kind exist at every level of the Algerian bureaucracy, the most stable of those at the national level, in the *sociétés nationales* (public enterprises) the other state economic organizations (*offices nationales*, etc.), and even the various government departments, usually have their social basis in the regional fractions of the bourgeoisie.

6 Bureaucracy and Party

How then, are we to characterize the principal contradiction within the system of state capitalism as it exists in contemporary Algeria? The burden of my argument thus far can be summarized as follows: The development of state capitalism has entailed not only the massive expansion of the administrative apparatus of the state, but has also, at least initially, permitted a substantial development of private capitalist enterprise. The pervasive presence of patron–client relations within the bureaucracy, corollary of the backwardness of the Algerian state, has seriously interfered with the efficient management of the public sector. More important, the combination of this general feature of the bureaucracy with the specific mode of development of the regionally fragmented Algerian bourgeoisie has given rise to the far more acute problem of "clannishness"; that is, the incessant struggle between factions, which intervenes in the determination of administrative action at every level, but with particular effect at the level of the capital. While the general phenomenon of patron–client relations, particularly important at the lower levels of the administrative hierarchy, can to some extent be allowed for and discounted by the architects of government policy, that of "clannishness" poses a far more serious problem, since it characterizes administrative action at the highest levels of the hierarchy as well as lower down and intervenes in the functioning of the bureaucracy at crucial moments in ways which are inherently unpredictable.

The inefficiency and incoherence to which the management of the public sector has accordingly been prone could be and has been regarded by the government as an acceptable and, in any case, unavoidable price to pay for the state-directed primitive accumulation necessary for the construction of a modern industrial economy in Algeria. Once this primitive accumulation had been achieved, however, the case for the continuing domination of the state sector and the corresponding restrictions placed upon the private sector could be strongly challenged on the grounds of the superior efficiency and profitability of private enterprise.

Moreover, the phase of primitive accumulation has entailed, in Algeria as elsewhere, a long period of austerity and the comparative neglect of the consumption needs of the population, notably in housing. Social pressure on the government to pay greater attention to these needs has been building up since the early 1970s and the Chadli regime has made clear its intention to respond positively to this and has already begun to do so. But any significant shift in the relative importance accorded to the production of consumption goods as opposed to production goods must involve either a substantial expansion of the private sector, which has throughout been largely concerned with this type of production, or the development of a large state sector of light industry. The first option is likely to reinforce the social pressure for a more thorough-going economic liberalization of the kind which has been attempted in Egypt in recent years. Because of the unpredictable but probably disruptive social and political repercussions of such a development – quite apart from other considerations – this option is likely to be resisted by the political leadership. The second option entails the considerable expansion of the administrative apparatus of the state and, in view of the generally more complex nature of both the functions of management in, and the central planning of, light industry producing for the consumer market as compared with heavy industry engaged to a large extent in the production of capital goods, the capacity of the state to assume responsibility for this type of production would be gravely prejudiced by the persistence of the kind of irrationality and inefficiency which has tended to characterize its administrative apparatus until now. Accordingly, the choice of the second option is likely to be accompanied, if it is to be effective, by attempts by the political leadership to tighten its control over this apparatus, attempts which will, among other things, threaten the existing prerogatives of senior functionaries, and which are therefore liable to be strongly resisted by them.

The conflict between advocates of these alternative lines of development has a direct bearing on the continuing controversy within the regime over the role and prerogatives of the party, the *Front de Libération Nationale*. Since Independence the FLN has possessed neither the authority nor the technical competence to orient and supervise the activity of the administrative apparatus of the state. Its function has been rather to orient and control the population, through its control of the "mass organizations" – the trade unions, the peasants' union, the youth movement, the women's union and so forth. Neither armed forces nor bureaucracy have been subject to its authority. In a sense, therefore, the party and its ramifications could be regarded as part of the bureaucracy, performing essentially a public relations function on its behalf. Until recently the party apparatus was meagre in the extreme. It possessed neither central committee nor political bureau and no debates of substance took place within it, since it was not where power lay. Its job was to explain and justify decisions taken elsewhere, not to reason why.

But, if the Boumedienne regime actively connived at this state of affairs from 1965 to 1971, Boumedienne himself began to express increasing dissatisfaction with it thereafter. On 31 October 1972, in the early phase of the "Agrarian Revolution", he proclaimed the necessity of "a radical transformation of the FLN" both in its "modes of leadership" and in its "methods of action". Shortly afterwards, the conservative party chief, Kaid Ahmed, was sacked. No successor was named, however, until five years later, in October 1977, when Colonel Mohammed Salah Yahiaoui, a member of the Council of the Revolution and director of the Combined Services Academy at Cherchell, was appointed Co-ordinator of the Party. It appears that Boumedienne was relying on a new generation of activists committed to socialism to emerge in the course of the sustained popular mobilization which occurred from 1972 to 1977 over a series of government policies – the "agrarian revolution", the introduction of "socialist management" in the public sector, the launching of the national health service, the reform of higher education, the public debates over the National Charter in the summer of 1976 and the national mobilization over the Saharan crisis. Alongside Yahiaoui a number of other ambitious and influential figures were drafted into the party apparatus in 1977, their task being to prepare for a full-scale Party Congress, the first since 1964, scheduled to be held in late 1978. Boumedienne's death delayed the holding of this until January 1979, but the congress nevertheless went some way towards launching the party on its new career at the centre of the political stage, equipping it with a 160-man Central Committee and a Political Bureau of seventeen members, plus eleven commissions with responsibility for the principal areas of government policy.

In the struggle for the succession to Boumedienne, Yahiaoui appeared as the standard bearer of the left, advocating a hardline socialist perspective. He was opposed by Abdelaziz Bouteflika, Boumedienne's Foreign Minister, who was known to favour economic liberalization. Thus the two principal contenders for the presidency were publicly associated with the two alternative lines of development now open. However, neither of the tendencies within the regime favouring these alternatives was strong enough to secure the victory of its candidate. Instead, the army's nominee, Colonel Chadli Bendjedid, emerged as the compromise choice. Thus, if the divisions within the regime which were revealed in late 1978 suggest that Algeria had entered a period of crisis of the state-capitalist form and of the balance of forces which underlies it, Chadli's victory indicates that this period is far from over. Since taking office, Chadli has persistently tacked between the two wings of the regime, balancing certain measures of liberalization with selective tightening of political control in other spheres. He has also succeeded in clipping the newly fledged wings of the party, dissolving several of its policy commissions and reducing the Political Bureau to seven members, while further enlarging the Central Committee and thereby rendering it a less coherent and functional body.

These developments, combined with the elimination of both Yahiaoui and Bouteflika from the political scene, are evidence of the limits to which political polarization is possible within the current form of government of the Algerian state. These limits are ultimately determined by the political weight of the army, which has been the effective arbiter of the competition between factions within the national leadership since before Independence, and clearly does not intend to surrender this role. In acting, through its political representatives, to constrain the development of the party as an autonomous centre of power within the regime, the army has incidentally secured a new lease of life for bureaucratic irrationality in Algeria.

Revolutionary Iran and its Tribal Peoples

Lois Beck

Less than half of the total Iranian population of 35 million speaks Persian as a first language. Except for religion in the case of the 4 per cent of the population which is non-Muslim, language is used by Iranians as the main distinguishing feature of population groups. As the revolutionary process continues in Iran, distinctions between the Persian and the non-Persian populations, including tribal peoples, will undoubtedly have increasing political significance. Persians dominate all urban areas of central Iran and most of the plateau. Most high-level religious figures are Persians. National wealth and power are concentrated in Persian hands; the largest segment of the upper class is Persian. Persians fill most government positions, are the most highly educated and professionally trained, and are the most subject to Western influence. In addition, Persian language and culture, having been propagated from the centre, dominate the nation.

Iran's regional, tribally-organized populations, almost all of whom speak languages other than Persian as first languages, are regarded as national minorities. Many are located in strategic border, gulf and oilfield regions; others are in often inaccessible mountains. They include, in approximate order of size: Kurds, Baluch, Bakhtyaris, Lurs, Qashqa'i, Turkmen, Shahsevan, Arabs and many other smaller groups, such as Afshars, Basseri, Hazaras, Tajiks and Timuris. Iran's largest non-Persian population, the Turkic speaking Azeris (Azerbayjanis), along with the majority of the nation's Arabic-speaking population, are not tribally organized. A "tribe" is a sociopolitical formation brought about in response to state pressure and, as such, is often territorially based. Tribal membership is defined primarily by political affiliation to leaders. Tribal members often claim to share kinship bonds and common ancestors, and notions of cultural distinctiveness are also a factor. Prior to the twentieth century, Iran's tribes had economies based primarily on nomadic pastoralism. Now most tribal populations are settled in villages and towns, have mixed agricultural and pastoral economies, and have become increasingly dependent on wage labour.

Regional, tribally-organized populations played peripheral roles in the national effort to rid Iran of the Shah. The revolution was originally an urban phenomenon, and one that primarily

Table 6 *Tribal Populations*

	Estimated population in Iran[1]	Estimated population in other nations	Predominant religion[2]
Kurds	3,000,000	5,600,000-10,100,000[3]	Sunni Islam[4]
Baluch	1,500,000	3,500,000	Sunni Islam
Bakhtiyaris	570,000	–	Shi'i Islam
Lurs	500,000	–	Shi'i Islam
Qashqa'i	400,000	–	Shi'i Islam
Turkmen	315,000	1,385,000	Sunni Islam
Shahsevan	300,000	–	Shi'i Islam
Arabs	150,000[5]	millions	Sunni & Shi'i Islam
Basseri	20,000	–	Shi'i Islam
Others	200,000	–	Shi'i Islam

[1]Accurate statistics on Iran's tribal populations do not exist. Richard Weekes's *Muslim Peoples: A World Ethnographic Survey*, Westport, Conn, 1978, contains essays, written primarily by anthropologists, on these and other ethnic groups in Iran. The population estimates derive partly from this source.

[2]An estimated 6 per cent of Iran's Muslims are Sunni.

[3]The higher figure is that of Martin van Bruinessen, *Agha, Shaikh and State: On the Social and Political Organization of Kurdistan*, Utrecht, 1978, p. 22.

[4]There are a significant number of Shi'i Kurds, and many Kurds belong to Sufi orders.

[5]The estimated total Arab population in Iran is 615,000. For lack of statistical information, it is extremely difficult to determine the proportion of tribal to non-tribal people's among Iran's Arab population. The best estimate is that Iranian Arabs are about evenly divided between Sunni and Shi'i Islam.

involved Tehran and other cities. Tribal populations are not generally integrated into the urban religious institutions and the student and leftist organizations that were integral to the revolution; few demonstrations or other revolutionary activities took place in rural areas before the end of 1978. Tribal people working in the oil industry, as well as those who had migrated to Tehran and other cities for wage labour and education, participated in revolutionary activities along with worker and student groups, not as tribal representatives. These demonstrations were almost exclusively male, with exceptions in some cities in Kurdistan and in Shiraz, where young women in a tribal school demonstrated together in the streets, in tribal dress, with Turkic and Luric slogans.

Tribal Peoples and the Pahlavi Regime

Tribal populations had as much reason to detest the Shah and the Pahlavi regime as the more revolutionary urban Iranians. Their political and economic structures had been debilitatingly undermined by both Reza Shah and Mohammad Reza Shah. Since the 1920s tribal leaders had been subjected by the state to execution, imprisonment, exil and property confiscation. Through history, tribal leaders had mediated between tribe and state; in this century state action against tribal leadership was often the first and most important step toward political domination of the population. Under Reza Shah, nomadic pastoralists were forcibly settled. Mohammad Reza Shah provided no assistance to either migratory groups or those desiring to settle, and instead placed them under military control and restricted their movements and land use. Tribal populations, as well as many fellow citizens, were victims of incompetent and often corrupt government officials under both Shahs, and political activities were restricted, most effectively after the creation of SAVAK – the secret police – in 1957. Those of tribal affiliation were not usually represented in government, except for some tribal élites, most of whom did not represent tribal concerns, but rather their own class and personal interests.

Rural and tribal populations were subject to economic hardships in the 1960s and 1970s due to loss of land and work through pasture nationalization and national land reforms, increased capitalist penetration and high inflation. Much agricultural and pastoral production became unprofitable; the state increasingly relied on imported food, which it brought in under cheap tariffs and sold at subsidized prices. It became cheaper for many Iranians to buy imported food than to produce it themselves. Tribal peoples were among the nation's most impoverished citizens. As residents of the state's most isolated, marginal areas, they received scant benefits from rapidly increasing oil revenues. National services such as education, health care, water control and transportation were poorly developed.

Simultaneous with these destructive state policies were the heavily financed efforts of the Queen to glorify tribal and ethnic culture through arts festivals and handicraft production – both of which were oriented toward tourist and élite consumption. However, tribal populations, as well as all ethnic minorities in Iran, were denied many national rights under the Pahlavis and were victims of Persian chauvinism. National education, in which all students were required to read and write in Persian and in which Persian culture and civilization were stressed to the almost complete neglect of the contributions of other population segments, was culturally destructive. For tribal children who were offered formal education, most school teachers were urban Persians, as were almost all government officials in tribal areas. One exception was an innovative programme in Fars province which did provide tribal teachers for many of the region's nomadic children.

The Revolutionary Process

The nation's tribal populations joined the revolutionary process as significant forces only with the decline and then virtual end of central authority in late 1978 and early 1979. At this time many acts against the central government occurred in and around tribal areas; these were not directed toward the revolutionary aims proclaimed by the Ayatollah Khomeini and other insurgent forces as much as they were responses to weakening central control and to the change in the balance of power in provincial areas. Except at times in Kurdistan and Baluchistan, they were not generally organized through local religious leaders. Anti-government disturbances occurred at government offices, gendarme posts, army depots, and customs stations. Often caches of arms and ammunition were the incentives. As the gendarmerie and army became ineffective, tribal groups attacked government officials and their local patrons and supporters. For one tribal group, previously known for its state-threatening powers, the only reported "revolutionary" acts were attacks on two virtually deserted gendarme posts and the seizure of supplies abandoned by the French at an isolated mining camp on the day of the deposed Shah's departure from Iran.

The Khomeini regime has attempted to reinstate central authority in many areas through two new institutions which are under the aegis of the Revolutionary Council: Revolutionary

Committees (*komitehs*) and Revolutionary Guards (*pasdaran*). In contrast to many lower-middle and lower-class urban areas, where the two units often represent the class interests and cultural identities of the people for whom they are responsible, this is not the case in many provincial and tribal areas, and some populations have resisted their presence. Only in regions where settled tribal groups are in the majority, as in much of Kurdistan and Baluchistan, are some *komitehs* comprised of fellow tribal members and supporters and are not the threatening, exploitative forces they can be elsewhere. Activist clerics (and their supporters) who are closely allied with Khomeini and other clergy in Qum are at the core of most *komitehs*. *Komitehs* tend to represent existing wealth and power structures, which in provincial and tribal areas are dominated by large landowners, merchants and capitalist farmers and stockraisers. Along with the Revolutionary Guards, *komitehs* have taken over many governmental functions, including many gendarmerie functions. For that large proportion of Iranian tribespeople who are Sunni Muslims (see Table 6), involvement in local affairs by a Shi'i state through Shi'i revolutionary forces presents additional difficulties. As is the case with Iran's non-Muslim minorities, they express concern about what citizenship in an expressly Shi'i state will mean for their own religious (and political) freedoms.

Kurdish resistance to the imposition of Persian, Shi'i revolutionary forces in their areas in the summer of 1979 brought about a state military response. The resulting death and destruction helped to convince mány Iranians – tribal and nontribal – that Khomeini was not the kind of leader they had expected or desired. That he could send Iranian Muslims to kill Iranian Muslims so soon after his triumphant return from exile was a turning-point in his relations with the national minorities, and resistance to him and his associates spread. Some tribal people had boycotted the March 1979 referendum on the Islamic republic, and boycotts increased with the summer's election of the Assembly of Experts to draw up the constitution and with the fall's constitutional referendum. Some tribal groups reportedly supported local gendarmes against Revolutionary Guards sent from Tehran. Revolutionary Guards and Committees were driven out of some towns in tribal areas, and insistence that they be removed from others was commonly expressed by many tribal groups. Various high-ranking state officials and clerics were sent from Tehran and Qum to negotiate settlements. In order to prevent bloodshed in several towns in Fars province, tribal leaders and local clerics agreed independently – without government involvement – that tribal members would not brandish arms while visiting town if Revolutionary Guards would stay totally out of the countryside (and hence out of local tribal affairs).

In August 1979 the government produced and distributed wall posters which depicted Khomeini as the benevolent patriarch of the nation's tribes, represented by men and women in a diversity of tribal dress. Other attempts to gain or restore loyalty were also evident. Khomeini offered support for tribal groups (along with condemnation of Kurdish dissidents) in his speeches. But on 5 September 1979, in a televised speech in which he officially greeted a delegation of Turkmen tribesmen who had walked from nort-east Iran to Qum to present demands, he stated that all groups in Iran (and he named specific tribes) had suffered under the Shah and that none could expect immediate solutions to problems. Except for the Kurds, who were allocated a large sum for public works, those tribal groups formally requesting state assistance in such matters as land reclamation, roads, wells, schools, clinics and co-operatives received no response, and their early exhilaration with the revolution turned into a deepening resentment. Some tribal leaders have become quite nationalistic in their attitudes toward Iran in the face of what they jokingly say is "the second Arab invasion".

Tribal Peoples and the New Regime

Representatives of some tribal and ethnic groups, as well as some opposition and leftist groups, propose for Iran a federal political system with autonomous ethnic and provincial regions. The Khomeini regime has to date strongly rejected this notion, and there is no provision in the newly adopted constitution for regional autonomy. Some tribal populations, especially those which extend across Iranian borders into other states, demand local autonomy and self-rule and have formally presented their cases to central authorities. Others, particularly those whose leaders had been systematically removed by the Pahlavi regimes, have not effectively articulated a set of demands. No tribal groups demand total independence or secession from the Iranian state; most express the desire to contribute to and benefit from Iranian citizenship, including expected access to oil income.

The Kurds, who are the most organized in this regard, formulated the slogan "the self-determination of Kurdistan and democracy for Iran" at various sessions of the Conference on the

Self-determination of Kurdistan held in Sanandaj in the summer of 1979. Demands which they wanted legislated in the constitution included: Kurdish officials for the autonomous region, local police forces under local control, restrictions on the placement and activity of state army forces, constitutional safe-guards for the customs and traditions of all national minorities, teaching in the Kurdish language at all levels, a Kurdish university, economic development, improved facilities such as medical services and freedom of the press. Demands issued by some Baluch in the new Islamic Unity Party included regional autonomy, appointment of Baluch to positions in the provincial administration, teaching in the Baluch language and the right of free contact with Pakistani Baluchistan.

The establishment of productive links between minority populations and the government is currently impeded. Especially until the resignation of the Bazargan government in November 1979, a system of parallel governments existed in which the directives and understandings of officials from Tehran and Qum often differed. Both Prime Minister Bazargan and the Ayatollah Taleqani had agreements with Kurdish leaders about regional autonomy which were later ignored by Khomeini and the supporting clergy. In addition, revolutionary forces and self-styled vigilantes often act independently of either Tehran or Qum. Finally, political polarization within minority populations, especially between traditional leaders and young leftists, inhibits efforts to link populations with the centre.

Linkages among Iran's national minorities, which might facilitate common efforts, are also weak. In the spring of 1979 Naser Khan Qashqa'i proposed plans for a federation of southern tribes, and in January 1980 he spoke of a union of Iranian tribes, but to date no concrete steps in these directions have been taken. Effective political organization and capable leadership within single national minority populations could serve as a catalyst for broader movements. The Kurds and the Baluch, however, are the only tribal populations currently possessing formal political parties. The Kurdish Democratic Party was outlawed by Khomeini in the summer of 1979, and its leaders were sought by his revolutionary judge, the Ayatollah Khalkhali. Two other Kurdish political groups are the Marxist-Leninist *Komala* and the *Fedayi Khalq*. In 1979 a Baluch group formed the Islamic Unity Party, and the activities of political parties in Pakistani Baluchistan are increasingly having an impact on Iran's Baluch.

Results of the Revolution

For Iran's rural and tribal populations the major results of the revolution so far are the decline in central authority and certain local economic benefits. The revolution did not transform the nation's socioeconomic structure. New power figures tend to support the existing class system, although wealth and power are shifting from the control of the secular westernized upper class – much of which has left Iran along with its money – to the allied forces of the clerics and the bazaar bourgeoisie. For some rural and tribal people, decline in government authority has allowed acts of resistance to establish structures. Those populations politically organized and well armed are the most active in this regard. The resurgence of tribalism, rather than being the "survival" of an archaic form of organization, is instead a very contemporary response to current conditions of central weakness and to the centre's attempts to establish political domination.

Nomadic pastoralists are seizing pasturelands taken from them in the 1960s and 1970s, and expelling such non-tribal occupants as capitalist herdowners. Many who had been forced out of nomadic pastoralism have now abandoned their villages or urban jobs to resume migration. Many pastoralists and agriculturalists regard the deposed Shah's land reforms as illegal and illegitimate. There is competition among landowners – large and small, tribal and non-tribal – over land, as well as peasant revolts and general resistance to landlords, many of whom are out of Iran or afraid to visit their lands. Individuals and groups desiring to retain or seize land often seek tribal support for their actions. Some peasants take by force the land they sharecropped, rented or ought to have received under a genuine land reform, sometimes by simply harvesting standing crops or planting their own. There is also some resistance to and action against tribal leaders who attempt to retain or regain former privileges. Some tribal leaders under land reform were entitled to keep, as private property, formerly communal tribal land. Certain tribal groups are now demanding these lands for themselves, and some are successful. Small groups of leftists in some tribal areas are attempting to co-ordinate these actions, while Revolutionary Guards are acting to preserve the status quo.

One issue on which Revolutionary Committees and Guards have supported rural and tribal peoples against existing exploitative relations is in moneylending and commerce. Until early 1979, many moneylenders and merchants charged from 50 to 100 per cent yearly interest on loans and goods taken on credit; this was a primary cause of much rural poverty. With the establishment of the Islamic Republic, taking interest for profit was declared prohibited, and clerics and committees ordered that debts be recalculated to represent the actual amount of loans and purchases. Some of those who refused were publicly flogged or imprisoned.

Another local benefit of revolutionary conditions is greater economic productivity for many of the nation's tribal people. Soon after Khomeini's return to Iran, imported frozen meat was proclaimed unclean and ordered destroyed. Foreign suppliers are now said to be following proper Islamic procedures in animal slaughter, but meat imports are still reportedly much below that of pre-revolutionary times. Demand for meat and dairy products is high and the nation's pastoralists – many of whom are tribal – are able to find a good market. Many former nomads have resumed pastoralism, often on land that had been taken from them or others under the Shah. Flock redistributions within some tribal groups have allowed the impoverished to become economically productive. Many who were wage labourers or heavily indebted before the revolution are now able to assume greater economic independence.

But for Iran's agriculturalists (tribal and non-tribal) whose links with the land had been weakened or broken because of the economic disruptions of the 1960s and 1970s, return to production is more difficult. Many irrigation works are ruined, land abandoned and no longer cultivable, land-tenure systems disrupted, and kin-based relations of production undermined and altered by urban wage migration and the penetration of capitalist relations of production into rural economies. Agriculture demands a much higher capital investment than pastoralism, and many rural and urban Iranians are unable or reluctant to make the necessary financial commitment in these unstable times. The Khomeini regime's plans for an "Islamic" land reform have not resulted in action to date.

The State, the Tribes and the Left

Throughout much of Iran's history the state has played a direct role in tribal leadership by such practices as providing tribal leaders with resources and responsibilities (local law and order, tax collection, army formation) and attempting to install or replace tribal leaders. Part of this pattern continues in revolutionary Iran for a reason found also in history: the state's inability to control and administer its regional, politically organized, armed populations. In some areas the state entrusts local – and not just tribal – affairs to tribal leaders. On several occasions in the summer of 1979 Khomeini publicly attributed peaceful conditions in Fars province to Qashqa'i leaders. State authorities, in particulr secular officials and army gendarme officers whose forces are now weak, utilize tribal leaders as surrogate state officials and as mediators. One tribe's leaders are used to solve another tribe's disputes; the state has even transported leaders by helicopter to dispute locations.

Such use of tribal leaders can enhance and legitimize their regional and national position, inhibit local or leftist efforts to establish more egalitarian structures, and further undercut state authority and control. In September 1979 the prime minister issued an order demanding that the citizens of Fars province who were carrying arms submit them to state authorities within three days. The order was, however, first issued to a local tribal leader, who was expected to implement it. Nothing came of the order, other than an advancement of this leader's status. In another incident, gendarmes who were unable to end a fight between two tribal sections over pastureland stopped a tribal leader who happened to be driving to another location on other business and asked him to mediate the dispute. He agreed to the task, but was unable to fulfil the mission; one of the disputants killed him on the spot. Another tribal leader, long in exile during the Pahlavi regime, boldly claimed that he could, within ten days, end Khomeini's difficulties with the Kurds if Khomeini ordered him to take one thousand tribal warriors to Kurdistan. After he was condemned by fellow tribal leaders, he withdrew the offer.

An indication of the apparent ease by which the Western press accepts the Khomeini regime's explanations of provincial unrest is in the conflicting wire service reports on disturbances in the Gulf port of Bandar Langeh on 5-7 January 1980. The disturbances were first attributed to the presence of Qashqa'i and Khamseh tribesmen, then to disputes between resident Persians and Arabs, and finally to differences between Shi'is and Sunnis. Especially since the state's military involvement in Kurdistan last summer, Khomeini has attempted to blame tribal and other national minority unrest on leftist and foreign agitation. This draws attention away from minority group demands, increases tension between the state and its minorities, and increases the zeal with which Revolutionary Guards attempt to "restore order".

The extent to which national minorities and leftist groups are allied is not yet clear. Small leftist groups are found in most politically organized and active tribes, but they are having variable degrees of success in attracting support and developing common goals. Leftists who lack tribal origins have great difficulty in establishing rapport; this is especially the case for young, urban, Persians leftists. Where leftist groups have international affiliations some tribal members express concern that their tribes will be used opportunistically – primarily as military forces to aid a leftist regime's establishment – and that they would be denied national minority rights once the new regime was in power. The example of the fate of Muslim and tribal minorities in the Soviet Union is frequently cited, and the developing situation in Afghanistan between the Soviet-backed government and insurgent tribesmen is closely followed by (conflicting) shortwave radio broadcasts in Persian from many sources including Afghanistan, Great Britain, Soviet Union, Voice of America, Israel, Romania and Iraq.

Leftist sentiments and activities within tribal populations are found among the young generation, especially those who are formally educated and professionally trained. Some tribesmen who were military officers under the Shah in Dhofar (Oman) and Kurdistan – and who were radicalized by this experience – also have leftist inclinations. In south-west Iran it is especially teachers connected with a tribal education programme originally sponsored by the United States who are leftist. The leftist core of some tribal groups consists partly of sons and daughters of former or established tribal leaders. They are usually Western-educated, were active in leftist groups abroad, and have contacts with leftist movements within and outside Iran. As is true of many Iranian families whose members had different levels of revolutionary participation and who have different political affiliations, some tribal élite families are also politically split. In one case the father meets regularly with Khomeini in Qum, the son quietly seeks out opposition leaders who are underground in Iran or abroad and the daughter engages in grassroots activity in an urban shanty-town where she provides health services and classes in literacy and Islamic law to formerly nomadic, now settled and impoverished, tribal women and children.

At the time of this writing (early January 1980) it is increasingly apparent that the Khomeini regime's hostility to the demands of tribal and other national minorities and its charge of foreign and leftist intervention are distracting attention from the regime's stated goal: the transformation of Iran from a secular, dependent capitalist, Western-oriented, monarchical dictatorship into a popularly-supported, economically viable, nonaligned, Islamic republic. In refusing to grant Iran's many national minorities basic democratic rights, the regime creates further difficulties and postpones coming to grips with other tasks at hand. Disturbances in tribal and provincial areas are largely the result of the centre's continued intolerance of local desires for self-rule and its refusal to alter the Pahlavi policies of chauvinistic domination of the political, economic, religious and cultural life of the countryside.

Minorities and Political Elites in Iraq and Syria

Nikolaos van Dam

In publications dealing with the political situation in Iraq and Syria it is often suggested that the former country is ruled by an Alawi minority, whereas the regime in the latter is dominated by Sunnis and more specifically by tribally related people from the northern town of Takrit, who in their turn constitute a minority within the Sunni minority of Iraq.

Both situations would, at least statistically, be cases of so-called minority rule, because the Alawis are only about 11 per cent of the total *Syrian* population, a majority of roughly 70 per cent of which is Sunni, whereas in Iraq Shi'i Arabs are a majority of about 50 per cent; the Sunni Arabs and Sunni Kurds each making up for about 20 per cent of the population.

Some even speak about the Syrian "Alawi Ba'th" and the Iraqi "Takriti Ba'th", or about the "al-Asad family regime" and the "tribal Takriti clique". Many Western observers take over one or more of these labels of the Ba'thist regimes in Syria and Iraq, without critically testing their validity.

In this article I propose to investigate and analyse what the reasons are for the strong representation of Alawis in the Syrian Ba'thist regime, and of Sunnis, and Takritis in particular, in that of Iraq. In doing so I shall also try to answer the question of whether or not labels such as "Alawi, Takriti or Sunni rule" are justified.

1 Iraq

1.1 Traditional Sunni Dominance

It cannot be denied that Arab Sunnis have both before and after Iraqi Independence dominated the political scene, and that from a statistical point of view they have been strongly over-represented in Iraqi power institutions.

What accounts for this situation? When what is now Iraq was still part of the Ottoman Empire, the Ottoman government, itself composed of Sunnis, gave preference to co-religionists in appointments to the military, the bureaucracy and the upper echelons of the educational establishment which prepared young people for such posts. Arab Sunnis thus gradually came to dominate the army and the governmental bureaucracy, and had a disproportionate share of educational and professional advantages. The fact that the schools were at first mostly located in the cities and larger towns, only strengthened this trend: the Sunnis, forming the majority of the urban population, inevitably benefited to a greater extent that the Shi'is, who constitute the majority of the rural population; through education, many Sunni Arabs became teachers and army officers, key careers open to those without private means.

Since there is a natural tendency in any society for a dominant ethnic, religious or other social group to perpetuate its power, particularly if it has a disproportionate share of educational, professional and military advantages, it is only natural that Sunni Arabs remained over-represented in power institutions also after Independence, and notwithstanding the fact that no discrimination against the Shi'is and the Kurds has been practised, at least officially, since the Mandate.

1.2   Regional and Tribal Power Politics

As far as the post-monarchist period since 1958 is concerned, political factors go much further toward explaining the strong representation of Arab Sunnis in power institutions such as army and government. In the first place the Free Officers' movement which carried out the revolution of 1958 and dominated every regime up to 1968, when the Ba'th Party took over for the second time, contained no Kurds and very few Arab Shi'is, its members being mostly Sunni Arabs from the north. The intrusion of the army into politics put the Shi'is at a disadvantage, since relatively few Shi'is had reached as yet the top ranks of the military.

In fact the strong representation of Sunni Arabs in the army and governments since 1958 was not so much – as is often suggested – a result of sectarianism in the form of Sunni Arab discrimination and prejudice against Shi'is. It was much more a result of tribalism and regionalism playing an important role in Iraqi power politics. Military leaders tended to strengthen their grip on the army and to ensure their power positions in it by appointing tribal relatives or trusted friends from their home regions to sensitive positions. Since the population of Iraq is, from a religious point of view, not very much mixed geographically, and the Sunnis and Shi'is are mainly confined to specific areas (i.e. the Sunnis being concentrated mainly in the area of Baghdad and northward, whereas the Shi'is are concentrated in the south, both areas themselves having rather homogenous populations as to religion) regionalism or tribalism usually implies relying on co-religionists, without sectarian ties as such being important.

Typical cases of tribally and regionally narrowly based regimes were those of the Arif brothers (1963-8). Both heavily relied on officers, non-commissioned officers and men from their own al-Jumaylah tribe from the predominantly Sunni western province of Al-Ramadi. In the time of the second Arif regime the Iraqi government became, as Professor Hanna Batatu has described: "to a greater degree than formerly, a plaything of officers' groups, and as these groups were only nominally differentiated by ideas, but in fact revolved around self-interested persons or drew their nourishment from narrow regional loyalties, politics in the upper levels increasingly degenerated into a struggle of factions without issues".

It is true that the elder President Arif sometimes in his speeches made Sunni-coloured nationalist remarks (for instance, he particularly praised the Sunni Arab Umayyad dynasty) which Arab Shi'is considered as discriminatory against them. Arif's reliance on predominantly Sunni officers had, however, little or nothing to do with sectarianism, but reflected regional and tribal power politics.

1.3   The Quasi-relationship between being Arab Sunni and Arab Nationalist

A second factor which indirectly enforced the trend of strong Sunni Arab representation in Iraqi power institutions was the Arab nationalist orientation of the governments since 1963. Phebe A. Marr argues that

the major support for and leadership of the pan-Arab movement, both pro-Egyptian and Baathist, in Iraq has come from the Arab Sunni population, particularly that portion of it which inhabits the towns and villages along the upper Tigris and Euphrates between Baghdad and Mosul. These Arab Sunnis feel most in common with their coreligionists across the border in Syria and even in Egypt. The domination of the government since 1963 by the Arab nationalists and the Baathists, then, has meant Arab Sunni domination. Conversely, the pan-Arab orientation of these regimes, at least of their public professions, has drawn support from the Arab Sunni population and helped reinforce the presence of the Arab Sunnis in government.

So far so good, but has this strong representation of Arab Sunnis anything to do with their being Sunnis? And is there really a clear relationship between being Sunni and Arab nationalist? I would say not. The decisive factor here again turns out to be firstly regional. Many people in the northern (predominantly Sunni) Arab provinces traditionally leaned strongly towards pan-Arabism, inasmuch as they had in Ottoman times been economically (and in many cases socially) linked with Syria, and now suffered from the partition of the Arab areas of the Ottoman Empire and the obstacles of the new frontiers. "Indeed, it would not be going too far, to say that in the days of the monarchy the people of Mosul were closer in outlook and temperament to the Arabs of Syria or, more specifically, of Aleppo, than to the Arabs of central and southern Iraq."[2] This is partly a result of the fact that at the beginning of this century the major cities of Iraq differed in their economic orientation. The ties of Mosul were mainly with Syria and Turkey; those of Baghdad and the Shi'i holy cities with Persia and the western and south-western deserts; whereas Basrah looked mainly to the sea and to India. Until today many Iraqi Arabs living along the Euphrates west of Baghdad feel strongly related to the Arabs living across the border in Syria. This has little or nothing to do with the fact that both groups are mainly Sunni. Traditional economic and social orientations in the region are much more important. Nevertheless, the Shi'i Arab majority, in its bulk, particularly in the past when Arab nationalist ideology usually had a strong Sunni undercurrent, did not care to be integrated in what appeared in its eyes as an Arab unionist state of a predominantly Sunni colouring.

1.4   Secular Ba'thist Arabism

The secular Arab nationalist ideology of the Ba'th Party which assumed power in 1968, has generally made acceptance of Arabism easier for the Iraqi Shi'i Arab population. Secular Ba'thist Arabism considers Islam as an Arab cultural heritage, to which *all* Arabs, whether Sunni or Shi'i Muslim or Christian, are equal heirs apparent. Therefore, Arab heroes of Shi'i history are in Ba'thist ideology considered on the same footing as Sunni Arab historical figures. This point of secular Arabism has repeatedly been stressed by Iraqi President Saddam Husayn and by other Iraqi Ba'thists.

Thus, President Saddam Husayn, for example, recently stated in a speech in the Shi'i holy city, al-Najaf, that

> Iraq will fight and triumph against injustice everywhere with the swords of [Shi'i] Imam Ali, [his son) Husayn, Khalid al-Walid [chief general of the first Caliph Abu Bakr, and one of the key figures of the early Arab Islamic conquests], Salah al-Din [Saladin, the famous Kurdish Muslim commander from Takrit who recaptured Jerusalem from the Crusaders], all Arab strugglers and Islamic leaders of the land of Arabism and of the message of Islam.[3]

On another occasion, following the reported discovery in July 1979 of a plot against the Iraqi regime, President Saddam Husayn indirectly accused Syria of being involved in it by implicitly comparing the ensuing relationship between the Ba'thist regimes of Iraq and Syria with the historical seventh-century rivalry between Shi'i Imam Ali ibn Abi Talib, who controlled most of Iraq at the time, and Mu'awiyah, the Umayyad Governor of Syria, who challenged the former's claim to the caliphate. Notwithstanding his being a Sunni, President Saddam Husayn described the Shi'i Imam Ali as "a man of honour representing all meanings and spirit of the Islamic mission" who "always lived for honour, principles and the values of Islam and chivalry", whereas he simultaneously labelled Mu'awiyah, the founder of the Arab Sunni Umayyad dynasty, as a man "who was fighting for the sake of earthly temptations". Former non-Ba'thist Sunni presidents would probably never have made such positive remarks about Shi'i Imams like Ali when comparing him with Mu'awiyah.

1.5 Sunni and Shi'i membership in the Iraqi Ba'th

Notwithstanding its secularist orientation the trend towards so-called Sunni over-representation increased even further during the period following 1968 when the Ba'th Party took over power. In the new regime Ba'thists from Takrit played a key role. In the mid-seventies Ba'thists from Takrit held not only almost all the foremost posts in the party, army and the government, including of course the portfolio of defence, but also, among other things, the governorship and Security Department of Baghdad, and the commands of the air force, the Baghdad garrison, the Habbaniyah air base and the tank regiment of the Republican Guard.

What accounted for this anomalous situation? Originally, i.e. before 1963, the Ba'th Party in Iraq was quite different in composition of its membership. Whereas the officer-Ba'thists were in this period almost without exception Arab Sunnis who by birth or origina were preponderantly from the country towns of the upper Tigris and the upper Euphrates, the majority of the highest civilian leaders were Shi'is by extraction. Nevertheless, Shi'is and Sunnis were to be found in the major existing factions, and it can be said that up to November 1963, when the Ba'th was temporarily ousted from power, it had to a large extent the characteristic of a genuine secular partnership between the Sunni and Shi'i Arab nationalist youth. When the Ba'th made a come-back in 1968, the role of Sunnis, and of Takritis in particular, had risen sharply, while that of Shi'is had strongly decline. The Shi'is lost their numerical strength partly because many of them backed the Shi'i Iraqi regional secretary-general of the Ba'th, Ali Salih al-Sa'di, who together with some other Shi'i Party leaders like Talib Shabib and Hazim Jawad had filled both the military and civilian sections of the party apparatus with numerous personal followers, many of whom happened to be Shi'is as well. In many cases these members were admitted through irregular procedures, on basis of ties of mere friendship and according to personal inclinations. Thus, personal factionalism was encouraged in this period, and a kind of "wild growth" of the party apparatus undermined the position of the Ba'th Party in Iraq as a whole. Many of the members thus admitted were purged after the ouster of al-Sa'di from the party following his conflict with the military Ba'thists in 1963.

Another, perhaps much more important reason for the decline of Shi'is in the Iraqi Ba'th lay in the discriminatory practices of the police. Professor Batatu has observed that

Ba'thists belonging to this sect were, after the 1963 coup by Abd-us-Salem Aref, on the whole more systematically hunted than their Sunni comrades and, when nabbed, treated with severity, whereas the latter frequently escaped with lighter[er] sentences. The explanation for this is to be sought not so much in sectarian prejudice as in the fact that Sunni Ba'thists were often from the same town or province or tribe as the members of the police, for the departments of Interior and Security teemed with functionaries from the province of ar-Ramadi and the northern districts of Baghdad province, from which many Ba'thists also hailed. The situation was a carry-over from the days of the monarchy, when such directors general of police as Abd-uj-Jabbar ar-Rawi and Bahjat ad-Dulaimi – both by origin from ar-Ramadi – facilitated, it would seem, the entry of their kinsfolk and clansmen into the service under their control.[4]

1.6 Takritism

Though, as just mentioned, Sunni Ba'thists were on the whole less systematically hunted than their Shi'i comrades under the first Arif regime, the harshness of suppression of the Ba'th Party in general in Iraq should not be underestimated. Following the discovery of a Ba'thist plot to topple the Arif regime in September 1964, most party members were imprisoned, leaving those party members who had escaped arrest with the formidably difficult task of rebuilding and reorganizing the party apparatus, which as a result of internal splits and rivalries in 1963 had for some time been paralyzed in its activities. In 1964 leadership of the Ba'th in Iraq passed into the hands of General Ahmad Hasan al-Bakr and Saddam Husayn, who were both from Takrit, and were tribally related by common membership to the al-Begat section of the Al-bu Nasir tribe. Together they were responsible for reorganizing the military and civilian sections of the Ba'th Party apparatus which in 1968 assumed power. Due to political instability and the increasingly conspiratorial nature of politics, they, for security reasons, had to place a premium on mutual confidence. Those who could best be trusted, frequently turned out to be relatives, or friends from their hometown Takrit or its surrounding areas.

But this is not the whole story about the strong representation of Takritis in power institutions. Already before the rise of the Ba'th Party to power a great number of them was in the army. As Professor Batatu has pointed out:

> this fact is not unrelated to the impoverishment of the inhabitants of Takrit caused by the decline in the production of *kalaks* – rafts of inflated skins – for which their town was renowned in the nineteenth century. To earn their living, many moved to Baghdad and settled in what is known today as the quarter of [the Takritis] at – Takartah. Some found employment as railway construction workers or laboured on the K2-Baiji-Hadithah oil pipeline. Others, however were able to gain admission into the cost-free Royal Militay Academy.
>
> For this they had to thank Mawlid Mukhlis, a protégé of [King] Faisal I and a vice-president of the Senate under the monarchy[5].

Mukhlis, who was Takriti by extraction, and was married to a Takriti girl who was a kinswoman to Ahmad Hasan al-Bakr, was a man of the highest connections. Till his death in the fifties he used his influence in favour of Takritis in view of the many links that tied him to them, and he encouraged many young political aspirants of his poor and arid district to enrol in the army and police services. Similarly, politicians like al-Bakr and Saddam Husayn have used their influence to place Takritis during their rule in key posts, albeit on a Ba'thist basis.

To explain the rise of many Takritis to first rank in the Iraqi officers' corps, one has to refer also to the frequent comb-outs in the army. Since the Revolution of 1958 no fewer than three thousand officers have been pensioned off, among whom military royalists following the destruction of the monarchy; military supporters of the Qasim regime in 1963; the faction of Mosulite officers under leadership of General Abd al-Aziz al-Uqayli in 1966 and 1969; and finally the faction of Ramadi officers, who linked their fate with that of the Arif brothers or with the group of Abd al-Razzaq al-Nayif and Ibrahim al-Dawud, who only temporarily shared power with the Ba'th in July 1968 before being purged altogether. All these purges redounded to the advantage of Takritis.

Even during the reign of the Ba'th itself since 1968 the role of tribally related Takriti Ba'thists in military and civilian key positions was further accentuated and consolidated. This was partly a result of resentment which other prominent Ba'thists harboured against Takriti over-representation. For instance, Nazim Kazzar, the Shi'i Director-General of Internal Security, who felt excluded from real power, and reportedly resented Takriti dominance, only strengthened the trend he opposed, by trying to dislodge the most prominent leaders of Takriti origin from power in an abortive coup in June 1973. This may well have strengthened the conviction of the then President Ahmad Hasan al-Bakr and his then Vice-President Saddam Husayn that only by placing or maintaining some of the most reliable and tribally related Ba'thists from their home town, Takrit, in the most sensitive military and civilian key security positions they could ensure the survival of their regime in the longer run.

Nevertheless, the composition of the Iraqi Ba'thist élite is now gradually being broadened, away from regionalism and tribalism: more and more Ba'thists from other parts of the country, including the Shi'i south, have opportunities to reach high party and government posts, though perhaps only sporadically the most sensitive ones. And as long as the present high level of iron party discipline and absence of corruption in the Iraqi Ba'th upper élite is being maintained, this trend may well continue.

Taking all this into account it would be going too far to say, as Professor Batatu does, "that Takritis rule through the Ba'th party, rather than the Ba'th party through the Takritis"[6]. It is clear that Takritis are strongly over-represented in the most important power institutions. Nevertheless, I think it would be better to state that the present regime is in the first place Ba'thist, and that being a Ba'thist is decisive for being in power. The high-placed Takriti Ba'thists may consider themselves as a temporarily indispensable safety device, necessary to keep the present Ba'th leadership in power during a transitional period long enough to have Ba'thism penetrate deeply into Iraqi society and to broaden the Ba'thist élite's composition gradually, so as to finally win wider recognition in Iraq of its legitimacy as a ruling party.

2 Syria

2.1 Alawi Ba'thist Dominance

The present position of Alawis in the Syrian Ba'th differs considerably from that of Takritis in the Iraqi Ba'th. In Syria the strong over-representation of Alawis in power institutions was mainly the result of a long inter-Ba'thist struggle for power, in which sectarian, regional and tribal loyalties were exploited to the furthest limits, and played an important role ever since the Ba'thist monopolization of power in 1963.

Much of the present-day Alawi domination can be indirectly traced back to the more or less accidental fact that the leadership of the secret Ba'thist military organization – better known as the Military Committee – which seized power in 1963 happened to be in the hands of Alawi officers. In order to quickly consolidate their newly achieved power positions in the army, these officers called up numerous officers and non-commissioned officers with whom they were related through family, tribal or regional ties, so as to fill the gaps in the army resulting from purges of political opponents. Under these circumstances it is not surprising that the majority of purged officers were replaced by Alawis. Similarly the other places were filled to a great extent by Druzes, Isma'ilis and Sunnis from Hawran, due to the – again more or less accidental – fact that officers from these committees and regions were members of the Military Committee as well.

In a subsequent stage it was difficult for the Military Committee to get rid of ideologically unmotivated or other directed elements who were not on one line with the Ba'thist leadership, and nonetheless demanded their share of power as a compensation for their indispensable help during the first stages of the Ba'thist revolution. All this gave way to various kinds of factionalism and instability.

The Alawi-dominated factions in the Syrian army [owed] their powerful position partly to purges of other sectarian and/or regionally based military factions which resented their disproportionately strong representation in power institutions, but by their opposition to it helped to even strengthen the trend they opposed. In February 1966 some of the most prominent Sunni officers' factions supporting Sunni President Amin al-Hafiz were purged from the army following a Sunni-minoritarian polarization in the officers' corps; in September 1966 the major Druze factions were purged, following an Alawi-Druze sectarian polarization; and in the course of 1967, 1968 and the beginning of 1969 the remaining most important non-Alawi blocks in the Syrian army were eliminated or neutralized. In this period particularly some prominent Isma'ili and Hawrani Ba'thist factions lost power. All this resulted in a situation in which some Alawi officers' factions which had survived the preceding purges ended up in a supreme position. This found expression in the fact that the subsequent power struggle was mainly confined to members of the Alawi community themselves. In November 1970 power was more or less completely monopolized by the (mainly Alawi) officers' faction of Hafiz al-Asad, who became Syria's first Alawi President a few months later.

2.2   *Minoritarians in the Syrian Army and Ba'th Party*

When in 1963 sectarianism, regionalism and tribalism started to play an important role in the inter-Ba'thist power struggle in Syria, the minoritarian and rural officers of the Military Committee could count on help and support of many military men and other officers with similar social backgrounds, who were already present in the army and Ba'th Party before the leaders of the Ba'thist Military Committee had seized power.

As I have already extensively explained in my book on Syria,[7] the Ba'th Party in Syria counted many members from religious minorities and from the poor countryside as a result of the fact that the party at first recruited its initial members among rural migrants who had come to Damascus for further education. From Damascus the party organization spread spontaneously, and without any clear plans of action, through the traditional social channels to the communities of the first party members, many of whom happened to be Alawis, Druzes and Isma'ilis.

Its socialist ideals made it easier for the party to obtain a firm footing in the rural towns and in the poverty-stricken rural areas than in the greater cities, where the political scene was dominated by the local bourgeoisie and traders. Since in Syria Arabic-speaking religious minorities are mainly concentrated in rural areas and bigger cities are principally Sunni, it is not surprising that minority members predominated among the Ba'thists.

But whereas the socialist component of Ba'th ideology contributed only indirectly, i.e. because of an overlap between ecological and sectarian factors, to a disproportionately strong representation of minority members in the Ba'th Party, there was also a direct cause: the secular character of Ba'thist Arab nationalism. Since the Arab nationalist movement had - as I already mentioned - traditionally been Sunni-dominated and Sunni-coloured, allotting only secondary status to minoritarians, secular Ba'thist Arabism could appeal much more strongly to Arabic speaking minority members who may have hoped that the Ba'th Party would help them to free themselves of their minority status and the narrow social frame of sectarian, regional and tribal ties.

Finally, the minority members must have been attracted by the idea that the traditional Sunni-urban domination of Syrian political life might be broken by the establishment of a secular socialist-political system as envisaged by the Ba'th, in which there would be no political and socioeconomic discrimination against non-Sunnis, or, more particularly, against members of heterodox Islamic communities.

The fact that relatively many of the original Ba'thists came from rural and minoritarian backgrounds later formed a social impediment to the membership of urbanites, i.e. due to the traditional contrasts between urban and rural communities and between Sunnis and religious minorities. Such traditional social barriers impeded a normal country-wide expansion of the Ba'th Party organization also after it came to power in 1963.

Not only the Ba'th Party counted already many minoritarians in their ranks before 1963, but also the Syrian army. This was a result of, among other things, the French Mandatory authorities, who within the frame of a divide-and-rule policy favoured recruitment from the various religious and ethnic minorities, such as the Alawis, Druzes, Isma'ilis, Christians, Kurds and Circassians, in the Troupes spéciales du Levant, which later developed into the Syrian and Lebanese Armed Forces. A socioeconomic factor that even further accentuated the strong representation of minority members in the Syrian army was that to many people from the poor countryside (where most minoritarians live) a military career offered a welcome opportunity to climb the social ladder, and lead a life that would be slightly more comfortable than that within the agrarian sector. This incentive was of less significance for people from the larger cities which were mainly Sunni. Finally, people in urban areas frequently found it easier than their rural counterparts to avoid military service by paying a redemption fee.

After Syria became independent in 1946, entrants to the Military Academy at Homs increased strongly each year, mainly due to the vast expansion in the number of schools which opened up educational opportunities in hundreds of villages and small towns to the sons of the lower classes. Indirectly, this trend again helped to increase the number of (ex-peasant) minority officers.

Once having moved into command positions, these officers brought in relatives and others from their sectarian, regional and tribal communities, helping them to advance and tending to favour their applications to the army, navy and air academies.

2.3   Arab Nationalist Taboo on Sectarianism

Notwithstanding the fact that Syria is at present undergoing a serious internal crisis in which the country's national unit is severely threatened by sectarian tensions, particularly between Alawis and the Sunni majority of the population, the Syrian government and its mass media keep systematically denying that sectarianism could be of any determining influence on Syrian political and social life.

The following text of a press review on Radio Damascus may serve as a typical example of this complete denial:

> In today's comment, *Tishrin* cites the feverish psychological campaign waged against Syria by the Arab nation's enemies and plotters against our cause, saying that these enemies are playing the sectarian tune, attempting to stir up sectarian strife and giving sectarian interpretations to every incident, whether petty or significant, that takes place in Syria. *Tishrin* adds that the success of the United States and its allies in manipulating the sectarian issue

to serve their purposes in Cyprus and Lebanon recently, and in other parts of the world previously, has spurred them on to foment sectarianism in Syria through hirelings and agents as well as through instigation and fabrication. However, the imperialists' success in Lebanon and Cyprus were not only the results of cunning psychological warfare, but were originally due to the existence of psychological, educational, economic and political foundations for sectarianism. However, such foundations do not exist in Syria and never did, even during the occupation period. This is why all efforts exerted by the occupying colonialists to spread sectarianism and divide the people's ranks were doomed to failure, even when the colonialists divided Syria by force into sectarian statelets, since these statelets eventually gave way to the masses' national spirit and deep pan-Arab [*qawmiyah*] feelings.

After reviewing Syria's national and pan-Arab history from the French mandate to the present, the paper affirms that every attempt to diagnose Syria's problems by recourse to sectarian premises are mere fabrications against our people and must be resisted with force and determination, because our people, who have never experienced sectarianism, will form strong barriers in the face of all attempts to fake [?] the struggle waged by our masses and divert attention from the real enemies both abroad and within the nation.[8].

This example clearly illustrates the *taboo* which in Syrian and other Arab nationalist circles obtains an overtly speaking or writing about sectarianism as an important issue in political and social life. This taboo in particular makes it difficult for the scientist to obtain reliable information on the subject concerned. Political sensitivities prevent politicians from expressing themselves freely on a subject such as sectarianism, and foreign researchers into contemporary political and social developments often meet with distrust as to their real purposes, particularly if subjects like sectarianism, regionalism and tribalism are investigated.

Books on "Who's Who in Syria" or the "Arab World" simply do not provide complete details about religion, etcetera, certainly not where the presently ruling Ba'thists are concerned. One therefore has to find out for oneself, making statistical research on sectarian and regional representation in Syrian power institution not an easy task of just making mathematical calculations.

2.4   Sectarian Consciousness

The secretiveness which surrounds the subject of sectarianism in Syria nevertheless does not imply that many Ba'thists and others who publicly allege that sectarianism and regionalism are unimportant issues, would not know exactly what other people's religions or regional origins are.

This may be illustrated by a passage from an internal "secret" Ba'th Party document, issued in 1966, where it is stated that:

> Major General Muhammad Umran has said in front of the National Command that Mahmud Hamra cannot command his battalion because 70 per cent of the non-commissioned officers in his battalion are led by Ali Mustafa. The same applies to Muhammad al-Hajj Rahmun and Kasir Mahmud respectively. [Military] branch 60 considers this presentation [of things] as equivalent to a pure sectarian presentation [of the situation]. We [therefore] demand the expulsion of Major General Muhammad Umran from the Government and the Party, and we insist on this demand. The Branch likewise sharply criticizes sectarianism and regionalism and decides [to propose] even the death [sentence] for anyone who is proven to be under its influence.[9]

This quotation [shows] us various things. In the first place that sectarianism at the time played such an important role in the Syrian army that some Ba'thist officers found it necessary to propose death sentences for those who would be influenced by it in their dealings within the Ba'th Party and the army.

Second, it [shows] us that it is apparently taken for granted that all Ba'thists who at the time had access to the internal party document I just quoted were completely informed as to the sectarian backgrounds of their officer-colleagues mentioned by name. For only if one knew that Muhammad Umran, Ali Mustafa and Kasir Mahmud were Alawi Ba'thist officers, and that Mahmud Hamra and Muhammad al-Hajj Rahmun were Sunni Ba'thist officers, and when one fills in their religions as well as their military functions in the quotation I just mentioned, its deeper contents can become clear. It then reads:

> [The Alawi Minister of Defence] Major General Muhammad Umran has said in front of the National Command that Mahmud Hamra [who is a Sunni officer from Hama] cannot command his battalion [of the 70th Armoured Brigade], because 70 per cent of the non-commissioned officers in his battalion [are apparently Alawis and] are led by Ali Mustafa [an Alawi battalion commander in the same brigade, and supporter of Umran]. The same applies to respectively Muhammad al-Hajj Rahmun [who is a Sunni battalion commander] and Kasir Mahmud [an Alawi battalion commander].[10]

Third, this quotation shows us that the army command structure and discipline were at the time undermined by manipulation of sectarian loyalties. Thus, sectarian ties not only played an important role in the appointment of officers in high military positions, but also at lower levels. Some armed units came to be composed mainly of members of a specific religious community. Thus, some tank battalions, for instance of the 70th Armoured Brigade stationed near al-Kiswah south of Damascus, were mainly Alawi. The same applies today to the so-called Defence Companies (*Saraya al-Difa*) commanded by Rif'at al-Asad, brother of the Syrian President.

Apparently the appointment of Sunni officers at high military posts was sometimes principally intended to satisfy their Sunni army comrades, as well as to diminish their distrust of military men from religious minorities, most particularly Alawis. For such appointments might help to negate the impression that key positions in the Armed Forces were mainly occupied by members of specific communities. But to hold a high military function did not imply having independent power.

2.5 Sectarianism combined with Corruption and Lack of Party Discipline

Similar to the Iraqi situation, the most sensitive military and civilian key security positions in Syria are controlled by persons who are in many cases tribally and regionally related to the Alawi Syrian President Hafiz al-Asad, and thus belong mainly to the Alawi community. However, because of the fact that the Alawi-dominated party élite is deeply infected with corruption and lacks party discipline, a broadening of its composition seems to be hindered. Different from the Iraqi Ba'th the Syrian regime therefore seems to be caught in a vicious circle and its Alawi character becomes stronger and stronger partly also as a result of sectarian polarization in Syrian society, which endagers its very existence as well as that of many Alawis who have nothing to do with the Ba'thist regime. Officially the Ba'th Party pursues an ideology that wants to do away with sectarian, regional and tribal loyalties. But when it took power in Syria its leading officers found it necessary to revert to just those traditional loyalties in order to consolidate their positions and not to lose the strength that would be needed to realize that ideology. Thus, on the one hand, power was essential if the necessary drastic social changes entailing the suppression of sectaian, regional and tribal loyalties, were to be effected; on the other hand, maintenance of that power entailed dependence on those same loyalties, thus temporarily hindering their suppression for a period long enough to broaden the Ba'th élite's composition, and create a Ba'thist inspired political community in Syria. But, as I already said, mainly as a result of a combination of corruption, sectarianism and lack of party discipline, the necessary broadening of the Ba'thist élite's composition could not be realized.

3   Sectarian, Regional and Tribal Overlap

Sectarian, regional and tribal categories can easily overlap, making it difficult to determine which play a role in a particular situation. In the event of such overlap, there is a danger of interpreting tribal and regional loyalties as sectarian loyalties, for instance, or vice versa. Overlap may be due to the regional concentration of particular religious communities and tribes in specific areas or provinces. Examples are the Sunni Arabs inhabiting northern Iraq and Shi'i Arabs in its southern part; the Alawis living mainly in Syria's north-western Latakia and Tartus regions; and the Syrian Druzes, concentrated in the southern "Jabal al-Duruz". Overlap may be further due to the fact that tribal groups as a whole usually belong to the same religious community (there are exceptions); and to that tribal and sectarian elements are sometimes inseparably linked to one another. In this respect the compact religious minorities in Syria, notably the Alawis, Druzes and Isma'ilis, and the tribes belonging to these minorities, serve as clear examples.

Sectarian, regional and tribal groups may in turn partially overlap with socio-economic and ecological categories. For example: the compact religious minorities in Syria live mainly in the poor countryside, whereas the cities are predominantly Sunni; in Iraq the majority of the rural population is Shi'i, whereas the urban population is predominantly Sunni. Thus, both in Iraq and in Syria urban-rural contrasts partly overlap with sectarian differences.

All this potentially implies that in cases of overlap of regional, tribal, sectarian and socioeconomic factors, social or political tensions may find an outlet through one or more of the existing social sectarian, regional, tribal or socio-economic channels. A class struggle can for instance be directed and stimulated through sectarian channels, in case socioeconomic and sectarian contrasts coincide.

4 Conclusion

In countries like Iraq and Syria reliance on regional and tribal ties at present appears to be preconditional for staying in power. Regionalism and tribalism do not, however, necessarily give rise to sectarianism, also not when there is theoretically a strong overlap between the three.

The Iraqi case may show that sectarianism can be curbed and may gradually fade away, notwithstanding outside (and particularly Iranian Shi'i) efforts to encourage Shi'i sectarianism in Iraq for [Iran's] own political purposes. Success depends, however, to an important extent on continued party discipline, absence of corruption and gradual widening of the party élite's composition; and subsequently democratic reforms and educational development.

This does not mean that sectarianism (i.e. the Sunni/Shi'i dichotomy) does not play any role in Iraqi internal politics. We have seen that the disproportionately strong representation of Takritis in Iraqi power institutions had little or nothing to do with Sunni sectarian solidarity, but was a result of tribalism, regionalism and socioeconomic factors. All this does not prevent the possibility however that Shi'is opposing the Ba'th regime can nevertheless perceive it as a Sunni regime, or that Shi'i (and even Sunni) opponents of the secular Ba'th regime can exploit the sectarianism issue for political purposes, so as to undermine its position. In the latter case one can say that political ideas create their own realities, and sectarianism may start to lead its own life, irrespective of whether or not the dominant political group derives its power from sectarian solidarity.

The Syrian case shows how regionalism and tribalism have given rise to and have stimulated a destructive kind sectarianism, due to over-emancipation of formerly discriminated-against Alawis, combined with corruption and lack of party discipline. It remains questionable whether President al-Asad will be able to solve these problems which have pervaded greater part of the Syrian regime and have had an effect of sectarian polarization on Syrian society which seems extremely difficult to reverse in the short term.

Just like two years ago, the recently announced second anti-corruption campaign seems to be doomed to failure from the very beginning because some high-placed military officers in the direct entourage of President Hafiz al-Asad who constitute an indispensable part of the hard core of his mainly Alawi officers' faction, in which his brother Rif'at plays a central role, seem to be deeply involved in corrupt practises. To purge these officers from the army, or to take severe disciplinary action against them would inevitably directly undermine the position of al-Asad's faction and consequently of the whole regime itself.

It seems therefore likely that present resentment against so-called "Alawi-rule" in Syria will continue to grow, together with the accompanying terrorist violence of Sunni opposition groups who through premeditated sectarian polarization hope to wrest power from the ruling Alawi minority.

In practice, this so-called "Alawi-rule" appears to be limited, however, to a rather restricted tribally and regionally related section of the Alawi community, from which many other Alawis, falling outside this section, have been able to profit on more or less sectarian grounds, therewith strengthening the Alawi sectarian character of the regime. David Hirst of *The Guardian* even goes so far – and as long as only part of the Alawi community is meant here I do not think that he is going too far – as to say that "the Alawites adopted Ba'athism as their instrument of supremacy", and further that

> it is not, in any real sense, the Ba'thists who run this country. It is the Alawites . . . In theory they run it through the party, but in practice it is through their clandestine solidarity within the party and other important institutions . . . Behind the façade, the best qualification for holding power is proximity - through family, sectarian, or tribal origins - to the country's leading Alawite, President Assad.[11]

As long as the just mentioned Sunni groups and their temporary Sunni allies have no dependent control over large quantities of arms and strategically important army units success for schemes to end Alawi domination seems unlikely.

Therefore, if President al-Asad fails to realize the necessary reforms, present-day so-called "Alawi rule" in Syria together with all its negative effects may in this stage only be ended with the help of Alawi officers themselves, however contradictory this may sound. For it is probably only Alawis "who, privy to the inner workings of the system, command the resources of organisation and information to launch a clean-cut coup",[12] be it with or without the help of officers from other communities.

Landownership, Citizenship and Racial Policy in Israel

Uri Davis and Walter Lehn

. . . The state of Israel was established on 14 May 1948 with the unanimous adoption of the "Declaration of the Establishment of the State of Israel" by the People's Council in ceremonious session at 16.30 hours in the Tel Aviv Museum Hall. One of the most interesting debates in the history of Zionism was held a few hours earlier by the same Council to discuss the proposed Declaration.

The debate reveals an aspect of the Declaration which is rarely pointed out: On 14 May 1948 Israel was declared a Jewish state, not a sovereign, independent state. Indeed the document properly known as Israel's "Declaration of Independence" is not officially so identified; it is called the Declaration of the Establishment of the State of Israel by the People's Council in ceremonial session oversight. This point was explicitly debated in the meeting at 13.50 hours of the People's Council on 14 May. Meir Wilner, then as today a leading member of the Communist Party and a signatory of the Declaration, pointed out:

> Members of the Council: We are all united today in recognition of the significance of this great day for the yishuv [pre-state Jewish community in Palestine] and the Jewish people; the day of the abolition of the Mandate and the declaration of the independent Jewish state . . . The Eretz Israel Communist Party supports the proposed resolution of the declaration of the Jewish state, has reservations on a number of issues, and proposes a few amendments and additions . . . We propose, in accordance with the resolutions of the United Nations Assembly, to add the following paragraph:
>
> "The Council declares that a fundamental principle of its policy is that of the right of both peoples to self-determination and to independent states of their own."
> . . . In section 9, where it says, "Calling for the establishment of a Jewish state in Eretz Israel", we propose to add the word "independent," namely; "Calling for the establishment of an independent Jewish state in Eretz Israel."
> . . . At the end of section 11 it says:
> "We . . . hereby declare the establishment of a Jewish state in Eretz Israel." We propose to add the words "sovereign, indepen-

145

dent": thus "the establishment of a sovereign, independent Jewish state . . ."

Wilner's proposed amendments were not accepted. Yet the debate highlights the fact that those who formulated the draft consciously avoided words that would have specified the sovereignty and independence of the proposed state, emphasizing only its Jewishness.

Immediately after the establishment of the state, the following question was raised:

> Is the existence of the [World] Zionist Organization whose main objective has apparently been realized, still justified? Has the Zionist Organization not ended its historic mission and have not all its functions been handed over to the newly-born state?

It is from the ensuing debate that we discover why Israel was declared a Jewish and not an independent, sovereign Jewish state:

> Berl Locker (Chairman of the Zionist Executive): Today there is a need for a larger and stronger Zionist movement, more so than at any other time . . . The Zionist movement has not yet reached its final objective, and its right to exist has not changed. Though its functions have partly changed, especially in the territory of the state, the Zionist movement must continue its work, strengthen and expand it, in accordance with the new conditions now created . . . The Zionist movement is needed not only for the Jews who ought to come to the country, but for the very existence of the state . . . A Zionist movement – and I emphasize the word movement – is necessary, because the destiny of the entire people must be borne by them; it must not be the object of custodianship, not even that of the State of Israel. It is necessary that the Jewish people, for whom the State of Israel was created – and this state was created to be their homeland – themselves and through their strength forge their destiny and be the bearers of their own history . . .

Al Hamishmar (8 November, 1959), daily of the United Workers' Party (Mapam), spelled out the issues involved:

> We are only a part – though a pioneering part – of the people of Israel. The part cannot overshadow the whole. It is plain vanity to believe that we can tell world Jewry: "We do not need your advice. Please do not interfere in our affairs." . . . The mutual responsibilities mut be defined. The ways and the channels of influence must be determined through agreement, but the influence and authority [of world Jewry] cannot be challenged . . . Independence is independence vis-à-vis outside elements. Sovereignty vis-à-vis foreigners. A state is not independent in relation to its own people . . . A Jew who considers himself a Jew in the political-national

sense, who considers Eretz Israel . . . to be his homeland, is a partner with us in our enterprise. These are the Jews who constitute the Zionist movement, which is the representative of all Jews who belong to the Jewish people, to the nationhood of Jews, for whose independence, whose liberation this state is being built . . .

In short, the state of Israel was established as a Jewish state and not as a sovereign, independent Jewish state, because only under the former definition is it a state by, for and of the "Jewish people" throughout the world; under the latter definition it would be a state by, for, and of its Jewish citizens.

It is within this context that the Knesset passed in November 1952 the World Zionist Organization–Jewish Agency (Status) Law. It was the first step in regularizing the legal status of the various Zionist institutions in the newly established Jewish state of Israel.

The States Law makes the World Zionist Organization (WZO) responsible for "Settlement projects in the state" (section 3), and authorizes it to co-ordinate "the activities in Israel of Jewish institutions and organizations active in . . . development and settlement of the country" (4). Prominent among these Jewish institutions - "various bodies" (8), "funds and other institutions" (12) of the WZO – is, of course, the JNF, over which the WZO holds absolute control. In addition the law identifies the Jewish Agency (JA) with the WZO (3 and 7). This takes on added significance when the Constitution of the JA is recalled; Article 3 (d) and (e) states:

> Land is to be acquired as Jewish property, and . . . the title to the lands acquired is to be taken in the name of the JNF, to the end that the same shall be held as the inalienable property of the Jewish people. The Agency shall promote agricultural colonization based on Jewish labour, and in all works or undertakings carried out or furthered by the Agency, it shall be deemed to be a matter of principle that Jewish labour shall be employed . . .

Thus the activities of the WZO, the JA and the JNF are essentially specialized functions of one and the same organization, recognized as an equal of the state in Israel. In this way the state becomes a partner to the restrictive policies and practices of the JNF – for "persons of Jewish religion, race or origin".

The next step was taken in November 1953 with the adoption of the Keren Kayemeth Leisrael Law. This law authorized the Minister of Justice "to approve the Memorandum and Articles of Association of a company limited by guarantee to be submitted to him by the Existing Company [the JNF incorporated in England] for the establishment of a body incorporated in Israel with a view to continuing the activities of the Existing Company that had been founded and incorporated in the diaspora" (section 2). The new company's Memorandum and Articles of Association were approved by Minister of Justice Pinhas Rosen on 9 May, 1954, thereby establishing an Israeli company called Keren Kayemeth Leisrael. This name is virtually identical with that of the company incorporated in England, Keren Kayemeth Leisrael Limited. Since there is some confusion in the literature on this point, it needs to be emphasized the English company did not cease to exist; from 1954 on there are two companies with essentially the same name.

We shall examine below in detail the changes effected in the Memorandum of Association of the Israeli company, compared with that of the English company. In this task we are aided by a JNF document, "The Organization of the JNF as an Israeli Association", which was circulated as an internal discussion paper in mimeographed form in 1952. The introduction to this paper reads as follows:

> After the establishment of the State of Israel, the JNF Executive recognized that it was inappropriate that the national institution should continue to operate, legally speaking, as an English company subject to English law and the English legislative authorities in London. The time had therefore come for the Fund to reorganize as an Israeli company. The Executive of the JNF brought the matter before the Board of Directors, and in its meeting of April 9, 1950 a resolution was adopted to establish an Israeli company that would replace the JNF in its current form.
>
> Among the assets of the JNF, there are considerable areas of land in the Arab parts of the country, outside of the borders of the state. Should the English company, in whose name these lands are registered, be liquidated, then from the legal point of view this property would be lost. It was therefore proposed that the English company should not be liquidated, but that it should transfer to the new Israeli company all its property in land within the borders of the State of Israel, as well as all its capital assets in moneys and equities, and all the rights it holds. The new Israeli company will receive all the income from donations and fund-raising, as well as all new property in land which will hereafter be registered in its name. The English company will continue to hold the lands outside of the State of Israel and will also collect the moneys due to the JNF from bequests and living-legacies made to it prior to the establishment of the Israeli company.
>
> In order to add prestige to the institution of the JNF, the Israeli company will be established by a special law to be passed by the Knesset. A similar procedure is customary in England, and was

also customary in the country during the Mandate for important companies and institutions. We have already communicated with the Prime Minister on this matter and can assume that the government will agree to our proposal. The Executive is in contact with the government concerning the details of the matter.

The new Israeli company will replace and be the inheritor [in Israel] of the existing English company. In order to underline this continuity, it is proposed that the Memorandum of Association of the new company be identical to that of the existing company, with the exception of a few clauses which no longer correspond to the new realities. Following are the changes which will be introduced into the Memorandum:

1. Name of the Company

The law requires that some alteration in the name be effected in order that the new company can be effected in order that the new company can be distinguished from the English company which will continue to exist. Yet it is necessary that the new name be as close as possible to the current name so that donors and functionaries will know that they continue to work for the same institution with which they have been associated for many decades. It is proposed that the name of the new company be "Keren Kayemeth Leisrael", with the omission of the word Limited; the English company will maintain its present name.

2. Area of Operation of the Company

According to the Memorandum of Association of the existing English company as registered in London in 1907, the company is authorized to operate in the area identified as "the prescribed region". This term is defined in the Memorandum as the area of Eretz Israel [Palestine], Syria, and any other parts of the Ottoman Empire in Asia, including the Sinai Peninsula. Under today's political circumstances it is not desirable to continue with this definition, and it has therefore been proposed that the prescribed region for the purpose of land purchase by the new company will mean any area under the legal jurisdiction of the State of Israel.

3. Right of Leasing Lands to Jews only

In the Memorandum of Association of the existing company it is emphasized a number of times that the JNF is permitted to act for the benefit of Jews only. One clause specifies that the object of the company is to purchase lands for the purpose of settling Jews on such lands. Another clause specifies that the company is permitted to lease its lands only to Jews or Jewish companies, namely, companies whose shares as well as effective control are in Jewish hands. Another clause specifies the right of the company to make advances only to Jews in the prescribed region. Although the object of the JNF will continue to be to assist in the settlement of

Jews only, through the allocation of lands for their settlement, the need may arise to lease tracts of land to non-Jews or to an international company; further, should we allow this explicit prohibition to remain, *the undesirable impression might be created of so-called racist restrictions*, which are opposed by Jews throughout the world. It is therefore proposed that in the new Memorandum of Association the clause specifying the object of the company remain unchanged, as in the existing Memorandum: to purchase lands for the purpose of settling Jews. The other clauses will be modified so as to remove the prohibition against the leasing of lands or the allocation of cash advances to non-Jews.

One can assume that even without these explicit prohibitions, the JNF Board of Directors will know how to administer the work of the institution in accordance with the explicit object as specific in the aforementioned clause which remains unchanged.

Plus ça change, plus c'est la même chose!

A comparison of the clauses of the Memorandum of Association of the English (1907) and the Israeli (1954) companies suggests that they fall into three groups: (1) Clauses which are identical, or of which the differences appear to be simply a consequence of one company being incorporated in England and the other in Israel; e.g. the "registered office" of the English company is "in England" (clause 2), of the Israeli "in Israel" (clause 2). (2) Clauses which exhibit differences; and (3) those which are in the Israeli, but for which there is no equivalent in the English Memorandum; there are no clauses in the latter for which there is no equivalent in the former.

In 1907 the JNF was registered as Juedischer Nationalfonds (Keren Kajemeth Le Jisroel) Limited (clause 1). In 1921 this was changed to Keren Kajemeth Le Jisroel Limited and in 1925 to that currently used by the English company, Keren Kayemeth Leisrael Limited. The name of the Israeli company is Keren Kayemeth Leisrael (clause 1).

. . .

As distinguished from the Memoranda, the Articles of Association of the two companies display fewer differences. Many of them are the same; where differences exist, they appear to be simply consequences of one company being English and the other Israeli, or are consistent with, hence derive from, the differences between the Memoranda discussed above.

Shortly after the establishment of the Israeli company, in July 1954, the Covenant referred to in the WZO-JA (Status) Law was signed by Moshe Sharett for the government and Nahum Goldmann and Berl Locker for the Zionist Executive. The

Covenant is identified as "A Covenant between the Government of Israel (hereafter, the Government) and the Zionist Executive, also known as the Executive of the JA for Eretz Israel (hereafter, the Executive), 1954."

On the signing of this Covenant the government and the Executive exchanged formal letters, all dated 26 July 1954 confirming and acknowledging the agreement, and specifying the position of the Executive's functionaries in official ceremonies; e.g. the chairman of the Executive ranks "immediately after the members of the cabinet", and the rank of the members of the Executive is "equal to that of the members of the Knesset". The letters confirm the impression that the WZO and its several institutions constitute legally and effectively an equal of the government, hence virtually a state within the state of Israel.

. . .

Although the relationships between the government and the WZO in Israel were clarified by the 1954 Covenant, it still remained necessary to define the role and activities within Israel of the JNF, the largest and most influential Zionist institution. The initiative in this endeavour was taken by the JNF, whose Board of Directors meeting jointly with the JA Executive on 13 March, 1955 adopted a resolution calling for the establishment of a 'common institution for national lands". With the official blessing of the Twenty-Fourth Zionist Congress (Jerusalem, 1956) the JNF and the government eventually agreed on the wording and intent of the "Israel Lands" laws, the role of the JNF in the implementation of these, and the relationship of the JNF to the state. The most significant result of these several developments was the extension of the JNF's restrictive landholding and leasing policies to all state lands – now identified as Israel or national lands – a consequence for which the JNF takes, and in our view deserves, the credit.

These negotiations between the government and the JNF were concluded by the signing of the 1 August 1960 Memorandum signifying agreement in principle "to observe the regulations of the Covenant to be signed by the government and the JNF, the formal endorsement of which will be effected after the clarification of certain legal problems relating to the status of the JNF". This Covenant (to be distinguished from the 1954 Covenant between the government and the WZO), which details the agreed terms of implementation of the Israel Lands Law adopted by the Knesset in July 1960, was signed in Jerusalem on 28 November 1961. It is an agreement "between the State of Israel, represented for this purpose by the Minister of Finance, and the JNF – with the sanction of the WZO – represented for this purpose by the Chairman of the Board of Directors of the JNF".

. . .

Through deliberate and conscious legal formulations predicated on the manipulation of the meaning of terms such as person, nation, etc., the state of Israel has succeeded in presenting to Western intellectual and public opinion its far-reaching apartheid legislation as progressive social democracy. This manipulation is predicated on the rather different meanings ascribed to these terms in Zionist usage, where "person" is read as "Jewish person", "public" as "Jewish public", "the people" as "the Jewish people", "Nation" as "Jewish nation", and "Israel" as "the people of Israel" (i.e. the community of adherents to Judaism, to be distinguished from the citizens of the state of Israel, and even from the Jewish citizens of the state).

These "translations" emerge from the lengthy presentation and ensuing debate in the Knesset of the Lands Law. The three laws – Basic Law: Israel Lands, Israel Lands Law and Israel Lands Administration Law – passed by the Knesset in July 1960, were presented in August 1959 for first reading by the Minister of Finance, the late Levi Eshkol, under the titles; Basic Law: The People's Lands, The People's Lands Law and The People's Lands Administration Law. In view of the significance of the occasion, Eshkol reviewed the history of JNF activity in Palestine as well as the motivation underlying the proposed laws:

> With the establishment of the State, it may seem that the JNF mission of redeeming the land [from aliens] has been completed . . .; this mission, entrusted to it by the Fifth Zionist Congress, has been completed for it. On the other hand, by the force of the new reality, the weight of the second mission of the JNF – the redemption of the land from desolation – has increased . . .
>
> Meanwhile the decisive fact has been established that the land in the State of Israel is concentrated largely under two owners: the state and the JNF . . . This situation necessarily results in certain duplication of activities in administration of the land-leasing, exploitation, preparation, afforestation, and other development works . . . Against this background, the Prime Minister in July 1957 appointed a committee to examine the activities of the JNF in the lands domain in the light of the needs of the state, and to present – if they deemed necessary – recommendations to the government . . .
>
> I think it appropriate that I read to you the conclusions of the committee in order that you understand that what we propose is

not something that has casually entered someone's head. The committee gave the matter thorough examination; their conclusions are based on three assumptions:

1. The mission entrusted to the JNF by the WZO at its Fifth Congress was to redeem from aliens the land of Eretz Israel, the property of the nation, which shall not be sold for ever, the aim being the settlement of olim from the diaspora. This mission the JNF fulfilled . . . with perseverance, faithfully striving toward the Zionist aim – a Jewish state. This mission was almost completed in the War of Independence, when the Israeli army liberated the greater part of the land within the boundaries of the state.

2. With the establishment of the state, the mission of the JNF was transformed; the redemption of the land from people became the redemption of the land from desolation, a mission hailed by the Jewish public in the country and in the diaspora. In the fulfilment of this mission . . . the JNF demonstrated during the first decade of the state perseverance, loyalty and executive capabilities in the reclamation of lands and afforestation of hundreds of thousands of dunums . . .

3. The love and respect with which the Jewish people and their diaspora, encompassing all parties from small to large, have regarded the JNF before the establishment of the state have not ceased after the change in the mission of the JNF. The Jews abroad, who direct their eyes to the State of Israel, consider the JNF a popular institution which weaves daily ties between themselves and the country, and the state also, through the traditional donations and the Zionist-Israeli education that this institution spreads among them . . .

On the basis of these assumptions, and in order to strengthen the JNF in the fulfilment of its future mission in the country and abroad without duplication in the administration of the national lands in the state, the committee arrived at the following conclusions:

1. The principle established as the basis of the JNF, that land purchased by it is owned by the Jewish people in perpetuity, and shall not be sold forever, will be established as a principle applying to state lands. For this purpose the Knesset will adopt a basic law which will determine that the land owned by the state, with the exception of certain areas, cannot be sold but only leased under fixed conditions to promote effective use and exploitation.

2. (a) The administration of the national lands – the lands owned by the state and the JNF – will be concentrated in one lands administration headed by one of the ministers of the government.
(b) The present legal ownership of the lands – the ownership of the JNF of its lands and the ownership of the state of its lands – will be maintained also in the future. All the government and JNF offices that deal today with land affairs will be abolished and replaced by a single Administration which will administer, lease, and supervise

the lands and execute the ownership rights. (c) The Minister, in consultation with the JNF Board of Directors, will appoint a Director of the Administration. (d) The Administration will have authority to execute the national lands policy and all that it legally implies.

3. A Covenant between the government and the JNF Board of Directors will be made according to which the Administration will administer JNF lands . . .

4. (a) The JNF Board of Directors, as an independent institution of the WZO, will act within the Jewish public in the country and in the diaspora to collect money for the redemption of land from desolation, for land reclamation, development, and afforestation. The JNF will also act to promote information and Zionist–Israeli education in the diaspora and among the Jewish youth abroad in order to draw them closer to the idea of Jewish colonization (itnahalut) in the homeland. (b) The Administration will make available to the JNF every assistance in its information activities in Israel and abroad. The JNF Board of Directors will decide, as the need may arise, to purchase lands . . . The administration of the new lands . . . will also be the responsibility of the [Israel] Lands Administration . . .

5. The project of land reclamation in its various aspects and of afforestation in its various aspects will all be concentrated in the Land Development Administration of the JNF. Whereas we have transferred the centre of gravity in matters of land ownership and administration to the government, the centre of gravity of afforestation, development, reclamation and terracing is with the JNF . . .

6. The unification of the offices for lands administration as well as of those for reclamation and afforestation will be carried out by mutual consent with the aim of maximal possible reduction of the number of employees . . .

These conclusions are, as noted earlier, the fruits of long negotiations and the result of careful and scrupulous discussions with the Chairman of the JNF [Board of Directors], Dr. Granott, and with Joseph Weitz, as representatives of the JNF . . .

These recommendations and conclusions of the committee constitute the basis for the resolutions of the government, the JNF Board of Directors, and the institutions of the Zionist movement concerning the principles of land policy and the coordination of activity in the administration of the land and its development.

These resolutions have been formulated into laws dealing with land policy in Israel and are herewith brought before the Knesset.

The Third Knesset debated the proposed laws in its Six hundred and ninety-second session, 6 August 1959. The legislation was passed in first reading and handed over for final formulation to the Finance Committee. When the laws were brought before the Fourth Knesset on 19 and 25 July, 1960 for second and third (final) reading, they were, however, renamed – Basic Law: Israel Lands, Israel Lands Law and Israel Lands Administration Law. The reasons for the changes in name provide insights into the workings of Israeli-style apartheid legislation.

Minister of Religious Affairs Zerah Wahrhaftig, Chairman of the Constitution, Law and Justice Committee, presented the proposed Basic Law to the Knesset in the following terms:

> The reasons for this proposed law, as I bring it before you, are as follows: to give legal garb to a principle that is fundamentally religious, namely, "the land shall not be sold forever, for the land is mine" (Leviticus 25.23). Irrespective of whether this verse is explicitly mentioned in the law, as one proposal had it, or whether it is not mentioned, the law gives legal garb to this rule and principle in our torah. This law expresses our original view concerning the holiness of the land of Israel, "for the land is mine" – "the holiness of the land belongs to me", says Gemara [Talmud] in "Tractate Gittin", page 47a. And Ibn Ezra explains why the land should not be sold for ever: "for the land is mine" – "this is a most important reason". And Nachmanides says, "and the intelligent will understand". I also trust that the educated will understand; therefore I will not further explain the reasons for this principle . . .
>
> Concerning the name, we gave this law the name Basic Law: Israel Lands. There were a number of proposals about the name. MK Harari proposed to name it "The People's Lands". On the face of it, I do not see any great difference between the two names. I admit that neither name hits the target. What is it that we want? We want something that is difficult to define. We want to make it clear that the land of Israel belongs to the people of Israel. The "people of Israel" is a concept that is broader than that of the "people resident in Zion", because the people of Israel live throughout the world. On the other hand, every law that is passed is for the benefit of all the residents of the state, and all the residents of the state include also people who do not belong to the people of Israel, the worldwide people of Israel.
>
> MENAHEM BEGIN (Herut Movement): This is not expressed [in the law].
>
> ZERAH WAHRHAFTIG: We cannot express this. Whatever we write, Israel lands or people's lands, from the strictly legal point of view, the reference is necessarily to the people resident in Zion only. Every law is valid only in the area under the jurisdiction of the state, and therefore it makes no difference what we write . . . We thought it would be better to write "Israel" rather than "people". It is also a question of tradition, of habit . . .

MK Meridor was wrong when he said that there is no legal innovation in the law. There is therein a very significant legal innovation: we are giving legal garb to the Memorandum of Association of the JNF . . . As for the JNF, the legal innovation is enormous; it gives legal garb to a matter that thus far was incorporated only in the JNF's Memorandum.

Nevertheless, in spite of this vindication of JNF principles and their extension to state lands, the JNF remained unwilling to transfer to the state title to its lands. Some insight into the reasons for this may be afforded by the explanation given to the Twenty-third Zionist Congress (Jerusalem, 1951) as to why the JNF, and not the state should acquire title to the abandoned lands made available through "the triumph of the Haganah and the flight of the Arabs". The JNF "will redeem the lands and will turn them over to the Jewish people – to the people and not the state, which in the current composition of population cannot be an adequate guarantor of Jewish ownership".

As a consequence of the 1960 Israel Lands Law, the 1960 Memorandum of Agreement, and the 1961 Covenant between the government and the JNF, "the State of Israel adopted the JNF guidelines for all publicly-owned lands, i.e., for over 90 per cent of the area included in Israel's borders at that date". This claim by the JNF appears to be – as we have seen from the Knesset debates above – not only warranted, but in full accord with the intent of the land laws; the debates also explain why the wording of the laws is not explicit on this point. Effraim Orni, an official at JNF headquarters in Jerusalem, also explains what is meant by "guidelines" and "adopted": "JNF agrarian principles have been incorporated in Israeli legislation and are binding for over 90 per cent of the total area of the state." As for the agrarian principles, only three are mentioned prominently: (1) "public ownership", (2) "inalienability of the soil", and hence use of the land only through (3) "hereditary leaseholds" which "run for period of 49 years and can be automatically renewed." Less prominent is another JNF principle, (4) "the stipulation of Jewish labour on JNF land". Not made explicit at all – it rarely is in Zionist literature – is a fifth principle: the lessee must be Jewish (see the 1952 JNF paper cited above).

The fourth principle – Jewish labour – is mentioned by Orni only in commenting on "the Arab propaganda lie that Jewish settlement created a landless class in Palestine" – ' a fabrication of unnamed "Arabs" and "Arabophiles," "inflated" by official Commissions of Inquiry. Among the latter he singles out the one headed by John Hope Simpson, whose "views were definitely inimical to the Zionist cause", evidenced by the fact that "he took exception to the JNF principle of inalienability of the land" and "also opposed the stipulation of Jewish labour on JNF land". Orni of course denies that Zionist colonization helped to create a landless class in Palestine; he does not, however, deny that the JNF prohibited the employment of non-Jewish labour; he observes only that leaseholds were small, and thus there was little need for hired labour. From the latter fact derives the codeword for Jewish labour commonly found in JNF literature – self-labour or self-help, positive and innocuous labels, which, as Orni quite correctly notes, have their "roots in Zionism's fundamental ideology." It is also worth recalling that the size of the leasehold was fixed at the 1920 Zionist Conference in London as the amount the lessee and his family could cultivate without hiring help, in part to keep him from having to employ Arab labourers, recognizing that Jewish labourers were not likely to be available.

There is no question that Jewish labour was and remains a cardinal JNF principle. It is in fact included as a standard clause in JNF leasehold contracts; e.g. a 1953 contract, clause 10, reads: "The lessee undertakes to execute all works on and in the holding – improvement, ploughing, sowing, planting, construction, and the various works in the buildings, groves, etc. – only and exclusively with Jewish labourers." The same or very similar wording, including the final restrictive phrase, occurs in JNF leasehold contracts of various dates, e.g. 1930 (clause 23), 1936 (25), and 1964 (13.4a). The immediately following subclause in the 1964 contract specifies further that the lessee is responsible for adherence to the stipulations of 13.4a by "all members of his family, his tenants . . . or any person residing on the leasehold; . . . in case any of the aforementioned violates any of the said stipulations, the lessee himself will be held to have violated the said stipulations" (13.4b).

The phrase "over 90 per cent" occurs repeatedly in JNF sources when referring to public or national or Israel lands; (the denotation of these adjectives in a Jewish state needs to be kept in mind). A more precise figure is given in the Report of the Israel Lands Administration for 1961–2. We quote from the preface (see overleaf):

Table 7

LAND OWNERSHIP

Land ownership in Israel is divided into four categories: state, Development Authority, JNF, and private. Private ownership is in turn divided into Jewish and minorities.

State and Development

	dunums
Authority lands	15,205,000
JNF lands	3,570,000
[National lands total]	18,775,000
Privately owned lands	1,480,000
TOTAL	20,255,000

It follows that national lands concentrated under the administration of the Israel Lands Administration represent 92.6 per cent of the total area of the state.

Based on this information we conclude that privately owned lands now represent at most 7.4 per cent of the area of pre-1967 Israel, the majority of which is reportedly owned by Arabs. The Arabs, however, are excluded by law from most of the area of Israel, from the 92.6 per cent designated national lands.

The so-called national lands are those whose ownership, lease or control is restricted by the "Jewish" clause, prohibiting their lease or sublease to non-Jews, as well as the employment of non-Jews in their cultivation or maintenance. One might assume that at least the 7.4 per cent of land that is privately owned is not similarly restricted. That this is not necessarily so is suggested in the Report cited above, where the distinction is made between Jewish and minorities (i.e. Arab) private ownership.

Part III

Structures and Processes

Introduction

Part III contains four longer texts on a variety of topics which cannot usefully be fitted into any of the existing models employed to analyse or explain changing social processes. This is partly because of their special mix of factors, partly because they involve processes which are not controllable at the level of the state and thus cannot be reduced to objects of bureaucratic management or national class struggle. These topics are: different types of agricultural transformation viewed from the perspective of the village, the changing relationship between urban leadership and localized violence in certain Middle Eastern cities, the political and economic marginalization of the Palestine refugees after 1948 and the conflicting attitudes of a ruling élite towards its own country's past as shown by its policies towards the medina or "old" quarter of its capital city.

The study of such subjects has certain specific advantages. They focus attention on the limited opportunities for choice and for reallocating resources open to quite small groups of people. They raise questions concerning existing modes of explanation at what is, generally, a modest and realistic level. For these reasons they are subjects which allow - and even seem to encourage – fresh thinking and new methods of conceptualization.

Keydar's text is a first attempt to classify the process of structural change within the agricultural sector according to the dominant trend of development within a variety of different types of villages. Using five case histories he is able to show that the intensification of Turkish capitalism, the growth of agricultural production after 1950 and the accelerating process of rural outmigration provided a new set of opportunities which were made use of in a number of analytically separate ways. He also goes on to suggest that the ability to take advantages of these opportunities was affected by a set of variables including the pattern of migration, the nature of the soil, the average size of agricultural holdings, the distance from markets and, just as important as everything else, the time at which particular opportunities presented themselves. The result was the emerg-

159

ence of a diversity of rural structures which is very much at variance with the common assumption that the process of development takes a predominantly unilinear path.

One of the great advantages of Keydar's method is that it breaks away from the conventional but often sterile and confused discussion which take the rural household as its primary unit of analysis.* As he himself argues, it is the social structure of the village which mediates the impact of social and economic change on any particular family. But this method of analysis presents something of a handicap when he addresses himself to the different problem of analysing rural social differentiation and the emergence of different classes or strata within each village. While it allows him to make a number of useful suggestions as to future developments at the national level - in terms of the economy-wide division of labour - he cannot identify the mechanisms which allow particular village families to improve their economic position at the expense of others within the local community.

Johnson's text focuses on a particular type of urban context in which the divisions of the population into well-differentiated classes has not proceeded very far and in which the combination of a predominantly service economy and a low level of government services permitted the development of a system by which national leaders associated themselves with local strong-arm men in a general exercise of personalised control over the popular quarters of Beirut. He then goes on to show how this system came under increasing pressure from the 1960s onwards as the strong-arm men in the predominantly Muslim districts were able to exploit new sources of power independent of their national patrons, through their links with the Military Intelligence organization (the Deuxième Bureau), outside governments like the Libyan or the increasingly independent Palestinian groups. The result was an immediate politicization of the struggle between the rival local leaders during which each sought to recruit followers by the use of more overtly ideological slogans to such a point where their conflicts could no longer be mediated or controlled at the national level. Another feature of this process was the growing differentiation in patterns of leadership and control between the predominantly Muslim areas of Beirut and those where the Christian militias (actively supported by Israel) exercised a more institutionalised form of hegemony.

The great advantage of Johnson's analysis is that it provides a

* For a strong defence of the household as a basic unit see Wallerstein *et al.* (1982).

systematic explanation of such features of Beirut's social life as its "individualism", the important attached to personalized rather than institutionalised relationships and, since the Civil War of 1975–6, the very different types of political process in the two halves of the divided city. Where it is less convincing, as the author clearly recognizes, is in demonstrating that the type of relationship he characterizes as that of leader and strong-arm man (*za'im* and *qabaday*) was indeed the predominant one in post-Independent Beirut and can thus be used to provide a paradigm for urban leadership and social control in general.

Sayigh's text provides an analysis of the political and economic maginalization of the Palestinian refugees as they were forced to try to make a life for themselves in the countries to which they had fled. Even in those places, like Jordan, where they were granted citizenship this conferred few rights. Every kind of barrier was placed in the way of their obtaining more than the most menial jobs. In additional, until the resuscitation of the PLO after the 1967 war, they were deprived of any consistent political leadership and the best they could do to protect themselves was the use of the weapon of the strike or of passive resistance whenever a government or the United Nations Relief and Works Agency (UNRWA) pressed them too hard. In these circumstances the refugees had to learn to make what use they could of small opportunities for individual advancement or betterment and as Sayigh clearly demonstrates, the role of chance or of sheer persistence often provides as good an explanation of success as family ties or economic position or anything else. She also shows how difficult it is to build a socioeconomic profile of the Palestinian refugee communities, partly because of the absence of information, partly because concepts like 'class' are too large and clumsy to describe their particular set of economic and social relationships. Sayigh's method has, of necessity, to be somewhat impressionistic. It provides a good way of listening to the true "voices" of a particular set of disadvantaged historical actors. It can help to clear the ground of any number of misleading misperceptions. But it is much more difficult to use as the basis for a new set of concepts which might act as a guide to future researchers.

Finally, Micaud's text traces the changing perceptions of a section of the Tunisian élite towards the medina (or "old" quarter) of Tunis. In particular she shows how much such perceptions were dominated by sets of ideas which sprang directly from a wider historical experience: first the idea that colonialism was responsible for all major social ills, second that areas like the medina were simply tiresome problems when viewed from the perspective of plans designed to promote a particular view of modernity and to develop the country's tourist potential. It was only after a decade or so of numerous studies and investigations that planners began to see the medina not as an embarrassment, but as a specific urban quarter performing useful economic functions and housing a sizeable minority of the city's population. As a result of this approach Micaud is also able to open up a variety of larger subjects – for example, the conflicting attitudes of a number of social groups towards their own urban heritage and how to make us of it, and the way in which the promotion of tourism leads almost inevitably to a point of view which sees a country's heritage primarily through the eyes of a European hotelier or a European holidaymaker.

The possibility of a style of development employing local initiative, and adapting local resources in a productive way, is nicely brought out in Micaud's conclusion. But it is important to remember that such development plans are conceived and put into effect by people who are subject to a variety of social constraints - local, national and international - and not merely by decision-makes with good or bad ideas. If cheap alternative technologies (in housing, or agriculture, or energy, or whatever) fail to catch on, this is due more often to political economic forces beyond the control of local communities than to ignorance of physical techniques. The need for understanding these forces is therefore always a matter of the utmost importance.

Paths of Rural Transformation in Turkey

Cağlar Keydar

I Introduction

In any discussion of agricultural transformation in Turkey it is necessary to establish that agriculture has been a dynamic sector, especially during the last two decades. It is true that the social organization – the mode of production – does not seem to have undergone the (mistakenly) expected changes. This, however, does not indicate a stagnation or "blockage". Agricultural production may increase with significant technological change and greater integration into the social division of labour despite the persistence of small family farms. Unlike in industry, larger scale does not necessarily imply increasing efficiency in agriculture.

The development may be observed in rising output and productivity figures. Moreover these increases have occurred together with a considerable amelioration of the consumption levels of agricultural producers which is readily visible. Annual growth rate of agricultural output (in real terms) was 2.4 per cent in the 1960–70 period, and 3.4 per cent between 1970 and 1977. Since population engaged in agriculture has been declining in absolute terms in the last few years, productivity of agricultural labour is obviously increasing. Other calculations indicate an average annual increase in productivity of 4.2 per cent between 1967 and 1977. This performance indicates that after Greece and Netherlands, Turkish agriculture's transformation has been the most rapid among the OECD countries.

It is not the intention of this paper to argue that quantitative change has occurred without structural change. The structural change which seem to have taken place has, however, followed a considerably more complicated pattern than the unilinear path some theorists have expected. This is an attempt to describe the multiplicity of development paths which can be observed at the present stage in the transformation of agriculture.

The breakthrough in agriculture could be dated to the early 1950s when a number of developments coincided to form a unique conjuncture. Among these were the reconstruction of the world economy with Turkey's peripheral role in it; capital flows and financial aid advanced within this pattern of reconstruction which helped to implement the integration of agriculture into the national economy (roads); rapid technology and scale change (tractors leading to land reclamation); the Korean War price boom which helped to change the terms of trade in favour of agriculture and thus created incentives for investment in that sector; political developments internal to Turkey where a peasantry-supported party came to power and, through inflationary policies, postponed the impact of the post-Korean recession on agriculture. It is our contention that this conjecture lasting until the middle of the decade largely determined the later structuration and differentiation of the agricultural sector. Large landholding exploited through share-cropping arrangements, which had been declining steadily in importance since the 1858 land legislation, now received a decisive blow when tractor technology replaced labour-intensive grains production and as former sharecroppers could occupy newly reclaimed – albeit inferior – land. This trend towards the entrenchment of the small family farm was further aided by a government scheme through which newly reclaimed land, amounting to one-third of the total increase in land under cultivation, was distributed to the landless and the poorest owners. The recipients, who were mostly former tenants now technologically unemployed, numbered more than 200,000 families.

We might express these developments in a different terminology. It was during the early 1950s that capitalism began to irreversibly dominate Turkish agriculture. This domination, which is not to be confused with the installation of capitalist relations of exploitation, created not an increasingly homogenous structure, but on the contrary reinforced and accommodated an increasingly identifiable differentition. Before the onset of this process, rural structures were more homogeneous in all of Turkey and differences could be identified on a regional basis. Different regions could be characterized by the domination of different social structures, and inside a given region most villages would exhibit a homogeneous picture. Now a diversity of rural structures could be observed, interspersed within the same geographical area.

Our research which grew out of posing such questions led us to determine the various paths of rural transformation under the impact of capitalism. The identification of such a typology seems to be the most readily accessible method towards observing the implications of agricultural transformation on the economy-wide social division of labour, and towards predicting the modality of proletarianization (the installation of capitalist relations of production) at the level of social formation. More specific questions to be derived from the same problematic would include the nature of the existing relations of exploitation; differential developments as to crops, technology and commercialization; and perhaps most importantly the patterns of labour demand in various structures-in-formation which lead us to a better understanding of both permament and seasonal migration.

The following will present only a preliminary conceptualization of the research which has so far been conducted on more than thirty villages. Among these villages we have been able to identify both recurring patterns and cases which might reasonably be construed to represent movements along the same path. As a result of these empirically observed patterns interacting with our prior conceptualizations we have been able to come up with a working typology. Below, this typology will be presented in the form of a description of five representative case histories. Each case is a particular village which we believe to represent a conceptually distinguished type.

II Description of Cases

1. The village of Yeşildumlupınar in Çankırı [north-east of Ankara] is an old settlement, dating to early Ottoman times. With the lack of primogeniture land has been and is being continuously fragmented. Despite the introduction of fertilizers and machinery, the tired soil provided yields that may in fact be among the lowest in all Turkey. Although the potential means of integration into the national economy exists, the degree of commercialization is weak. The village enjoys a paved road, and is about 20 km from the provincial centre. It has had the status of municipality which allowed for the establishment of junior high school and hence for the inflow of civil servants. It seems therefore that the low degree of commercialization might in fact be due to the lack of agricultural surplus and to the difficulty in finding a commercial product suitable to local conditions.

The overwhelming economic activity is the cultivation of grains: wheat and barley. Sheep are raised for intermittent cash needs, and no household specializes in animal husbandry as a commercial activity. There are almost no side activities adding to the incomes of the households.

Both the land and the sheep are distributed fairly evenly, with two-thirds of the families owning between 30-100 dönüms (1 dönüm = 919 square metres). There are no landless households although there is incidence of land rentals which bring about a more even distribution of cultivated land. Most households own between 10 and 20 sheep and market them as cash is needed. There seems to be no absolute shortage of land or pasture as what villagers consider to be marginal land remains uncultivated, because "the yield will not be worth the effort". However, only about one-tenth of the households are actually self-sufficient. The rest seem to be subsidized from outside the village. To describe this mechanism we have to investigate the dynamics of migration.

Even before the 1950s the village of Yeşildumlupınar used to yield a small seasonal labour force to especially Ankara. In the 1950s and increasingly in the sixties migration came to attain a permanent character. At the present time both in Ankara and in Istanbul there are well-established groups of former Yeşildumlupınar inhabitants. This means that every single family in the village has one or more relatives living and working in the big cities. These migrants, however, have not yet lost contact with the village as their kins of an older generation continue to cultivate the fields. They themselves spend their leaves – which usually coincide with harvest time – in the village. The children of the third generation are sometimes left in the village at least until school years. There are also a number of retired functionaries and workers who have returned to the village. The economic impact of this outmigration has been twofold. On the one hand there is a gradual decline of the village as a viable economic unit. The age composition of the population remaining in the village is a telling testimony to this: it is mostly the older and the youngest who are the present inhabitants with the generation in the working age missing. There has also been a slow decline in the total population, presumably as the remaining members of a family are deceased. It is possibly this opportunity of outmigration and the availability of "exernal subsidies" which have precluded an alternative path of specializing in a different commercial activity (there are cases of neighbouring villages which are beginning to introduce new crops with commercial prospects). On the other hand the village is clearly subsidized from the outside. Each household receives an additional income from the "remittances" of those who work in the cities, and this allows inhabitants to sustain an elevated level of consumption.

Under the present dynamics, the long-term tendency for the village would seem to be towards extinction. Even now there are uncultivated fields which have no takers. The village has outlived its function as a permanent source of outmigration since the child-bearing population has mostly already migrated. In the absence of the working age population, the probability of a commercial transition through the adoption of a new crop is also negligible. Thus, the village might remain as a residential settlement with some subsistence activity, but is gradually forfeiting its economic viability. This outlook might only change if the urban economy undergoes a severe depression forcing recent migrants who maintain close contact with the village to return.

There are villages similar to what we have described in the Black Sea region as well as scattered around the interior regions of Anatolia, especially along the principal highways. Their common characteristics are insufficient commoditization of a low level of production and the relatively ready availability of outmigration opportunities.

The next village we shall consider started from a comparable situation, but due to the introduction of new activities, and the almost full commoditization of the economy, succeeded in becoming a viable economic unit.

2. The similarities between Uşak's Yayalar village and the previous village we have considered are evident. Yayalar also is a village of old settlement with a not very fertile soil, and a similarly even distribution of land. The resemblances, however, end there. Yayalar is obviously a viable and even thriving economic unit with a considerably higher level of per capita output in spite of smaller per capita land availability. Up until the late 1940s it would have been possible to conjecture that Yayalar would follow the same path as Yeşildumlupınar. In fact even during the 1950s population was stagnant and permanent outmigration was common. What began in the late 1940s was the introduction of new activities leading to greater specialization and commoditization. The most common of such activities was seasonal migration whereby villagers would travel to near-by Manis and Aydın to work in the harvesting of tobacco and cotton. While seasonal migration is the most commonly found extra source of income in all of Turkey, as villages begin to diversify their own economies, it loses its relative importance. In Yayalar too, as new crops and activities were introduced, especially since the late 1960s, seasonal migration came to affect the lives of a fewer number of families. In the last ten years tobacco-growing, opium, maize, poplars, grapes, chick peas, vegetable gardening, sheep husbandry have become important activities. In addition to seasonal migration and local agricultural production, inhabitants of this village also

engage in various commercial activities such as the transport of vegetables, and there is a growing – although still small – domestic industry in the form of cloth-weaving through a putting-out arrangement. The village is on its way to becoming a small economic centre as evidenced in the reversal of population trends: it has been receiving rather than yielding migration in recent years.

Almost every family is engaged in at least two of the activities listed above, so much so that instead of specialization, time and [the] management [of their economic assets] seem to characterize their economic decisions. Their activities are arranged according to complementariness. A family, for example who offer their seasonal labour in the harvesting of tobacco do not themselves cultivate the same strand of the crop in order to be able to efficiently manage the family labour potential.

The extent to which subsistence production has disappeared and commercial activity has become predominant is a good index of the degree of economic diversification. Even bread is obtained as a commodity through an arrangement with the nearby town centre. The village as a whole is deficient in bread grains as the composition of its output has tended towards what might be termed cash-crops.

Within this commercial nexus there is some sort of specialization according to the size of land cultivated by each family. All the hundred families (out of nearly three hundred) who themselves own less than five dönüms, rent small amounts of land and cultivate tobacco. It seems that the so-called self-exploitation of the family labour is most efficient with the highly labour-intensive tobacco technology. (Larger than five-dönüm plot of tobacco would require additional hired labour and the advantages of family labour would cease.) Only the very large owners predominantly cultivate grains on the least fertile land: there are three who own more than 200 dönüms – to a total of 800 – who are in this category. About 200 families regularly supply seasonal labour for agriculture while another 20-30 families yield winter labour to cloth-weaving workshops in the near-by town centre.

Although this village provides an extreme example of economic diversification, the addition of new sources of income to traditional activities is quite common. This is especially true with the availability of seasonal employment which tends to allow families to remain in the village and preserve a traditional structure. In villages of petty subsistance production such as Yeşildumlupınar, the traditional structure becomes absolute under the impact of permanent outmigration and elevated consumption patterns.

When, however, petty subsistence production yields to a high degree of commoditization additional revenue sources postpone the dissolution of the village structure. This is commonly the role played by seasonal employment opportunity, especially in eastern Anatolia. In the village we have described, new revenue sources have developed to such a degree that the village has gained a new and viable economic momentum essentially based on its traditional structure.

It is tempting to speculate on the initial causes of the separation of development paths between a village like Yeşildumlupınar and one like Yayalar. There does not seem to be a regional determination, as villages of both kinds might be found interspersed within the same geographical locus. Neither is it the case that the quality and the fertility of the soil are different. There is, however, a difference in the amount of land available to especially poorer households. The considerably smaller plots that Yayalar peasants have to survive on must have constituted an early incentive toward side-activities and economically more efficient utilization of the land. In Çankırı, on the other hand, subsistence-providing plot sizes which combine with migrant's remittances to allow rising consumption levels seem to have induced a relative laziness. It seems therefore that earlier integration into commercial channels and the "entrepreneurial spirit" of those who had to supplement a sub-subsistence primary output, were, in all likelihood, instrumental. This terminology indicates that factors which would be difficult to account for in a macro perspective such as ours, play a significant role.

3. The village of Karayavşan in Polatı [west of Ankara] is a recent settlement, dating to the late nineteenth century, situated on relatively fertile plains. At the start there were eighty households who were given equal amounts of land. Now, after a century of change, there are forty households with a degree of polarization which leads us to believe that there will be a further decrease in the number of households. Thus, the average amount of land per family is substantially higher than in the case of our two previous examples. The factor which has disrupted the even distribution at the beginning has been fragmentation through inheritance. The families which used to remain in the village despite being left with a small amount of land, have since the 1960s begun to migrate to the city. The process starts with what seems to be a temporary arrangement, with the family renting out their small plots while they themselves leave the village to find employment elsewhere, and terminates with the final sale of the land. Ten families have left the village in this

manner within the last decade.

The villagers cultivate grains to the exclusion of any other crops. There are thirty tractors and six combines, figures which indicate that all of the fields in the village are cultivated with a uniform technology. As this technology is machinery-intensive, there is no alternative source of employment within the village. On the other hand, all the families who own more than the "subsistence" level of around sixty dönüms, enjoy an accumulation potential. This potential has so far been utilized towards accumulation inside agriculture in the form of land and machinery purchases. Given the predominance of grain cultivation, this accumulation seems to be tending towards an optimum size and technology of family farms. This pattern of land concentration around family establishments we shall term the "kulak pattern". .

The extent of the operation in such a situation is determined by family size, since employment of outside labour remains at a minimum. There is no market for either permanent or seasonal work, thus the village does not receive any migration. On the other hand, although seasonal outmigration by poorer families is conceivable, in this particular case where such employment is not available in the vicinity and where permanent emigration is a tradition it does not seem to provide an alternative. An additional factor increasing the attraction of permanent outmigration is the existence of a market for land. Since families in the process of becoming kulaks are willing to purchase land towards the attainment of their optimal size, it is always possible to sell and thus to be able to arrive at the city with a supply of ready cash. In effect the unfolding of this kulak pattern is the only situation where concentration of the principal means of production occurs exclusively through the workings of the market.

It might be conjectured that the higher yields of relatively more fertile plains which facilitate accumulation are a necessary precondition of kulak development. Of course, the pattern most obviously obtains in the cultivation of grains where the widespread technology of today allows for the exclusive use of family labour. Other cases which are similar to Polatlı may be observed in the predominantly grain cultivating areas of Konya; and more and more in the plains of Bafra and Amasya where a former pattern of labour-intensive commercial crop farming seems to be yielding to the use of higher technology in the cultivation of grains and to the concentration of land around the kulak size.

4. The village of Tuzburgazı in Söke is another example of the kulak pattern where the majority of the households ae well-to-do, primarily utilizing their own labour. Tuzburgazı is a recent

settlement where former nomads were sedentarized on marsh land in the middle of the nineteenth century. Other nomadic settlements at the turn of the century and the exchange of population after the First World War modified the population mix in the village. The last major incorporation has been the gradual settlement of nomads who used to previously have winter encampment privileges. On top of what must have been an even distribution of land in the very beginning, two major land grant schemes in 1952 and 1960 have contributed to form the present picture. At the moment, out of 175 households, close to two-thirds own between 30–80 dönüms with only two families owning more than 150 dönüms (totalling 450 dönüms). About 10 per cent of the families are completely landless, but find employment either as fisherman or in the nearby forest administration, while some households owning less than thirty dönüms supplement their incomes through seasonal employment.

Ninety per cent of the village land, which is mostly irrigated, is cultivated under cotton. While every single household grows cotton, the smaller households also own olive groves which require intensive labour during the picking season. The distinguishing characteristic of cotton cultivation within the kulak pattern it the predominant use of family labour. Although outside help – usually within the village – might be resorted to, the proportion of labour expended by the family members far exceeds the external component. For farmers growing cotton in smaller fields, outside help takes the form of a village-wide arrangement where especially the younger members of all such families come together during the harvesting season and jointly pick the cotton in one small family plot after the other. Because the plots are small, the village as a whole does not organize to import migrant labour. Rather, workers in the adjoining villages are contracted to supplement the indigenous labour supply.

It appears, however, that the seemingly small scales of operation are still sufficient for accumulation on a widely spread basis. Tuzburgazı is a rich village where all the households enjoy electric power and at least a third own TV sets. Although cotton technology does not necessitate tractor usage to the same degree as grains, over a hundred families own tractors, used for a variety of purposes including that of pumping water for irrigation. This accumulation potential does not lead to a significant change towards concentration of land. Except for the case of the one large landlord who consolidated his holdings in the 1960s, land distribution has remained fairly constant. Renting acts as another process tending to equalize land under use. Most important transfers occur in the form of farmers engaging in non-agricultural activities (fishing) or renting their land out to the landless or to the small-holders. This pattern of distribution and, perhaps more importantly, the local availability of employment induce villagers to remain in the village and permanent emigration does not become an attractive alternative. Accordingly the population of the village has been increasing, parallel to the natural growth rate.

This second example of the kulak path characterizes certain development patterns along the Mediterranean and Aegean littorals. Its crucial characteristics are the preponderant use of family labour and the evident stability of the land distribution pattern. Since land is generous, labour-intensive cultivation of cotton, and increasingly of vegetables, allows for family-size farms which yield sufficient output for accumulation.

5. The last village we will consider is situated in the most backward region of the country, and despite (or perhaps because of) this location it is the only one where "capitalist" farming takes place. The village of Sinan in Bismil (Diyarbakır) is a formerly tribal Kurdish settlement whose social structure was disrupted after the Seyh Said incidents (1926). The tribal chief cum landlord was able to register the entire village grounds as his private property after his return from a short exile. Until the 1950s the land was cultivated in a tenancy arrangement with every family in the village having access to more or less equal amounts of land. In addition to the rent-in-kind which usually amounted to 80 per cent of the product, there was also an insignificant corvée obligation through which the small domain of the landlord was cultivated. With growing commercialization and the wave of land reclamation in the early 1950s the landlord incorporated what used to be pasture land into his private domain. At the same time the labour-rent arrangement became obsolete due to the use of tractors. The first wave of enclosures occurred in the late 1950s when the landlord succeeded in both decreasing the area of land rented to the tenants and in driving a number of families out of the village.

Mechanization, enclosures and class struggle attained an increased momentum during the 1960s. Despite the conflicts, the landlord gradually advanced toward the realization of his goal. At the moment he owns twelve tractors and two combines, and is trying to convert the entire village into a private farm. Class struggle, however, has intensified to such a degree that families do not readily leave the village despite the use of force. The landlord has to pay a significant sum of money (commutation in reverse) to be able to induce households to permanently emigrate. Twenty households took this option last year (1979). Fifty of the families who remain in the village are refused the rental of land because the landlord finds them "troublesome", and would like to force them out of the village. The remaining families who are allowed to rent land have access to subsistence size plots, but their only obligation consists of a nominal (10 per cent) rent-in-kind. The landlord employs thirty families as permanent labour, as tractor operators, mechanics and servants.

This degree of mechanization and formation of a capitalist pattern is fairly recent. Only in 1976 did the landlord invest in an irrigation project. Thus, although the transformation in technology is complete, there is still a large ground to cover in enclosures and a commercial adaptation with more flexible market response is yet to begin. The landlord still cultivates wheat to a large extent although a slow transition has begun towards tobacco and cotton. Of course to switch to these labour-intensive crops which require seasonal labour, would cause further problems with the not-yet-enclosed households in the village. Therefore it would seem that commercial transformation will take some time.

The process of capitalist transition through enclosures and expulsion of the tenants is transparently visible in this village. It is, therefore, a significant example of the genesis of a particular path (a path, we might add, which was thought to be the general rule for all of agriculture). Cases which are further along in this pattern of development are readily observable in other provinces of the south-east and in the Çukurova region. The point of arrival especially in cotton-growing Çukurova is the full enclosure and disappearance of a village where only a few families in the permanent employment of the landlord remain, and where seasonal migration provides the main source of labour. The commercial switch accompanying this development is towards greater adaptability to market conditions.

III Conclusions and Observations

On the basis of these case histories, we shall propose a typology consisting of basically three categories. We must at the outset mention that our methodological choice has been a classification based on village types. Instead of looking at particular patterns of land exploitation and arriving at a classification which takes as its units farms, we have chosen to classify villages according to the dominant developmental tendency within them. It is this dominant tendency which determines the transformations that the remaining households within the village will undergo. The impact of social and economic change on individual households is primarily mediated by the social structure of the village. Therefore, it would be impossible to predict differential developments based on adaptations to socioeconomic change on the basis of individual households. We believe that in understanding social transformation, in analyzing the formation of classes in agriculture and in the society as a whole, and especially in the determination of social and economic complementarities on regional lines, we need to pursue a classification based on the transformation of village structures.

The five divergent cases we have described may be reduced to three basic types. The first type is that of villages dominated by petty commodity production. Our cases 1 and 2 represent two variants of this type. It is from within this group that we might expect proletarianization of the insufficiently commercial producers (case 1) or semi-proletarianization of those who find in seasonal migration an extra source of income. While the poorest villages in this category, unable to diversify their activites, seem to be doomed to economic extinction, the rest (such as case 2) will certainly survive. These latter are completely integrated into the national economy through commercial channels. Of course, as they consist exclusively of small producers utilizing family labour, commercial exploitation of unpaid labour is predominant in these villages. Thus, their function in the national economy is primarily that of producing cheap commodities (including labour power), while their livelihood derives from a multiplicity of activities. In the case of seasonal migration the advantages of this variety are evident: a greater part of the reproduction of the labour force is not due to wages received, but is undertaken in the village; simultaneously the existence of an extra wage income allows for depressed prices of the produced commodities. In case of predominantly subsistence farming supplemented by seasonal migration it will be the difficult-to-predict "degree of commercialization" which will determine whether the village becomes economically viable, or dissolves through the negation of seasonal by permanent migration.

Our second category is the kulak village as exemplified in the Polatlı village (number 3) and possibly by the village in Söke. The term "kulak" refers to the rich petty producer who is in a position to accumulate his own surplus and bring his technology up to contemporary standards. The kulak village consists of several kulaks to the exclusion of poorer families because the principal source of labour is the family members. If the American and European experiences provide a guidance, the kulak village might be a transitional form which will dissolve into isolated farmsteads. In the process of its formation the kulak-dominated village yields permanent outmigration. However, since these households leave the village with a supply of cash – obtained through the sale of their land – they are not readily proletarianized as is the case with migrants out of a type I village. Our case number 4, which in terms of income would fall into the kulak classification, is nevertheless different, because of the seasonal employment of outside labour. For this reason case 4 falls in between types II and III.

The really capitalist type complete with enclosures, driving off of former tenants, and proletarianization *in situ* is exemplified by case number 5. Here non-wage labour is at a minimum and the defining relations of exploitation are properly capitalist. As we had mentioned above, it is not accidental that the village in our sample which describes type III is located in the least developed region of Turkey. It was here that feudal-type relations of exploitation survived for the longest period, until the 1960s. Integrated into a capitalist market, these relations underwent the historical transition toward capitalist enclosure. Since we believe that the dominant tendency in the distribution of land is that of fragmentation rather than concentration, the pure capitalist type is to be observed its genesis and immediately thereafter. In its developed form it may already be on the verge of disintegration. . .

We shall now turn to the relative stability of these types. It has already been mentioned that within petty commodity-producing villages those resembling our case number 1 are bound to disappear in the long run unless they achieve a transformation into case number 2. It is also conceivable that a type I village may transform into a kulak village. This transformation would require a considerable amount of land appropriation by the would-be kulaks through the market mechanism. That is why it is a difficult development especially when a market for land does not traditionally exist. By contrast the formation of a kulak pattern out of the dissolution of a large ownership situation or from among already well-to-do producers is more likely.

The kulak category, as is demonstrated in abundant historical evidence, is the most stable among our types. Technology and the advantages of family labour combine to prevent a move towards greater concentration which would require the employment and costly management of outside labour. On the other hand, the relative wealthiness of the family prevents the fragmentation of the farm through inheritance since younger children may be sent to the city to be educated, and thus be offered alternative employment opportunity. It must be mentioned here that the advantages of family farming are evident and irreversible only if we assume the continuity of the present conditions – especially of labour use. At the present time (January 1980) agricultural labour in Turkey . . . enjoys political freedoms and consequently a high rate of remuneration relative to either South Asian or Latin American examples. It is in these latter "underdeveloped" situations that classical relations of wage labour and capital are the most prominent. In the United States, for example, proper capitalist agriculture only exists as a function of a severely dual labour market, where "agro-business" primarily employs illegal immigrants. It seems, therefore, that in the case of "free" labour with relatively high wages, only family farms using non-wage labour are efficient enough to remain in a market where suppliers in widely divergent technical and social conditions produce identical goods. Given the present conditions in Turkey, we therefore think that a transformation of kulak villages into pure capitalist types is a very "improbable possibility". On the other hand, the dissolution of a capitalist landholding to yield a kulak-dominated pattern is much more frequently observed, and indeed predicted as the national integration of the labour market progresses. The ostensible reasons for such a dissolution are mismanagement of the farm and fragmentation through inheritance which leads to the sale and dispersion of the land. Thus a reversal of the concentration which has culminated in the capitalist type always remains a possibility.

It must also be mentioned that the stability and transformational possibilities of these types depend on external conditions. Relative prices of the crops have an obvious impact as crops requiring labour-intensive techniques may replace machine-intensive ones, causing a change in the pattern of labour use. This change would in turn influence migration potentials as well as determine the availability of extra sources of income. Another example would be the economic conjuncture which determines the demand for labour in the cities. A sufficiently serious downturn, for example, would discourage and might in fact cause a reversal in permanent migration out of type I villages. We have so far implicitly treated permanent migration to be solely determined by the social structure of the migration-yielding village. We believe that availability of employment in the cities would gain importance only through drastic changes in economic conjuncture. A general crisis (such as the one Turkey is experiencing now) where most of industrial production comes to a stop, and growth remains around zero, would be such a conjuncture. It is also possible to trace out the probable impact of various state policies, including land distribution, employment creation, credit and support prices, on the likelihood and stability of our development types. Support prices, for example, have a differential impact on primarily subsistence producers who need to supplement their output with cash income, and on surplus producers of grains. If the relative price of petrol to tractor owners is allowed to increase, this might raise the rental price of machinery, and might cause a return to more labour-intensive techniques, especially in the case of small producers. Such a change would in turn curtail their opportunities for seasonal migration.

We can also point to one particular institutional change at the supra-national level which would have an important impact on development potentials, and on labour use. A greater integration into the EEC, where restrictions on Turkish exports would be gradually lifted, will certainly induce a rapid transformation of the entire coastal area in the temperate Mediterranean zone. If the change is towards labour-intensive vegetable-growing, family gardens might emerge as one other development to cause a fragmentation of the land, and to prevent rapid outmigration. Beginnings of such a development are already visible especially in the Mersin area.

We undertook this research to discover the impact of capitalist domination on the agricultural sector. Our findings so far indicate that substantially different developments than those suggested by theoretical excursions – either of unilinear orthodox or bipolar dependency type – are in order. We believe, for example, that the properly capitalist model, which is most prominent in the most backward regions, is not a terminus but mostly a transitional situation.

Popular Movements and Primordial Loyalties in Beirut

Michael Johnson

This paper seeks to explain some of the complex interrelations between class, clientelism and confessionalism in Beirut. It argues that a clientelist system of control operated in Lebanon to contain class and confessional (or religious) conflict, but that this system broke down in the Civil War of 1975–6 to allow the emergence of popular movements independent of the control of the Lebanese state. A major concern is to discuss the conditions under which primordial loyalties were partially transformed into a kind of class consciousness amongst the Muslim poor or "crowd" – that social category described by Hobsbawm as the "menu peuple" (Hobsbawm, 1971, p. 113). Ultimately, primordial loyalties reasserted themselves, but at the height of the Civil War it looked to some as though a social revolution was taking place in Lebanon. The reasons for that revolution's failure are too complicated to discuss here, but the paper does indicate the limits of the popular movements which emerged in the 1970s and hopefully represents a starting-point for understanding the social conflicts which led to the destruction of the Lebanese state.

Clientelism as a System: Class Formation and Confessionalism 1943-70

What is particularly striking about Beirut in the modern age is the persistence and sophistication of the socioeconomic and political structures which had emerged under the Ottomans and French. The service-based economy developed such that Beirut became the banking and trade centre for the Arab Middle East. The relative decline of Lebanese agriculture, coupled with the emergence of capitalist farming in what were previously neo-feudal estates, led to an increasing migration to the city. A small and dependent industrial sector remained subordinate to the interests of commerce and finance, and thus did not provide work for significant numbers of immigrants who simply swelled the ranks of the semi-employed sub-proletariat.[1] The small size of the industrial proletariat and the weakness of socialist organizations contributed towards the persistence of mob action and gangster-ism among the urban poor, rather than the growth of class consciousness. And in order to contain the powder keg of the crowd, parliamentary representatives of the commercial–finan-cial bourgeoisie established sophisticated political machines which bound the "menu peuple" into clientelist systems of social control. These machines made use of the *qabadays* [*qabadyat* – strongarm, and often criminal, leaders of the street], who in return for protection from arrest and imprisonment, delivered votes to their *za'im* (*za'im* – political boss, pl. *zu'ama*) in elections and mobilized supporters and armed men for factional confrontations. A very repressive system developed which both responded to the "menu peuple's" individualism and encouraged its persistence by an insistence on personalized contracts between the za'im and his clients. Trade unions, syndicates and societies had great difficulty in negotiating concessions or services as groups because the zu'ama would usually help the "menu peuple" as individuals and not as members of class or interest organizations. Unions and syndicates which did emerge were often controlled by the zu'ama as extensions of their machines, and groups that developed some autonomy or stepped out of line could be terrorised back into compliance by strongarm and gangster retainers (Johnson, 1977)

Clientelism was thus transformed from the rather more philan-thropic variety of the Ottoman period into a developed system of political and social control. This system bore a close resemblance to that which operated in a place like Naples, where political bosses also used gangs to organize a clientele amongst the sub-proletariat. Allum's analysis of Neapolitan politics describes the local society as being "transitional" between a "simple agrarian" and a "complex industrial" one (Allum, 1973). In this transitional society, classes were in a process of formation; social relationships were no longer predominantly communal or *gemeins-chaftlich*, but neither were they yet fully *gesellschaftlich*. Political organizations were not based on that peculiar mixture of "coer-cion" and "consent" which characterizes the relations between a landlord and his peasants, nor were they fully developed into political parties and interest groups. Rather, they were composed of a political boss and his machine – an organisation designed to win elections in order to gain access to patronage which could then be distributed to the clientele.

There were, however, a number of differences between the clientelist systems in Beirut and Naples. First, industrialization in northern Italy had influenced the politics of southern cities and towns. In Lebanon, on the other hand, the politics of Beirut were more determined by the neo-feudalism of the countryside and the confessional divisions amongst the population. The za'im was not part of a national political party, but was essentially a local, communal leader with no disciplined organization behind him. His leadership rested not only on what Allum calls the "coercion" and "manipulation" of the machine (Allum, 1973, p. 10), but also on the consent of many of his clients who perceived him as a communal champion. Nor was the za'im dependent on state power and patronage to the extent that the political boss in Naples was. Due to their strong local bases, zu'ama could survive for a number of years in opposition to a particular government by relying on local sources of patronage, and could also, as in 1958, mount insurrections against the regime in power. Finally, whereas the Neapolitan boss was usually a "lesser professional man" (Allum, 1973, p. 10) like a lawyer with no particular social rank, one of the resources of a za'im in Beirut was the notable status of his family – usually built up over generations of mercantile and political activity.

Up until the Civil War of 1975–6 the clientelist system worked remarkably well. It is true that the lack of political parties and national political structures meant there were few arbitrating mechanisms which could control local conflicts. This resulted in costly local feuds between notables, and contributed to the outbreak of a full-scale Civil War in 1958.[2] But the system was flexible enough for enemies to become reconciled. In addition, the factional squabbles between zu'ama usually served the interests of the dominant social class, for a weak state could not interfere in trade and finance. The most serious danger to the Lebanese commercial-financial bourgeoisie was the prospect of social unrest among the urban "menu peuple" and sub-proletariat. So long as the zu'ama could control these people, the persistence and reproduction of the social formation was not endangered.

The success of the clientelist system was, however, predicated on the continued availability of patronage, particularly with regard to the provision of employment, promotion and career opportunity. Furthermore, given the strong social attachments to religious primordial loyalties, the distribution of this patronage had to be fairly shared between the confessions. In the early years of independence these conditions appeared to be being met, but as time wore on fundamental problems emerged which led ultimately to the revolutionary climate of the 1970s. The rate of unemployment rose, and it became increasingly obvious that the Muslim community – and especially the Shi'ite sect - was underprivileged as compared with the Christians.

As banking, trade and other services in Lebanon expanded, agriculture went into a relative decline and industry remained stagnant. Whereas, in 1950, agriculture accounted for 20 per cent of GDP, by 1970 its share had dropped to 9 per cent. During the same period the industry and construction sector failed to increase its share of around 18 per cent, while the tertiary sector grew from 63 per cent of GDP to 73 per cent (Lebanon, Ministry of Planning, 1971, pp. 426–7). This increasingly 'lop-sided' structure of Lebanon's economy had differential effects on the country's various communities (Khalaf, 1971). The high level of education on Mount Lebanon meant that those sons of the predominantly Maronite Catholic peasantry, who were forced off the mountain as a result of land shortage and increasing fragmentation of holdings (Khalaf, 1971, pp. 14–15), could at first find employment as clerks, managers and entrepreneurs in the expanding tertiary sector. That this was so indicated by the low level of migration from Lebanon to other countries after the Second World War. Emigration had been the traditional response of Lebanese faced by unemployment. When the silk industry first declined, over 7,000 people had left annually and it was estimated that between 1900 and 1914, 100,000 people – representing a quarter of the local population – had emigrated from Mount Lebanon (Ruppin, 1916, p. 194). By comparison, emigration from independent Lebanon (with an obviously much larger population than the mountain region) averaged less than 3,000 persons per year during the 1950s (IRFED Mission, 1960, p. 49).

If the Christians of Mount Lebanon were easily absorbed by the government bureaucracy and the commercial and financial firms of Beirut, the predominantly Shi'ite immigrants from the peripheries of Lebanon were less fortunate. Tenants, sharecropping peasants and agricultural labourers of south Lebanon and the Biga' were gradually forced off the land as the result of high rents, low wages and, particularly in the later 1960s, increased mechanisation on the large estates. Lacking the education of the mountain Christians the Muslims from the peripheries were less able to find employment in the service sector where the demand for unskilled labour was relatively low; and lacking financial resources, they were prevented from setting up businesses on their own account or emigrating abroad. They also had to compete with the indigenous Sunnis of Beirut, who were favoured by local communal patrons in recruitment to jobs. As a result, Muslim migrants to the city tended to swell the ranks of the semi-employed sub-proletariat in the *bidonvilles* and suburbs (Nasr, 1978, p. 10).

Given the lack of reliable statistics, it is difficult to estimate the unemployment rate in the 1950s and 1960s, but there is little doubt that it increased. In 1970 a government sample survey put the rate at 8.1 per cent of the active population (Lebanon, Ministry of Planning, 1971, p. 135), but this seems an underestimate, particularly when it is considered that the number of people who emigrated in that year was nearly 10,000 (Lebanon, Ministry of Planning, 1972, p. 83). Whatever the accuracy of the unemployment figures the increasing level of emigration suggests the inability of the service sector to absorb the *educated* unemployed. What data are available, coupled with my own impressions formed while living in Beirut, suggest that Christians continued to find it easier to be recruited into clerical and other jobs in the tertiary sector. The Muslim salariat of Beirut complained bitterly during the 1950s, for example, about their weak representation in the ranks of the government bureaucracy . . . and this goes a long way towards explaining why they were active supporters of the insurrectionary zu'ama and their private armies duing the Civil War of 1958. Though, after the war, some positive discrimination was extended to Muslim applicants for positions in the bureaucracy, Christian dominance within the commercial–financial bourgeoisie meant that it was still difficult for the Muslim salariat to enter the private sector. The clientelist system worked in such a way that patrons preferred to help their co-religionists, and as the Muslim bourgeoisie was relatively small, Muslims usually faced more problems in finding work.

As classes developed in Lebanon the relationships between them and confessional categories became clearer. In the countryside the Maronite freeholding peasants and farmers on Mount Lebanon contrasted greatly with the neo-feudal landlords and sharecropping peasantry in the Muslim peripheries - predominantly Sunni in the northern 'Akkar region, and Shi'ite in the north-eastern Biqa' and south Lebanon. The class structure of the mountain did not exhibit significant changes during the period presently under discussion, but in the peripheries capitalist relations further developed during the 1960s as a result of mechanization and a decline of share-cropping (Nasr, 1978, pp. 6-9; Dubar and Nasr, 1976, pt 2, ch. 3). It is the city of Beirut which concerns us, however, and here the dominance of a largely Christian bourgeoisie is one of the most important characteristics. A glance through a publication like *Annuaire des Sociétés Libanaises par Actions*[3] reveals the overwhelming predominance of Christian names amongst the directors of banks and joint stock companies. And in a sample survey of 207 leading businessmen in the early 1960s, only one-sixth were Muslim, outnumbered in ratios of 10:2 in industry, 11:2 in banking and 16:2 in services (Sayigh, 1962, pp. 69–71). The petty bourgeosie and salariat also tended to be largely Christian, while the proletariat and sub-proletariat were mostly Muslim. These latter assertions are supported by a survey of the active population conducted in 1972.[4] In an admittedly small sample of 152 people, roughly equally balanced between Christians and Muslims, those in "middle-class" occupations – such as civil servants and clerks in the private sector – were predominantly Christian. Workers and sub-proletarians, on the other hand, tended to be Muslim.

As this confessionally influenced class structure developed, so the Christian and Muslim crowds became more sharply differentiated, both socially and organizationally. In the eastern, Christian half of the city, some *qabadays* continued to organize the "menu peuple" right up to the recent Civil War, but due to the predominantly petty-bourgeois character of Christian Beirut, and perhaps particularly the existence of a large educated salariat intent on defending its privileges, the crowd became more and more influenced by the disciplined "Kata'ib" party (*Phalanges libanaises*) originally founded in 1936 and modelled on the militia structure of European fascist parties (Entelis, 1974). In western Beirut, by contrast, it was the large sub-proletariat which set the tone of popular politics within the Sunni Muslim community, and it was the zu'ama political machine which controlled these politics by making use of strong-arm leaders of the street.

The Politicization of the Gang Leaders in Sunni Beirut: 1960-75

All zu'ama in Sunni Beirut used *qabadays* to help in recruiting political clients from amongst the "menu peuple" and more importantly to organize and control the clientele – usually in sub-units based on the various quarters which made up the Muslim half of the city. As a result of the zu'ama's assistance, some of these street leaders had become prosperous businessmen in their own right. Others operated protection, prostitution and smuggling rackets. These were protected from the law-enforcement agencies by their za'im patrons, who because of their positions as parliamentary deputies or members of government could bring influence to bear on the police and courts (Johnson, 1977). During the 1960s, however, a new type of clientelist relationship developed between some *qabadays* and the state.

Rather than being the clients of individual zu'ama, these *qabadays* were directly protected by the law-enforcement agencies themselves,. most notably by the military intelligence apparatus of the "Deuxième Bureau".[5] This practice fitted in with the general strategy of President Fu'ad Shihab to weaken the popular base of the zu'ama, whose Byzantine and internecine factionalism had contributed to the outbreak of Civil War in 1958. During the regime of Shihab's successor (1964–70) the Deuxième Bureau continued to offer a number of *qabadays* protection and other types of assistance, including direct payments of regular sums of money. This was part of an attempt to influence general elections in order to bring about the re-election by parliament of Fu'ad Shihab in 1970; and in Muslim Beirut the Bureau's activities were largely directed against Sa'ib Salam, the major Sunni za'im who had helped lead the opposition to the "statist" and reformist policies of "Shihabism".

Thus during the latter 1960s, two groups of *qabadays* could be distinguished in Sunni Beirut. One was composed of strongarm businessmen loyal to Sa'ib Salam. These included Hashim 'Itani in the quarter of Musaytiba. A member of a large family or clan composed predominantly of menu peuple, 'Itani, with Salam's, help, had risen from being a small coffee-shop proprietor to become a director of companies owning cinemas, restaurants, bars and cafés in the more fashionable parts of the city. Another "businessman-*qabaday*" was Faruq Shihab ad-Din in the quarter of Basta, which with its environs formed perhaps the most celebrated district in Beirut, having an epic reputation as a Sunni stronghold, a major seat of local and national leadership, and a centre of factional turbulence. In keeping with local tradition, Shihab ad-Din worked in the port where he and his brother had a family transport business which had been handed down from their grandfather.

The second group of *qabadays* was Shihabist and was protected or paid by the Deuxième Bureau. These leaders of the street were more committed than the Salamists to the popular ideology of Arab Nationalism. They were at least nominally Nasserist and had remained loyal to Cairo after Sa'ib Salam had changed his own allegiance to Saudi Arabia. The most important and influential *qabaday* in this group was Ibrahim Qulaylat from the popular quarter of Tariq al-Jadida. A somewhat mysterious 'Robin Hood' character, Qulaylat was generally considered to be an agent in the pay of Egyptian intelligence or the Deuxième Bureau, and probably both. In the late 1960s he was unsuccessfully prosecuted for the assassination of a right-wing and pro-Saudi newspaper editor.[6]

The election of President Sulayman Frangieh (Faranjiyya) in 1970 brought about a change of regime. Sa'ib Salam became Prime Minister and, with his President's blessing, set about disbanding the Deuxième Bureau. Principal officers were put on trial and others were removed from positions of influence. The new internal security agency was staffed by officers loyal to the Frangieh-Salam regime, and although these men were competent they lacked an access to the intelligence networks which had been assiduously built up since 1958. As a result the regime lost control of the political underworld and was unable to prevent or solve the mystery of a series of bomb attacks in 1972 (Salibi, 1976, pp. 57–60). These were directed against political targets such as the pharmacy owned by Pierre Gemayel (Jumayyil), the leader of the rightist Kata'ib party, and the offices of leftist and Palestinian organizations.

More important for our immediate purposes, however, is what appeared to the Lebanese state to be an increasing anarchy among Beiruti *qabadays*. During the Shihabist period (1958–70) the Deuxième Bureau was able to tolerate some minor excesses on the part of the racketeers, while at the same time keeping them under a tight political control. After the dissolution of the Bureau, these Shihabist *qabadays* were able to operate more independently. While some pro-Frangieh *zu'ama* were able to recruit certain criminal *qabadays* and bring them under state control by offering a continued protection from the law, other street leaders were able to build links with powerful patrons outside the Lebanese clientelist system. These patrons were principally the Palestinian organizations and the Libyan and Iraqi governments.

By the beginning of the 1970s a number of Palestinian gangs, largely recruited from the refugee camps, had developed smuggling and protection rackets of their own and were emerging as competitors of the indigenous Lebanese gangs. Through their connections with commando organizations the Palestinian criminal networks were well armed; and as the Cairo Agreement of 1969 allowed the Palestinians to enforce their own laws in the refugee camps of Lebanon, the gangsters had a secure base from which they could operate. The competition between these new gangs and the Lebanese *qabadays* led to armed clashes and vendettas. In March 1970 a clash occurred on the edge of Beirut between Palestinian commandos and a gang of smugglers who were supporters of a Lebanese Muslim *za'im*. A number of smugglers were killed, and others captured and murdered (Salibi, 1976, p. 54). In July 1974 a quarrel between two smugglers, one a

Christian Lebanese and the other a Palestinian, resulted in two days of fighting between the local Kata'ib militia and the refugee camp of Tall az-Za'tar (Salibi, 1976, p. 80). And in August 1974 a member of a Shi'ite *"qabaday* family" or clan was kidnapped, murdered and stuffed down a well, apparently by a group of Palestinians who held the *qabaday* responsible for killing a friend of theirs. After a militant funeral (during which members of the clan fired their Kalashnikovs in the air) a bloody vendetta was narrowly averted by the Palestinian security agencies handing over one of the alleged culprits to the Lebanese authorities. It is not certain what lay at the roots of these confrontations between Palestinians and Lebanese, but the *za'im* protectors of the *qabadays* were powerless to prevent such incidents, and were often unable to bring the Palestinians to justice. Revenge was exacted through vendettas which exacerbated the existing state of tension.

Some of the Muslim racketeers dealt with the new situation by working in partnership with Palestinian gangs, and it appears that the commando movement itself took control of some *qabaday* networks. The Shi'ite clan mentioned above, for example, was reported to have had as many as a hundred of its members enrolled in the ranks of commando organizations.[7] Palestinian and Muslim Lebanese gangs were also brought closer together as a result of their common opposition to some of the Christian gangs. There was a traditional rivalry between the communal champions of Muslim and Christian Beirut – a rivalry that was usually contained as a result of the mediation of *zu'ama* and notables from both communities. It seems that in the 1970s one of the objections of parties like the Kata'ib to the armed Palestinian presence in Lebanon was that it was upsetting this delicate balance of the political underworld.

Of perhaps greater concern was the fact that some Muslim *qabadays* were becoming more overtly political than the normal type of racketeer. By mid-1973 the propaganda war between Egypt and Libya had begun to affect the Lebanese Nasserist parties (*L'Orient–Le Jour*, 24 July 1973). A year later Najah Wakim, a lawyer and leader of the Nasserist Union of Popular Labour Forces (*at-tanzim an-nasiri-ittihad qiwa ash-sha'b al-'amil*), complained that Libya and Iraq were trying to subvert his organization by buying off its leaders. In a prophetic statement he charged the two radical regimes with sending hundreds of agents into Lebanon in order to "drown the country in blood" (*Arab World*, 21 June 1974). In part this statement was directed against the *qabaday* leader, Ibrahim Qulaylat, who after the death of Nasser (Jamal 'Abd an-Nasir) had switched his allegiance to Arab paymasters more radical than President Sadat and had founded his own organization called the Independent Nasserist movement (*harakat an-nasiriyyin al-mustaqillin*). Probably, at this stage, Qulaylat's support base was largely confined to his own locality, but he was clearly intent on extending his control over the Nasserist movement as a whole.

The populist ideology of Nasserism was attractive to such "primitive rebels" (Hobsbawm, 1971), appealing particularly to their political identification with Islam. It was during the 1950s that it had first provided a populist expression of the Sunni "menu peuple's" discontent, and many of the more powerful *qabadays* had established themselves in the 1958 Civil War as the communal champions of their quarters. Qulaylat, for example, was sixteen years old at the time and he, like other Sunni *qabadays*, fought for the "Nasserist" insurrectionary *za'im*, Sa'ib Salam. The adoption of Nasserism by Salam and other *zu'ama* reduced the already limited, revolutionary potential of the ideology, incorporating it and the *qabadays* into the clientelist system. After Salam broke with Egypt in the 1960s, the Nasserist *qabadays* were brought under the supervision of the Deuxième Bureau. Again the radical element of the ideology was controlled, possibly more effectively this time, by the apparatus of a quasi police state. Whereas the intellectual Nasserists of the Arab Nationalist Movement (*harakat al-qawmiyyin al-'arab*) had developed into Marxists and revolutionary socialists (Kazziha, 1975), popular Nasserism remained moribund as an ideology which could mobilise the subproletariat and other "menu peuple" as a political force independent of the controls of the clientelist system. Manipulated first by the state itself, Nasserism provided a framework for socializing the urban poor and their *qabaday* leaders into an acceptance of the status quo. The end of Shihabism, however, provided an opportunity for freeing the ideology from the control of the state and liberating its populist appeal.

The Breakdown of the Clientelist System of Control: 1975–6

The radicalization of popular Nasserism was a gradual process, and it became a significant political force only when state authority finally collapsed in Beirut during the fourth "round" of fighting in September 1975. The controls of the clientelist system operated reasonably well in Sunni Beirut during the early part of

President Frangieh's regime, and even during the first three rounds of the Civil War (April–June 1975) the *zu'ama* seemed to have had a moderating influence over their clienteles. Although rapid inflation and icnreasing unemployment caused widespread unrest and strike action from 1972 onwards,[8] these popular manifestations were subject to a set of controls in the quarters of west Beirut which were it not for factors outside the relatively closed world of Sunni politics, could have contained the situation until the economic crisis ended. Popular disturbances were blatantly manipulated by *zu'ama* in order to gain factional advantage over their rivals, such that during the period 1973 to 1975 no fewer than four cabinets (under the premierships of Sa'ib Salam, Amin al-Hafiz, Taqi ad-Din as-Sulh and, finally, Rashid as-Sulh) were forced from office. This parliamentary game of musical chairs, in which *zu'ama* vied with one another for control over state patronage, was crucial for the overall stability of the clientelist system. The appointment by Frangieh of each new Prime Minister created a temporary climate of optimism and, more importantly, provided the deposed Premier with an opportunity to rehabilitate himself amongst his clientele.

The case of Sa'ib Salam is instructive here. At the time of his resignation in April 1973 he was widely and generally opposed by the Sunni "menu peuple" of west Beirut because of his repressive handling of the strikes and demonstrations of 1972-3.[9] But within a month or so, as a result of President Frangieh's sending in the Lebanese army and airforce to bombard Palestinian positions in Beirut, Salam was able to re-establish his leadership by posing as a communal leader determined to defend the rights of the Lebanese Muslim community which on the whole identified with the Palestinian struggle. I was living in a popular quarter of Sunni Beirut during this period and was daily astounded by neighbours and friends who, having vehemently opposed Salam during his premiership, by June 1973 were claiming him as a champion of Arab nationalism. On reflection such changes of attitude should not surprise us. Popular Nasserism had always laid greater emphasis on appeals to the nationalist and confessional sentiments of the Muslim urban poor than to their potential class consciousness. Consequently, the ideology was open to manipulation by the Sunni *zu'ama*. From the moment he resigned, Salam used conservative themes to regain control over his clientele. In alliance with Rashid Karami (the *za'im* of Tripoli) he became closely associated with the Mufti of Lebanon (the spiritual head of the Sunnis). Together these men began to press the traditional demands of their community, specifically for more powers to be given to the Sunni Premier *vis-à-vis* the Maronite President, and second, for Friday – the Muslim day of prayer – to be accorded the status of an official holiday along with the existing holiday on Sunday (Salibi, 1976, pp. 72–8).

During the Civil War the Sunni establishment was again able to demonstrate its loyalty to the Arab nationalist and Muslim cause when President Frangieh formed a predominantly military cabinet after the first round of fighting between Palestinian commandos and Kata'ib militia. This short-lived "military government" was strongly opposed by the Sunni *zu'ama*, especially as it included as Minister of Defence the army Commander-in-Chief, a man widely held to be far too partial to the interests of his own Maronite community. Such a provocative appointment led to a second round of fighting and brought the Muslim establishment into a temporary alliance with the National Movement (*al-haraka al-wataniyya*)[10] against the Lebanese state. The fighting ended only after the resignation of the government and the appointment of Rashid Karami as Prime Minister at the end of May 1975 (Salibi, 1976, pp. 97 ff. and *MERIP Reports*, 44, 1976).

Throughout the first three rounds of the Civil War, the quarters of Sunni Beirut remained relatively free from the fighting. Barricades were erected around some quarters and there were cases of kidnappings, mutilations and murders, but there was no heavy fighting as there was in the suburbs. The Sunni establishment only lost control of the situation in September when the Kata'ib militia began to bombard the western half of Beirut's commercial centre in an apparent attempt to force Karami's government to send in Lebanese troops to restore order (*MERIP Reports*, 44, 1976).

Already unpopular within his community for agreeing to use the army in Tripoli, Karami was unable to move troops into Beirut. Such an action would have risked reprisals by Palestinian commandos and would almost certainly have led to fierce resistance from the militias of the National Movement. Thus the fighting was brought into the centre of the city. The state was then unable to prevent it spreading into the quarters along the northern coast of west Beirut which included hotels, foreign embassies, the local headquarters of several foreign firms and the homes of foreign residents. Limited actions on the part of the security forces made the situation worse and brought the fighting into the heart of Sunni Beirut. On the evening of 19 October, for example, the mutilation and shooting of a Muslim taxi-driver led to shooting across the Damascus Road which divided west (Sunni) and east (Christian) Beirut. Security forces shelled both sides in an effort to stop the fighting, but the strong resistance offered by Muslims forced the army to move west into Musaytiba (Sa'ib Salam's quarter) and from there north-west into the coastal quarter of Ras Bayrut (*Arab World*, 20 Oct 1975).

Many of the gunmen fighting the security forces on the night of 19 October were local *qabadays* fulfilling their traditional duty of defending their quarters against outsiders. Such clashes mobilized the Sunni sub-proletariat and "menu peuple", and helped to establish the strong-arm men as local leaders independent of the *zu'ama*. If the latter had had some difficulty in controlling their clienteles since the early 1970s, the Civil War now made such control impossible. Criminal gangs and local militias – many with Palestinian support and training – were able to operate at will. Looting and smuggling increased, and up to the beginning of October 1975 the Sunni *qabadays* seemed still to have been mainly concerned with pillaging in the area around the battlefront (*Arab World*, 18 and 22 July 1975 and 9 Oct 1976). By the end of the month, however, Ibrahim Qulaylat's militia, the "Murabitun", had become involved in a strategic battle which earned Qulaylat the right to be considered as one of the foremost leaders of the National Movement.

On 22 October fighting again broke out along the 'confrontation line' which divided west and east Beirut, and later spread westwards along the coast from the commercial district towards Ras Bayrut. The Kata'ib and other Christian rightist militias were attempting to control access to the port, and as part of their strategy they occupied the high-rise building of the Holiday Inn. Opposing them were a number of leftist and Muslim militias under the overall leadership of the Murabitun. Both Muslim and Christian militiamen looted hotels, shops, offices, and private homes. The looting of the Qantari quarter, in particular, caused embarrassment to the National Movement, but the Muslim militias inflicted a significant defeat on the Christians, and the Murabitun demonstrated that it was a relatively well disciplined and powerful fighting force. In the fifth round of fighting, in December, Ibrahim Qulaylat again achieved notoriety when he led another attack on the Christian strongholds in the hotel district, and forced the predominantly Maronite militias out of the Saint George and Phoenicia hotels. The Kata'ib continued to have a small force at the top of the Holiday Inn when a fifth ceasefire was imposed in mid-December, but the area between Qantari and the commercial centre was more or less completely under the control of Muslim-leftist forces (Salibi, 1976, pp. 97 ff; and *MERIP Reports* 44, 1976).

Before the hotel battles of October and December, Qulaylat's Independent Nasserist Organisation had been just one of many Nasserist and populist groups in Sunni Beirut. Although it had supporters in the suburbs, its militia had not been one of the most significant in the National Movement. As a result of the bravery and success of its fighters at the end of 1975, however, the Murabitun militia became an influential force in Lebanon's political mosaic. This period marked the final collapse of the *zu'ama's* clientelist system in Sunni Beirut. Men like Ibrahim Qulaylat would never again be beholden to their traditional patrons. Although Sa'ib Salam, for example, made persistent communal appeals to the Muslim community, forming a new political party based on the "teachings of Islam" and condemning what he called the "destructive left" (*MERIP Reports* 44, 1976), the initiative had already passed to the new Nasserist leaders. In contrast to 1958 the war of 1975 brought about the establishment of a popular movement in Sunni Beirut completely independent of the *zu'ama* and the clientelist system.

Conclusion: the Origins and Limitations of Popular Movements in Sunni Beirut

In assessing the nature of this independent popular movement it is important to emphasize that it developed under very special conditions. Only after six months of fighting in the suburbs did the Sunni "menu peuple" of western Beirut become actively involved in the war. Had it not been for the radicalism and determination of the Palestinians and their predominantly Shi'ite allies in sub-urban Beirut the war might well have been contained within manageable limits. This raises the question as to why controls operating in Sunni Beirut did not extend to the suburbs and Palestinian camps; and part of the answer – not properly recognized in the literature on the war – lies in a consideration of the limits of the clientelist system.

Neither the Palestinian refugees nor the Shi'ites and other immigrants in the suburbs were part of the system. Although many Palestinians had been living in Lebanon since 1948, few were enfranchised citizens of the country. They therefore had nothing to offer *zu'ama* and were denied those services which politicians could perform as a result of their control of governmental and private exchange. Excluded from the Lebanese political system, with its exchanges of services for political support, the Palestinians formed their own political society within the refugee camps and the framework of the Palestinian liberation movement – a movement influenced by the emergence of socialist and Marxist tendencies in the early 1970s. The immigrants to the suburbs, although Lebanese citizens, were similarly cut off from the clientelist system. Most were Shi'ite Muslims from southern and north-eastern Lebanon who continued to maintain relatively close ties with their villages of origin and with the political patrons or *zu'ama* of their home districts. Few had registered to vote in Beirut, and at election times their *zu'ama* provided them with transport back to their villages where they would vote for their traditional leaders. Since they spent most of the year in Beirut, only returning "home" for short visits during the summer, these immigrants were gradually divorced from the patron–client structures of control which existed in their villages. No longer sharecroppers beholden to their neo-feudal lords, they were absorbed into the small proletariat or large sub-proletariat of Beirut. No effective structures of political control were established to deal with the steadily expanding population in the suburbs. Whereas the Sunni sub-proletariat lived close to their political leaders in the socially heterogeneous quarters of west Beirut, and were in contact with the *qabadays* who acted as Lieutenants to the *zu'ama*, the immigrant sub-proletariat were geographically distant from the control of their former lords and were thus susceptible to the radical appeals of Nasserist, socialist, and, very significantly, Marxist organizations. As the immigrants were not registered to vote in Beirut, the local *zu'ama* refused to perform services for them, and their own *zu'ama* were singularly inept in dealing with the changed nature of their clienteles. As a result, organizations like the Communist Action Organization (*munazzamat al-'amal ash-shuyu'i*) and the Communist Party of Lebanon made considerable gains in the suburbs and provided an ideological pole of attraction which transcended the limits of popular Nasserism.[11]

The co-operation between the Lebanese left, with its relatively strong base in the suburbs, and the Palestinian movement, with its arms and expertise undoubtedly had a radicalizing effect on the Sunni "menu peuple". But there were, nevertheless, serious limitations to the Nasserist movements in Sunni Beirut. Although influenced by socialist ideology and organizations, these movements did not achieve their position of strength simply as a result of a class struggle between the urban poor and the commercial–financial bourgeoisie. The type of person recruited into the *qabaday* networks and then into the Nasserist groups was what

Hobsbawm calls a "primitive rebel" and not a revolutionary socialist. Criminals and other members of the sub-proletariat had originally taken up arms as *qabadays* to carve out a place for themselves on the margins of the Lebanese economy. They had some idea they were exploited, but did not usually interpret that exploitation in class terms. The Maronites and the Presidency became identified as their oppressors and as the enemies not simply of the Sunni poor, but of the whole Arab nation. As Ibrahim Qulaylat said in a press statement in January 1976:

> Lebanon's Arab character cannot be the subject of doubt or discussion . . . Our movement rejects the nonsense about sovereignty [put forward] by the leaders of the isolationist parties .
> . . and regards it as a prelude to . . . the destruction of the Palestinian resistance.
>   . . . The existing regime, with its decayed institutions based on political confessionalism, which has made Lebanon a country of privileges for the Maronite community is utterly unacceptable.[12]

Thus the popular rebellion in Sunni Beirut was expressed in a religious and nationalist symbolism, which until the outbreak of the Civil War could be manipulated by the established Sunni leaders. Some *qabadays* resented their dependence on *zu'ama*, but while the latter controlled the state there was little that could be done except co-operate with the clientelist system and work for individual economic advancement. The war between the Palestinians and the predominantly Maronite militias, and the gradual extension of the fighting into Sunni Beirut, presented the Nasserite *qabadays* with a situation where they could use their armed strength to promote themselves as more effective leaders than the *zu'ama*. The latter had co-operated with the Maronite leadership in the past and were now incapable of persuading the Maronites to accept even a mild compromise:

> The isolationist groups' rejection of the superficial and fatuous solutions that have been called "common denominators" is a slap in the face for the traditional Muslim leadership, which has tried to ride the wave of a popular mass upsurge . . . in order not to lose their position of leadership . . .
>   . . . their thinking has continued to rotate around the crumbs of privileges which have been allowed to them by the regime, and, but for such a regime, they would have disappeared from the political scene and been brushed aside by the masses.[13]

The moment had arrived for the popular leaders of the street to wrest the leadership role from the *zu'ama*. The question remained, however, as to how far the *qabaday* leaders were committed to a reformed political system. Could their aim simply have been to establish themselves as a new generation of *zu'ama* at the head of a clientele? Subsequent events have shown that the post-war political system in Muslim Beirut collapsed as a result of internal and external pressures. The potential of the National Movement in 1976 was not realized and the clientelist system continued to operate, though now in a much more anarchic form. The continuing vitality of clientelism owed much to the inability of many of the "leftist" militias to transcend their primordial loyalties to confession, clan and quarter. As "primitive rebels" they were able to act independently of their former patrons, but ultimately they could not overthrow the system against which they rebelled.

Palestinians in Camps: The New Reality, 1948–65

Rosemary Sayigh

Brutal Awakening

Hijra and Humiliation

Even while still in Palestine, peasants who had taken refuge in safe villages near their own in the hope of returning as soon as the fighting was over, began to feel their new status. The Israelis issued them with ID cards stamped "refugee" and in the course of time deported them. Once over the border there began the hassle with permits and papers that has been a basic feature of Palestinian life every since. [A] woman from Kweikat who, as a girl, used to creep back through the Israeli lines to "steal" flour for her family, recalls the next stage in their odyssey after their expulsion in March 1949:

> We stayed in Nablus for fifteen days, then my father got us permits to go to Amman. The Jordanian police stopped us on Allenby Bridge, they said our papers weren't right. They made us sleep on the ground by the bridge, and if a woman hadn't got bread to feed her children, they'd die of hunger. My father went back to Nablus to fix the permits. Then we went on to Amman.[1]

This family was well off by peasant standards, since they could afford to hire transport, unlike the vast mass of refugees who trudged the whole *hijra* on foot. After staying for a week in a mosque in Amman, they hired an uncovered truck, along with two or three other families who had been driven out of Abu Sinan at the same time. Their plan was to reach Hawran in Syria, but first they had to pass the police post on the Jordanian/Syria border. It was exceptionally wet and cold that winter:

> At Irbed crossroads it started raining. Then the police post at Ramtha wanted to send us back to Amman because they said our papers weren't right. I remember that one of the women who was with us jumped out of the truck, in the rain and the mud, and she cursed the police and all the Arabs. She was so mad that she got hold of her nine-month-old grandson – his father was dead - and

almost threw him at the police post, screaming, "You sons of pimps, are we Jews? We are Arabs!"

There should have been a Tolstoy at hand to describe the *hijra*, a leaderless trek of thousands of dazed and panic-stricken villagers, their bundles of bedding dropping by the wayside, families separated, old people dying of exhaustion, children carrying younger children, babies dying of dehydration. Survivors remember eating grass and drinking their own urine (it was high summer when the majority left). Settled peasants, many of whom had never been outside their sub-district, they were suddenly expelled into an alien world in which others would look upon them as different, threatening, or even contemptible: "refugees", "displaced persons", "strangers". As [a] man from Saffouriyeh who lost his daughter said: "In twenty-four hours we were changed from (a state of) dignity to humiliation." It was particularly hard for self-respecting peasants to beg. Accustomed to a high level of generosity, they were shocked at the Lebanese selling them water: "They even wanted to sell us the weeds in their fields", said a woman who remembered she had been refused a glass of water for her five children because its price was 3p and she could only offer 2½p. . . .

First Days in the Camps

. . . The majority of refugees did not stop in the villages of south Lebanon, but made straight for the cities of the coastal plain, mainly Tyre and Sidon, where they would be more likely to meet others from their village and hear news of missing family members. Conditions in the first, improvised camps were at their worst, but the refugees, even then, resisted arbitrary relocation, attempting to stay in large groups and as close as possible to Palestine. The man from Saffouriyeh remembered: "We went on until we reached Tyre, and in Tyre started a life which none of us had imagined or dreamt of. There were three, four, five families to a tent. We had to go a long time without washing. Dirt increased. We lived a life that I am ashamed to describe, even if it's necessary." Another man who had been in Tyre commented: "Abu Hussain is ashamed to say that we had lice, and he is ashamed to say that we used to live waiting for a sunny day so as to get rid of them. We lived like animals."

A man whom the others addressed respectfully as *mrabbi* gave a more elaborate version of the first year of living in a refugee camp:

We gathered, not less than fifty or sixty villages, in a large mass at Bourj al-Shemali, east of Tyre. Life was difficult. As many as seven families to a tent, sometimes from different villages. Sharing a tent with strangers was painful for us because of our traditions. There weren't enough tents for everyone so some families had to live in caves. There was sickness and overcrowding. Many old people and children died because of the bad conditions.

We spent the winter there, and then in the spring they forced us to leave. We tried to refuse because Bourj al-Shemali was close to Palestine, and we wanted to stay close to our country. Often four or five young men would risk death to go back over the border to our villages to get food.

The Lebanese police came and told us we had to leave. They promised to settle us in better places, and said they would struggle with us so we could go back to our homes. But after our experience with the Jaysh al-Inqadh we knew it was all lies.

We were people from sixty different villages and we insisted that we should all be moved together. But they distributed us, some to 'Ain Hilweh, some to North Beka', some to Anjar and Kar'oun. The sixty villages refused to be separated, so the police beat our old people and fired in the air to frighten us and force us to get into the trucks. They beat us with sticks and rifle butts.

Our fate was to go to the barracks of Kar'oun. We found some of our kin from Saffouriyeh already settled there. They told us that many had died that winter because the snow there reached a metre or more. Provisions from Zahleh had been cut off. There had also been fighting between them and the neighbouring villages, when they'd gone out in the snow looking for a mouthful of bread.

At the end of the summer we made a strike with the refugees in Anjar to force the authorities to let us leave the Beka' because of the hardness of the climate. This is something which we have to thank our parents for, that they forced them to allow us to leave Kar'oun. So they moved us to Nahr al-Bared camp.

I remember that the day we arrived in Nahr al-Bared it was raining. There were women who had given birth to children in the trucks taking us from Kar'oun to Nahr. We found tents there, and they distributed us among them.

. . . Apart from the harsh conditions of the first few years, there was the psychological trauma of separation from homes and property. The village – with its special arrangement of houses and orchards, its open meeting places, its burial ground, its collective identity – was built into the personality of each individual villager to a degree that made separation like an obliteration of the self. In describing their first years as refugees, camp Palestinians use metaphors like "death", "paralysis", "burial", "non-existence", "we lost our way", "we didn't know were to go, what to do", "we were like sheep in a field". Thirty years after the Uprooting, the older generation still mourns, still weeps as it recalls the past. The passion of their attachment is shown in the way old people make their children promise to re-bury their bodies in Palestine, after the return. The same word, *hajj*, is used to visits to Palestine/Israel as for the pilgrimage to Mecca.

For more than a year after the Armistice Agreements, the refugees went on believing that they would soon go home. As survivor remembers, "We used to encourage one another by saying "Next month we'll be back". Anxious to hide the depth of the defeat of 1948, the Arab governments kept issuing encouraging statements. As we saw when the Lebanese police removed refugees from Bourj al-Shemali to the Beka', the authorities had already adopted the practice of deflating Palestinian anger by promises of support for the struggle, or a speedy return. In addition there were the traditional peasant values of patience and acceptance of God's will which, along with a strong streak of healthy optimism and toughness, kept the mass of refugees from despair, however black their present situation and uncertain their future.

Ambiguities of being Refugees

The same question, bitter and ironical, that the woman screamed at the police camp at Ramtha, "Are we Jews? We are Arabs", recurs in most camp Palestinians' description of their situation as refugees. It arose from the ambiguity of Arab attitudes towards the Palestinian people and their struggle, in which theoretical support was often combined with unconcern in practice. It also arises from a fundamental difference of definition. To themselves, the Palestinians were a people who had struggled, and who would have resisted expulsion if they had not been starved of arms; at worst they were victims of an imperialist Zionist alliance too powerful for them, or any other Arab people, to defeat. But to many other Arabs, the refugees were a burden and a problem, as well as a reminder of national humiliation.

There was an immediate, spontaneous surge of sympathy for the refugees amongst large segments of the Arab public, but it was a sympathy that often did not have political staying power. Arab ignorance of what had happened in Palestine was widespread; and the fact that the élites and press of the Arab world were still, in spite of Arab nationalist sentiment, susceptible to European influence meant that the Zionist version of the Palestinians' flight, which passed unchallenged in the West, came also to be accepted by some segments of Arab public opinion. It was easier to believe that the turbulent, destitute refugees were themselves to blame for their situation – that they had sold their land, or fled in needless, cowardly fear instead of standing up to the Powers that protected Israel. Also, from the perspective of the host governments, the refugees were a threat to stability and order; the immediate need was to stabilize their presence through restricted areas of residence – the camps – and through special regulations controlling their actions.

When the host governments had opened their borders to the refugees, they assumed like everyone else that their stay would be temporary, and they were not prepared to assume the economic cost of supporting them. Unable to force Israel to repatriate them, the only couse left to the Arab governments was to put every possible pressure upon the international community, represented by the United Nations, to shoulder responsibility for keeping the Palestinians alive. This was easier because of the internationalization of the "Palestine problem" which had preceded the War of 1948. The UN was already heavily involved in Palestine, and the establishment of an Agency to aid the refugees, first UNRPR, then UNWRA, was merely a logical continuation of this involvement.

UNRWA: the Contradictory Assumptions

From the outset the states that made the largest contribution to UNRWA (the very same states that supported Israel) intended that it should be used to phase out the "refugee problem". The Clapp Mission's report of 1949, which provided UNRWA's blueprint, made two major proposals: that the burden of supporting the refugees should be passed on as soon as possible to the host governments; and that UNRWA's funds should be mainly used to integrate the Palestinians into the host economies. Thus a three-cornered struggle developed: between UNRWA and the host governments over the issue of responsibility for refugee support; and between UNRWA and the refugees over the issue of "resettlement". The Arab governments succeeded in winning their argument that the refugees were an international, not an Arab, responsibility. As for the refugees, one of the first struggles through which they manifested their continued existence as a people was their resistance to permanent resettlement outside Palestine. UNRWA was forced to drop the projects that came to be known as *towteen* (implantation), and focus instead upon relief, education and ·health.

> An activist from the Tripoli area recalls this early period: We felt that UNRWA had a certain policy that aimed at settling us. They wanted us to forget Palestine, so they started work projects to give us employment. This was part of the recommendations of the Clapp Report. They used to give loans to people to set them up in small businesses such as shoe-mender or carpenter; then they'd take away their ration cards. More dangerous was the way they tried to encourage emigration to Australia or America. They'd give a man a ticket, and take away his ration card. We opposed all this, through publications and secret meetings, night visits and *diwans* – these weren't prohibited. Politically conscious people used to go to these gatherings, and take part in the conversation. We opposed these projects because we felt that, living in poverty, we would stay attached to our land.

The camps set up to shelter and contain the mass of refugees epitomized the ambiguity of their situation. Politicized Palestinians saw the camps as part of the machinery of dismemberment and dispersion, separating them from each other and making them easier to control. At the same time the camps offered rent-free housing and minimal services (garbage collection, water, health care, education). While registered refugees who qualified for relief and/or services[2] were not forced to live in camps, most preferred to stay close to the distribution centres. Moreover, whilst the camps made it easier for the authorities to control the refugees, they also made possible the continuation of Palestinian village relationships and values. They became foci both of oppression and of Palestinianism.

Although Palestinian national institutions had not been totally effaced by the Disaster,[3] they had no political force until 1964 when the Palestine Liberation Organization (PLO) was set up. The Mufti and the Arab Higher Committee continued to have contacts with the people in the camps, shoring up the traditional leadership of family and village elders, and abstaining from contesting the authority of the host governments. In Lebanon it is alleged the Mufti was used by the authorities to pacify refugee discontent. Possibly this function was a condition of his permit of residence.

The Refugees and the Host Countries

There was no attempt by any of the host governments to train the refugees for liberation struggle,[4] and strict control over the camps made it impossible for the refugees to initiate their own training. In any case, for the first decade, the masses were too crushed, by the struggle to survive, to have energy left for national struggle. For many, this appeared deliberate: "UNRWA and the host governments intended that we should be absorbed in seeking our daily bread and never have time to work seriously to regain our country" (an ex-UNRWA school teacher).

To the militant minority who demanded a role in the struggle the host authorities would say exactly what the Arab governments had said in 1948 to the Palestinians in Palestine: "Leave it to the Arab armies."

The political and economic systems in which the Palestinians now found themselves were those of neo-colonial states still tied by formal treaty or habit to the imperialist powers. The ruling classes were still composed predominantly of large landowners and merchants. Religious dignitaries still had great political influence. The experiments in democracy championed by the Westernizing upper and middle classes had become discredited. There were still no truly mass political parties whether rightist, leftist or liberal; indeed parties were little more than city-based cliques of students and intellectuals. The merchant class, small and large, was still a political force, and the cities predominated as centres of power and resources over the neglected and impoverished rural hinterlands. Both government income and expenditure on public works were extremely low, but in all three host countries government was an important economic sector in itself, employing a high proportion of all employees. Everywhere the agricultural sector was stagnant and depressed. Industry was in its infancy.

Jordanization

The way each government defined the refugees varied with their policies towards the "Palestinian problem". Jordan pursued an energetic policy of integration, with its newly acquired half of Jerusalem as the priceless asset in its tourism plan. Jordan refused to recognize a separate Palestinian identity; the authority of theWest Bank notables was carefully preserved; and Palestinians were recruited in vast numbers into the army and government services. But though Palestinian "ultras" were well rewarded with ministerial posts, popular discontent was ruthlesly suppressed and the camps kept under close surveillance. Someone who attended a camp school between 1958 and 1967 remembers how armed patrols would aurround the camps on days commemorating national events:

> The camps were always more supervised on certain dates, for instance May 15 (the establishment of Israel). When we were children in school, before 1967, the tanks would surround the camps so that no demonstration could take place against the Uprooting. On those days they would make the school children walk in single file, three or four metres apart, and we were forbidden to talk together. When we reached our street each one of us had to go straight to his home and stay there. We weren't allowed to listen to the Voice of the Arabs from Cairo or to Damascus (Saudi Arabia, Amman and Israel were permitted). Soldiers filled the camp all the time and used to listen at the windows to hear which station we were listening to. People used to put blankets over their windows to stop the sound going out.

Equal Rights in Syria

In Syria, the most Arab nationalist of the three host countries, Palestinians were allowed equal rights with Syrian citizens, while keeping their own identity. As in Lebanon (but not in Jordan), a Directorate of Refugee Affairs was set up, directly linked to the Ministry of Interior and to the Intelligence Services, and whose function was to issue Palestinians with the papers needed to carry on normal life. Those who wanted to travel were issued with a *laissez-passer*, renewable every two years. These were harder to get than ordinary ID cards, and constituted a useful form of pressure. Unlike in Lebanon, Palestinians in Syria could join the army and work in government service. Promotion opportunities and salaries may have been lower for Palestinians than for nationals, but discrimination seems to have been least in Syria. There was no need for work permits, and Palestinian professional people could practise as freely as Syrians. Because of their slightly higher level of education, Palestinians found city employment more easily than rural Syrians, many of whom had to migrate each year to work in Lebanon.

Ambiguous Status in Lebanon

Lebanon differed from the other two main host countries in several ways. Lebanon has a European as well as an Arab face; Palestinians were placed in an indeterminate category, neither "foreigners" nor "nationals", and were excluded from joining the army or entering public service. The authorities' stance towards the refugees was dictated by two fears: first, that they would upset Lebanon's delicate sectarian equilibrium (in reality its Maronite hegemony); this fear was particularly acute during the rise of Nasserism in the fifties. The second fear was of Israeli retaliation against *fedayeen* action; this fear grew after the break-up of the UAR, and the beginning of Resistance Movement operations inside Israel.

Because the Lebanese labour force was more highly skilled than that of Syria or Jordan, there was direct competition between Palestinian and local workers, taking place in a framework of lop-sided development, chronic unemployment and gross inequality. As a result, Palestinians were excluded from all public and many kinds of private employment[5] as well as being forced to apply for work permits. A Palestinian lawyer describes the Palestinians' situation in Lebanon:

> The policy of the Lebanese authorities regarding ID cards and travel papers has always fluctuated, depending on the political situation at the time. The same was true of work permits. There have never been any specific texts applicable to Palestinians as regards travel, work, or residence. There was never anything clearly defined in law. Granting any kind of permit depended on "discretionary powers" and was thus a form of pressure which had no control, and against which there was no appeal.
>
> To take a specific example: travel documents are issued by the Directorate of Refugee Affairs via the Sûreté Générale which issues passports to Lebanese, and which is a part of the Ministry of the Interior. According to the political interests of the moment, the Sûreté Générale would be helpful or difficult about issuing travel permits. At one time Palestinians wanting to go to Damascus would have to wait two or three weeks for a permit; at another time – which lasted for several years – the Deuxième Bureau also had to give its OK. If the D.B. said "No", there was nothing a Palestinian could do about it. This lasted through the regime of President Helou. They never said to someone, "We forbid you to travel because you did such and such", it was simply a "No" without any reasons.
>
> Of course this kind of harassment was directed particularly against Palestinians who were active politically, but the number of suspects was always very high. The D.B. would keep lists of people who attended meetings in camps; such people would be considered suspects and their requests for travel permits refused.
>
> In regard to work, Palestinians were regarded as non-nationals and had to apply for a work permit from the Ministry of Social Affairs. Here, too, there was fluctuation. In periods of tension the

number of permits would decrease, even though President Chehab
once said in an official speech that Palestinians ought to be treated
like Lebanese. But when we asked that this should be applied, or
that there should be a law which would regulate employment of
Palestinians, the authorities always refused to present a text to
Parliament. They would tell us, "It's true that you are treated as
foreigners, but you have *priority*." Palestinians were always able to
get low-level jobs: masons, labourers, concierges. But if they tried
to do something more ambitious it was very difficult to get a work
permit. . . .

In all three host countries there exists a solid core of "legitimate" refugees, Palestinians who registered with UNRWA when
it was first set up, who had documentary proof of property in
Palestine, and who were enumerated in early censuses. They had
a certain minimum security: they could not be deported. But there
was another category of refugee who belonged officially nowhere.
Palestinians expelled from Israel *after* 1950 could not register with
UNRWA and had to find other ways to stabilize their existence.
There were cases of people successively thrown out of Israel into
Lebanon, from Lebanon into Syria, from Syria into Jordan, often
to end in prison. Political crisis added to the number of second and
third time refugees; after Black September in Jordan (1970), a
large number of Palestinians took refuge in Lebanon, but their
residence there, though not forbidden, remained highly insecure,
and they had no right to travel permits or ID cards. Increasingly
now, all the host countries are refusing entry to any but "their
own" Palestinians; for instance, entry into Syria now depends on
having a relative inside to apply for a visa. The same is true of most
of the Arab countries to which Palestinians migrate for work.

The never-ending hassle with permits that arises from their
statelessness has been no small part of the oppression of
Palestinians in the *ghourba* [diaspora]. The comment of a laundry
worker in Bourj al-Barajneh camp is strikingly true: "*Everything* in
our lives is struggle."

Economic Marginality

UNRWA relief meant that the refugees could not starve, but it
also created a false image of total dependence on international
charity, concealing the fact that, through the destruction of an
independent Palestinian economy, the Palestinian peasantry had
been transformed into a pool of landless labour. Aid also formed

an invisible subsidy to wages, this in countries where employment possibilities were so scarce that all have been exporters of labour over the last three decades. In fact UNRWA support per capita never exceeded 20 US cents a day. From the beginning it was hardly possible to survive without working[6] and the Palestinians' readiness to "do any work at any wages" provided the Arab economies with a zealous labour force.

Poverty in the Early Years

Recollections of the early period of exile reveal the conditions of exploitation in which Palestinian refugees worked. The first three speakers are from Nahr al-Bared camp, in north Lebanon, where even today a large proportion of camp-dwellers work as agricultural day labourers. They belong to the generation that was adolescent in 1948:

When we moved to Nahr al-Bared (from Anjar) I started working. First I worked moving sacks of onions for LL. ¼ a day, though because I was a kid I didn't even get paid my salary. Then I worked in a sugar factory, walking seven or eight kilometres to work. In those days the best worker, the *qabaday*, used to take from LL. 1 to LL. 1½ a day. At first it was just enough because people didn't want more than a mouthful of bread. If we ate meat once a year we thought it was great.

In 1948 I was twelve. From the time of the Partition Plan the schooling of my generation had been interrupted by the disturbances. When schools opened in Lebanon we were already too old, at 14 or 15 to attend. In any case, my family didn't have the means. I was the only son and I had to work. We weren't educated, we had no craft or skill, we couldn't write - so we had to work as labourers, at any wage, so as to be able to live. Most of us worked in agriculture because there's no industry near Nahr al-Bared. Agricultural work is seasonal, one month you work, the next you don't. There's more than one harvest, but there are also periods without any harvest. One day you work with the shovel, the next with the pruning knife. Changing jobs all the time, we had to work like donkeys to prove our worth to each new employer.

. . . In this early period women found work more easily than men because they were paid less. In spite of a strong dislike of women working outside the home, Palestinian women did enter the labour market, mainly in agriculture and domestic service. Families preferred women to work in factories because of its supervised, collective character, but this was only possible in the rare cases where factories were located near to camps. As for men of the *jeel Falasteen*, especially those who had never done anything but work their own land, the majority were unemployable. Only gradually, as a trickle of income began to flow into the camps, generated by the salaries of the first generation to go through school, did the small crafts, trades and services practised in the villages of Palestine reappear in the camps.

A study of the refugees carried out in 1951-2 gives a clear overall picture of their economic plight (Y. Sayigh, 1952). The average annual per capita income of all refugees, including the middle classes, was $21.7, or £P8.9, compared with £P41 in Palestine in 1944. When it is remembered that the average was artificially heightened by large sums paid in pensions and indemnities by the British government to ex-officials, as well as by the relatively high earnings of entrepreneurs and professionals, the destitution of refugees unable to find work can be imagined. Even those who could find casual labour, estimated as earning a yearly income of $15.2 in Jordan, $33.1 in Syria and $39.8 in Lebanon, would have had difficulty in feeding their families. Since working-class families were larger than middle-class ones, it can be seen how much lower than average were the actual per capita incomes of Palestinians in the camps.

The gap in income between urban middle-class Palestinians and the unschooled masses in the camps can be gauged from Table 8 (Y. Sayigh, 1952, appendix C, item V):

Table 8   *Incomes of Palestinian Refugees in 1951*

Source of income	Average annual income per earner ($)		
	Lebanon	Syria	Jordan
Private business	2,000	1,5000	840
Regular employment	1,000	1,000	140
Employment with government or security forces	–	–	403
Casual labour	60	75	37

Even casual labour was not readily available outside large cities, and conditions in camps like Nahr al-Bared, Wavell (near Ba'lbeck), Nabatiyeh and Tyre were so bad that it was painful for many to recall them. A woman whose father had been a prosperous farmer in Sohmata remembered their first years in Ba'lbeck. They had brought a little money with them from

Palestine and were able at first to rent rooms in the town. But the second year they had to move into the camp:

> Each section of the barracks had six families. Separating us there was only a thread and a blanket. Everything took place in public: eating, washing, sleeping. Those who had six children wouldn't have place to spread their feet at night.
>
> My mother didn't want us to work, me and my brother, so she went to work in the fields with the other women so we wouldn't feel that our lives had changed.
>
> When I got married we had nothing. I went to live with my husband in Tripoli. He had seven brothers, three sisters, his father and mother. We all lived in one room half the size of this one. He was the oldest, the only one working.
>
> In the old days it was the custom for every woman to have a chest, and I had one, with a mattress and a pillow. When we left his family, they gave me a quilt, an aluminium saucepan, and a baking pan. With this, we started our home.
>
> We moved back to Ba'lbeck where my husband was given a job as school director, at LL. 125 (£25) a month. For a while we lived with my family, and we brought one of his sisters to live with us, to lighten the load on his family. We used to send them LL. 25 (£5) a month, spend LL. 50 (£10) on feed, and every month we saved LL. 50 (£10) to buy something for the house.

Although the jobs that men of the generation of the Disaster could find remained marginal . . . schooling gradually began to improve the earning power of the young. The hunger of the peasant class in Palestine for schools for their children has already been described. In dispersion the hunger was sharpened by the feeling that there was no other way to survive. Illiterate parents had no more urgent message for their sons than success in school. A self-employed carpenter remembers: "I said to my sons, 'We have lost everything, our land and property is gone. You must go to school and get educated if you don't want to do hard labour all your lives.' So my sons worked hard, first to secure their future, then to get back our country from the enemy."

Education as a Way Out?

Fund-raising publicity for the refugees has often given the impression of an "educational miracle" through which the mass of refugees has been transformed into technicians, teachers, doctors and engineers. Though schooling has been the means to occupational change, there are two flaws in this picture: one is that the education provided to camp Palestinians by UNRWA has always been limited in quantity, so that camp families have to make sacrifices to keep children in school long enough to reach the diplomas they need for well-paid jobs.[7] The second is the suggestion that camp Palestinians' occupations and income levels have been drastically improved through education. The purpose of what follows here is to give some idea of the effort which camp Palestinians have themselves invested in the struggle to become educated; and to point out the structural limits to changes through educational improvement alone.

An extraordinary zeal was invested in education in the early period, both by students and teachers (who were all Palestinian). Schools were charged with a symbolic and emotional significance that went far beyond their job-creating potential. In the destitution and monotony of camp life, schools were generations of hope, windows to a different future. They were seen as the key to the improvement of the nation, to progress, science and the recovery of the homeland. Teachers became the leaders and guides in this community of exiles, consciously striving with small means to create a "new generation". Some idea of the conditions in which refugee children got their schooling comes through in this early account from the Tripoli area:

> I was among the first group of students from Nahr al-Bared school. There were 70 to 80 of us in the first tent school. There weren't any seats or school equipment – we'd sit on the sand or bring stones from the shore to sit on. Twelve of us managed to pass the *Certificat* and were transferred to the House of Education in Tripoli. There we really felt the depth of the Disaster, from our living conditions and the way they treated us. There we were, in torn clothes, sitting next to sons of Tripoli who had different clothes for every season, and pocket money. They put us Palestinians in the section for orphans, that way they got our rations from UNRWA as well as aid given by different charitable organizations that used to help the refugees.[8] In spite of all this, we had faith that there was no road but education. We used to go down into the street at night to study under the street lamps.

Any camp Palestinian from the *jeel al-nekba* who reached a diploma has a similar story of struggle. There were organizations and individuals ready to help, but the masses in the camps (particularly the rural camps) had no easy way to reach them. A thirty-year-old teacher in Bourj al-Barajneh told how he had managed, the only surviving male in his family, with a mother and two sisters to look after, to reach a teachers' training certificate. Like many others of his generation and class, he partly worked his way through secondary school, in summer harvesting, selling encyclopedias, giving private lessons. His mother and sisters had taken in sewing. In his race for certification, every year of education was a year of lost wages for his family, and it was thus a severe setback when he was refused a permit to go to Syria to sit for an exam. His story here is typical of the frustrations camp Palestinians face in their struggle for survival:

> I needed a travel permit from the Lebanese Sûreté to go to Damascus to sit for the *towijihiyyeh*, without which I couldn't get further training to become a teacher.[9] I went to the Sûreté on Saturday hoping my permit would be ready, for the exam was on Sunday. I waited until 1.30, and the Sûreté was about to close. I was desperate. I knocked on the Director-General's door, apologized for disturbing him, and pleaded with him to sign my permit. I told him, "Please Sir, one moment of your time can save a year of my life." He told me that if I wasn't careful I'd lose a year in prison. He didn't sign the permit, and I couldn't take the exam until the following year.

. . . It is true that Palestinians in general have an unusually high proportion of university graduates (Shaath, 1972; Hagopian and Zahlan, 1974), and that this reaching for higher education (which arises from the lack of their own independent economy) is also reflected in the camps, where as many as 0.2 per cent in Lebanon had university degrees in 1970-1, and many more are engaged in sandwich courses at Arab and Lebanese universities. But these figures, though striking, tell little about the struggle for qualifications and jobs of the mass of camp Palestinians. A mother expressed a universal worry when she said: "If I kiss a thousand hands I can't reach a job for my sons." Every year the hurdle of qualifications gets higher, the competition with other Arabs who have prior rights as "sons of a government" gets fiercer. Increasingly Palestinians have to go abroad (this is also true of Palestinians in Israel) to get training as well as jobs.

A look at UNRWA's educational statistics reveals some of the limitations of the "educational miracle". Enrolment (1970–1 figures) shows a marked fall-off at age 14:

years	%
6–11	88.4
12–14	67.1
15–17	37.3
18–20	8.3

The drop in school attendance from 67.1 per cent of the potential school-going population to 37.3 per cent is more serious because of the almost total absence of vocational training. UNRWA's technical and training college at Sibleen has a total intake of only 200 students and cannot be entered without first getting the difficult Baccalaureat. Beirut's suburbs teem with private establishments offering diplomas in everything from accountancy to aviation, but their fees are out of the reach of most camp Palestinians. This means that the mass of adolescent camp boys start working in repair shops, garages, small factories, with no hope of other training than learning on the job.

Changing Class Structure

The narrow limits of the occupational transformation of camp Palestinians is revealed in a Manpower Survey carried out by the Lebanese Department of Statistics in 1971. One clear indicator of economic marginality is the fact that 58.4 per cent of all employed camp workers are still paid on a daily basis; in contrast, only 8 per cent have long-term contracts. Sectoral distribution is another key indicator: 21.1 per cent are still employed in agriculture, with 13.6 per cent in building and construction, 11.8 per cent in industry, 2.4 per cent in transport and corporation services, 14.4 per cent in trade and hotels. But a massive 36.7 per cent fall into categories which the Survey euphemizes as 'other services' and "unspecified". Only 40 per cent of the working-age population is employed.

A recent study of Palestinians in Lebanon by Samir Ayoub (Ayoub, 1977) found that 62.9 per cent had a monthly income of less than LL. 500 (£100). Since the sample contained middle-class as well as working-class Palestinians, it can be taken that the proportion of working class families with less than LL.500 a month is around 80 per cent. Ayoub also found that a high proportion of families had debts; most said that their income did not cover their needs and that they wanted to change their jobs because they needed more money. The study provided clear evidence of a shift in the type of work done by Palestinians: whereas 68 per cent of the respondents' grandfathers had worked in agriculture, only 17 per cent of the sample now did and only 3 per cent said that this was their desired occupation. On the other hand, where only 22 per cent of grandfathers had worked in services, 74 per cent of respondents were employed in this sector and 78 per cent wanted to be. In contrast to the move into services, employment in industry showed less change (2 per cent of grandfathers compared with 9 per cent of respondents) reflecting the fact that industry in Lebanon is almost exclusively Lebanese.

Another significant change found by Ayoub's study is that whereas 76.4 per cent of respondents' grandfathers and 59.4 per cent of fathers, were self-employed, 79.0 per cent of respondents were employed by others. A people of small farmers, artisans and traders has changed into a people of clerks, accountants and administrators – *muwazzefeen*. Although no figures on occupational distribution are available for the Gulf it seems likely that a larger proportion of Palestinians work in government service or big companies than in construction and industry.

This mass move into services reflects a general Arab trend (Amin, 1974, pp. 24–8), but it also stems from the fact that Palestinians depend for a livelihood on economies they do not control and can only indirectly influence. A finding indicating Palestinians' job insecurity was that most of the sample had more than one occupation. Economic hardship was evident in the fact that the majority had more than one job at the time of the survey, while around 75 per cent expressed dissatisfaction with their current job, either on account of low pay, poor working conditions, or the employer's attitude towards them. One of the most interesting of Ayoub's findings was that 88 per cent of his sample said they thought it impossible for the Palestinian individual to change his class position.

The occupational categories used by economists – industry, services, agriculture – give little idea of the class level at which a given population participates in these sectors. "Services" in particular can mean anything from a cabinet minister to a nightwatchman. Hani Mundus's study of a single camp, Tel al-Za'ter (Mundus, 1974) is invaluable for its minute occupational breakdowns and concrete detail. Though one of the poorest of Palestinian camps in Lebanon, Tel al-Za'ter was unique in having a major proportion of its labour force (60 per cent) employed in industry, because of its closeness to the industrial zone of Mkalles. But what does "industry" mean in a country of underdeveloped capitalism? 80.4 per cent of all industrial units in Lebanon employ less than ten workers. Only the larger ones offer modern working conditions and benefits such as paid sick leave, paid holidays or compensation for accidents. Out of Tel al-Za'ter's 1,355 workers in the industrial sector, only 50 were in establishments of more than 50 workers, and these were mainly girls. Although a Lebanese employer who gave work to a Palestinian without a work permit could be fined, a great many did so because the difficulty of getting permits enabled them to offer lower wages.[10]

Mundus's study points out the basic features of Palestinian employment in Lebanese industry: a high rate of periodic unemployment and job insecurity, low wages, no benefits and no legal protection. In one respect, however, the situation of Palestinian workers in Lebanon is better than that of most ethnic proletariats in that the General Union of Palestinian Workers GUPW works closely with the progressive Lebanese workers' unions.

Dispersed through many small industrial units, Palestinian workers can only with difficulty be termed a "proletariat". Mundus places only 7 per cent of Tel al-Za'ter's work-force in this category, designating 85 per cent as "sub-proletariat" and 3 per cent "lumpenproletariat" (e.g. lottery-ticket sellers). The fragmentation of the Palestinian work-force is clearly shown by the fact that Mundus lists ten different main occupations, as well as seventeen miscellaneous ones. Further fragmentation arises from the small size of each unit (the same applies to agricultural labourers, employed on an individual rather than a collective basis, through long-term employer/worker relationships). The difficulty of organizing workers so dispersed is obvious. What gives them solidarity is less a developed class consciousness than their common insecurity as Palestinians, and the fact of living together in a camp. Their experience of exploitation seems to them to arise primarily from the fact of being Palestinian, only secondarily from the class structure of Arab society. Their difficulty in obtaining work permits and their exclusion from social security benefits reinforce their sense of national rather than class oppression.

Discrimination, job insecurity and poor work conditions in Lebanon have propelled an unknown, but large, number of camp Palestinians into job migration, but Mundus's Tel al-Za'ter study proves that this is only a feasible solution at a high level of skill. Few who go can save enough to change their situation radically. The details that Mundus gives of the conditions of Palestinian workers in Germany (more than half of Tel al-Za'ter's 900 migrant workers were there) make it clear why few stay there permanently. In the first place, residence and work permits are issued through a special office in Zerndorf, established with American assistance to place political refugees from communist countries. If they refuse this channel (as most do), Palestinian workers must go to offices that specialize in finding work for people without permits, taking 50 per cent of their wages. These kinds of jobs available to unskilled workers are: digging roads, building, cleaning, restaurant service, moving snow and unskilled industrial work. That Palestinian workers are ready to migrate to Europe, and put up with conditions like these, indicates the increasing difficulty of finding work in the oil-producing Arab countries, most of which operate informal quotas restricting Palestinian entry, as well as demanding increasingly high professional qualifications.

From the data available it is clear that, in spite of education and occupational change, Palestinians in Lebanon suffer from economic as well as political insecurity, and that large pockets of extreme poverty continue to exist, particularly in the rural camps. If we take even a relatively prosperous camp like Bourj al-Barajneh, which has benefited from its closeness to Beirut, we find that while some families have improved their economic situation sufficiently to move out of the camp and rent apartments in the near-by suburb, the majority have no hope of doing so.

At the very bottom level of poverty are a number of families who have lost their chief male wage-earners, and who depend mainly on help from the Resistance Movement, UNRWA's "special cases" programme, and the solidarity of kin and neighbours. The Civil War in Lebanon has greatly added to this category of family. Slightly better off than this "most miserable" category come the bulk of families in the camp, those with one unskilled or semi-skilled wage-earner, perhaps a nightwatchman or a concierge, earning around LL. 300 a month, on whom as many as ten children, a wife and two aged parents may well be depending. Some are self-employed artisans – carpenters, tile-fitters, plumbers – usually working under subcontract to larger building contractors, and highly vulnerable to economic fluctuations. Others are small traders in fish, fruit or vegetables, operating from barrows and bicycles. Slightly more prosperous, again, are the small shopkeepers – bakers, butchers, grocers – and the owners of laundries, TV and bicycle repair shops, or one-room sewing factories. When a camp family has a small regular source of income and one or two adult sons working, it can be said to have reached the highest level of prosperity that the mass of camp families aspire to.

To be able to draw an accurate class map of Palestinians throughout the *ghourba*, or even in one region, we should need much more accurate information on occupation and income than now exists. But certain broad trends are obvious: the massive move into services at low and medium-income levels; the only slight development of an industrial proletariat; the movement away from agriculture, even in a country like Syria where the potentially for an expanded agricultural sector exists; the attraction of the intellectual professions, especially teaching; the increasing flow of skilled workers and professionals to the Gulf; and the continuation of poverty amongst the families of unskilled workers.

Important as the acquisition of new skills has been, it is clear that there are structural limitations to further change. Those economic changes that have occurred do not seem to be great enough to eliminate Palestinian consciousness of their economic insecurity as an oppressed nation. Even the prosperous minority of professional people and entrepreneurs cannot wholly assimilate with the bourgeoisies of the Arab world because their political power does not match their economic position and therefore cannot protect it. For the less prosperous and the really poor, political oppression is matched by economic insecurity. National consciousness has been developed to the maximum by the present leadership of the Resistance Movement, capitalizing on the alienation of all classes of Palestinian in the *ghourba* and under Israeli occupation. Channelled into the goal of the Return, or of an independent Palestinian state on the West Bank, discontent is deflected away from existing Arab political and economic structures in the *ghourba*. Yet the inability of these structures to create the conditions for the Return (or even a truncated Palestinian state) ultimately must channel Palestinian discontent into attacking these structures too.

Urbanization, Urbanism and the Medina of Tunis

Ellen C. Micaud

Introduction

The medina of Tunis, which occupies 262 hectares or 6.5 per cent of the urban area while absorbing its highest population densities, is to many an archaic enclave.[1] Located dead centre of a rapidly growing and changing capital city, it appears at best a nuisance to be circumvented, at worst a reminder of poverty and lethargy, an eyesore that is an obstacle to rational urban planning. . . .

To those planners who know the city well the medina is a residential quarter still, housing nearly one-sixth of the population of Greater Tunis. Early results of the 1975 Census indicate that the 1966 total of about 140,000 residents in the central medina and its two traditional *faubourgs* (R'bat Bab Souika to the north and R'bat Bab al-Jazira to the south) has held steady.[2] The medina houses more poor people, of whom 60 per cent earn less than $80 a month, at less cost than could be done elsewhere in a booming city with an alarming housing shortage.[3] The central medina functions as well as a dispenser of services and goods, in some sectors even surpassing the economic activity of the adjacent *villeneuve*.

During the two decades since Independence, the medina has been the subject of scrutiny and recommendations by various planning bodies, each of which has sought to modify, or even entirely recast, the present vocations of the historical core. On the one hand, the medina has been the most faithful mirror of such by-products of independence as the upward mobility of the Tunisian bourgeoisie, the polarizing effect of the capital on all other urban centres, the neglect of tradition in favour of rapid modernization, and a general policy of *laissez-faire* urban planning nationwide. On the other hand, several of the many groups charged with urban planning in the capital have used the medina as a sort of magical mirror. Reflected are their visions of what the country has been or should be, never the image of what it is. Only the still vital historical core of a city can evoke so mixed and contradictory a series of perceptions and proposals for intervention. . . .

Our purpose, then, is to summarize the history of two decades or urban planning for the medina. While each stage of planning has drawn, to some degree, upon a heritage or urban planning reaching back to the colonial period, we can nevertheless discern three fairly distinct urban planning episodes since Independence in 1956. In each episode the medina has been viewed under a characteristic optique which led to urgent recommendations, their urgency unmodified by their variance with other plans.

A study of post Independence planning must begin with the apparently prevalent perception of the medina by the Tunisian élite. The historical core was apprehended as an obstacle that must be surmounted, both figuratively and literally, if the new country were to have a capital worthy of the active modernizing image being fashioned on all fronts. This perception will have a long life in many minds.

Then, with the rapid success of the tourist industry as the apparent catalyzing factor, there was a volte-face. From the late sixties Tunisians reappraised their medina and the consensus was that "la ville est malade". The search for cures led to international intervention via the "Projêt Tunis-Carthage pour la mise en valeur du patrimoine monumental en vue du développement économique". The results were paradoxical in calling for a return to an imaginary status quo ante while in fact compiling invaluable data as to the actual status of the quarter. This interesting period of intellectual ferment ended abruptly after less than three years.

Finally, since January 1973 those left in charge of the medina have entered a stage that might be characterized as one of retrenchment and realism. The term "renovation", which pervaded all recommendations in the previous stage, is now firmly opposed by a more modest call for rehabilitation. For the first time Tunisians alone are charged with the medina while foreign aid and expertise is channelled toward the District of Tunis, the high-level planning board that is to cope with the key problems of the capital: housing, transport, industry and municipal finances.

For the first time the contradictions of the medina, at once a witness to a vanished civilization of high urbanity and a centre-city ghetto, seem capable of resolution. The key lies in the acceptance of its dual nature; recognition of its historic and aesthetic value must be offset by good amounts of pragmatism. . .

From Indifference to Inquiry

It is often said that one must be a reasonable distance from things to see them clearly. The cliché seems to hold true in the case of Tunisian perception of the medina. Post-independence antagonism indicates a closeness to the phenomenon of a rapidly deteriorating historical core. As experts are hired to cope with the problem, antagonism gives way to the more passive state of indifference. And only after this stage has been allowed to run its course can the phenomenon be opened to reappraisal.

The fate of the medina became of interest to certain Tunisians only a good decade after Independence. The founding in 1967 of the Association Sauvegarde de la Médina (ASM) under the tutelage of the municipality and the presidency of the governor-mayor of Tunis is either the impetus for or the consequence of this renewed interest. The creation of such an association of interested parties to serve as a link between the inhabitants of the medina and the administration has nothing remarkable about it since such associations were provided for by statutes dating back to 1901. What was remarkable was that the ASM was rapidly expanded by an Atelier d'Urbanisme (AU) in order to prepare a master plan for the medina, and that it was encouraged to seek international aid to pursue an increasing number of aims.

This must be explained in the context of the political situation at the time. Minister of Plan Ahmed Ben Salah, was, with the concurrence of President Bourguiba, the most powerful man in the country from 1961 to 1969. In his hands Tunisia was pursuing economic development at an accelerating pace, a pace that would prove to be his downfall as he left too many in the population behind him. One of his few uncontroversial moves was the launching of tourism on a large scale. We may suppose that it was the actual presence of busloads of tourists in the medina that prompted the Tunisian élite to take another look at this quarter.

One of Ben Salah's close supporters was the governor-mayor of Tunis, Hassib Ben Ammar, son of an old Tunis family, and founder of the ASM. The preservation of the medina in the interest of economic development, which then meant in the interests of tourists, became the order of the day. Since this effort was beset with the ambivalence and ambiguity that both Westernized Tunisians and Europeans have always brought to the medina, it is difficult to analyze. The following factors may be examined in turn: the diagnosis, the remedies and the outcome of this first spectacular intervention in the medina.

Several factors brought about the first trip to the doctor. Among them were an influx of tourists to a capital city with a great history and only a neglected medina to show for it, some vague awareness of the consequences of such neglect, and a political situation favourable to inquiry and action. The diagnosis of urban malaise was quickly made. There was, however, some considerable confusion about both causes and consequences.

For many young Tunisian intellectuals, among them the first director of the ASM, the sole cause of the medina's ailments was colonialism. During that period the medina had one by one lost its functions as all vital urban activities slid into the new town. Somehow, in the process, the good Tunisian bourgeois became alienated from his traditional place of residence and business, of learning and worship, and he too slid into the new town.[4] We have seen that this slide toward the modern city was far from unconscious. It seems futile to berate colonialism for processes due to modernization, since Tunisians insisted on their share of the benefits of progress.

The more immediate and probable cause of the transformation of the medina from citadel of urbanity to marginal quarter was provided by sociological analyses of the medina. These showed how many traditional residences had been *oukalisé* as the old palaces were transformed into rooming houses for the profit of the absentee owners.[5] Densities are now 520 inhabitants to the hectare (or about 2.7 to a room) compared with an average of 219 in the greater Tunis area, and in some buildings they reach 1,000.[6] Numerous ASM studies show the degree to which this quarter has downshifted socioeconomically to serve a very different clientele than the one for which it was designed.[7] The consequences for the architectural *cadre* cannot but be disastrous, although the attempts of the present tenants to achieve privacy are sometimes as ingenious as they are pathetic.

The final diagnosis then is expressed in the title of a study by an ASM sociologist.[8] Eckert asks whether the medina of Tunis is a *faubourg* (an *extra muros* residential suburb like any other), or a *gourbiville* (a squatter settlement), and he allows the figures compiled from his inquiries to show that it is more nearly the latter. For him the key factor of degradation is that the constructions are not used as they were meant to be. Unlike many other researchers, he leaves colonialism, the battering-ram juxtaposi- of the *villeneuve*, the competition of manufactured products with traditional artisans and merchants and other marginal factors out of the equation to conclude that:

Constructed volume incorrectly used =
imminent degradation of the medina =
inevitable demolition =
new construction inappropriate to the medina.

While the best researchers among the international and interdisciplinary ASM team collected much-needed information, rather than indulging in speculations, or even suggesting remedies to the situations they set forth, or even suggesting remedies to the situations they set forth, the remedy was soon forthcoming.

The ASM had originally been charged with collecting all necessary data concerning the medina and its two traditional *faubourgs* to prepare a master plan for the area. The programme was to execute a complete socioeconomic, legal and architectural survey of the medina. Although it was carried out in some sectors to a minute degree, a master plan has yet to be formulated because its preparation was skipped over in the search for a means to restore the medina to its rightful place as a vital part of the capital.

Although the ASM would always declare that its sole preoccupation was the medina, international aid was acquired through a project linking the rehabilitation of the medina to that of Carthage, centre-point in an extended archaeological site (Punic to Byzantine vestiges) scattered the length of the suburbs on the north littoral of Tunis. Because of its cultural slant, the Projêt Tunis–Carthage (PTC) was channelled toward UNESCO by the Ministry of Plan. In 1969 consultants in economics, tourism, archaeology, urban planning and architecture prepared a nine-point project estimated at over $26 million. Seven parts of this project bore on the implantation of facilities for tourists, five in the coastal zones around Carthage. One was aimed toward making central Tunis, the ex-colonial downtown, a reception point of international standing for all tourists entering the country. And finally one was designed to make the medina a tourist attraction on a par with a renewed Carthage. Another project was to protect and develop the green belt between Tunis and the suburbs on the north littoral, and the final one concerned the creation of a supra-ministerial organization to accomplish all these goals.

Only in the preliminary document of 1969 can one get a clear view of the original aims of the Projêt Tunis–Carthage, since they became diffuse as soon as the first foreign experts began work in January 1970, at Dar Lasram, ASM headquarters in the medina.[9] The PTC worked in liaison with ASM for less than three years. During this period three general tendencies are fairly clear; first, a continued emphasis on tourism which would drag the urban planners in particular into studies spanning too much time and space – all of Greater Tunis through 1985 or even 2000; second, a tendency to reiterate and restudy several pet projects for the medina without ever moving closer to their realization; finally, a great enthusiasm for the Carthage part of the equation.

We may examine these in inverse order. Three years of activity yielded only one tangible result and that centred on Carthage. As summarized elsewhere:

> The only project coming out of Dar Lasram to have received the approbation of Tunisian authorities was a rezoning of the entire area . . . This is unfortunate. Again and again in the eyes of the world the monumental legacy of Tunisia is, not the Islamic monuments in which the country is rich, but what the Romans, and their mysterious predecessors, the Carthaginians, left behind on Tunisian soil. Even in the immediate area of Carthage, a real living treasure, the perched Turkish summer village of Sidi Bou Said, was neglected in favour of the "monumental zone" (Micaud, 1974).

In regard to the medina, ASM and PTC worked together to a degree that there was often considerable confusion about the division of rsponsibility. An ASM sociology team responsible for the sectorial survey of the medina would suddenly be sent to do an inquiry on the sociology of tourism nationwide or on the functioning of spontaneous markets on the periphery of Tunis. If certain broad projects for intervention in the medina seemed consistent and often well conceived - full restoration of a given number of historical monuments, establishment of several tourist circuits, renovation of parts of the Hafsia quarter adjacent to ASM headquarters and the preparation of a master plan – other goals were less consistent.

All those relating to a broad restructuring of the traditional economy, or, for that matter, addressing themselves to the problem of seeking new vocations and functions for the medina seemed at variance with the facts being brought to light each day. The medina had a function, that of low-cost housing for a high percentage of the urban population, and the traditional economy had adapted to serve this clientele with an increasing number of secondhand dealers and casual merchants.

In fact, in light of the then well-documented sociological makeup of the medina, many of the propositions regarding the implantation of tourist facilities of the European type seemed unrealistic at best. A goal of 3,000 beds was once heard, though it was subsequently adjusted to 300. The PTC technicians contributed to, if they did not cause, a general romantic mis-apprehension of the medina: "Dans ses palais et ses souks, résonne la "fête" permanente; celle-là que poursuit le voyageur à travers le monde, qu'il rencontre parfois, et dont son regarde emporte le souvenir. C'est là surtout que parle la Tunisie, et qu'alors le tourisme devient facteur d'humanisme."[10]

On the level of general urban planning the goal was to make up a Carthage–medina package for "cultural tourism" that would contribute to the economic development of Tunis by making it a first-class tourist attraction. The problem is that Tunis is not a first-class metropolis. It is, in fact, a curious mixture, both stylistically and in modes of functioning, of Western and non-Western models. The Planners found themselves more and more involved in grandiose parallel city schemes since the existing modern centre embarrassed everyone by its lapses from moderni-ty. To an increasing degree the economic and social realities of every part of the existing city were overlooked in aspirations to bring Tunis up to international norms while turning the medina into a museum city like Carcassone in southern France and Carthage into something like the roman campagna. The reci-pients of such extensive urban equipment could only be tourists of the sort not now attracted to Tunis and a small percentage of the Tunisian élite. According to figures given in the 1966 Census, Tunis had only the purchasing power of an American city of 40,000-50,000 people with a population fifteen times as great.[11]

First ASM, as it had been constituted, and then the PTC came to an official halt during 1973. Only one project had received official recognition. A second, for the renovation of the Hafsia area of the medina by the reconstitution of an ancient souk and the construction of some ninety-four units of low-cost housing, was to be approved within a year, but only as a speculative real estate venture.

The failure of the PTC to attain any of its goals was followed by a new stage in urban planning in Tunisia. The appeal to outside planning and financing for tourism that had brought about the PTC led next to the signing of accords with the World Bank in 1973 for a nationwide project for tourist infrastructures. The urban-planning dilemma of Greater Tunis led to the creation of another internationally staffed and financed organism, the Dis-trict of Tunis, in 1974. And, as the most direct result of this débacle, ASM was during 1973 reorganized in the interest of total Tunisification and sent back to its original tasks by the municipal-ity. While the *villeneuve* may yet be subject to the sorts of *folies de grandeur* to which too many occidental planners, heirs of the total planning tradition of Le Corbusier, are inclined, the medina has at last been taken in hand by Tunisians who are willing to accept it for what it is.

Retrenchment and Realism

Romantic idealism, disregard of socioeconomic realities, recourse to such abstractions as international norms or universal modes of function, emphasis on appearance are all characteristics of a by now somewhat dated occidental urban planning tradition. The medina, much of the older European city, the large squatter settlements that house nearly one-third of the urban population, and indeed most of the capital escape the comprehension of such planners. Such areas defy urban renewal which has come to mean extensive demolition, relocation of many thousands of people and then reconstruction for an imaginary clientele since modern construction cannot be scaled down to average Third World budgets.[12]

The shift in planning for the medina before and after 1973 can be characterized by two parallel sets of terms; with the medina folded back into itself under the tutelage of the municipally run ASM there is a conscious shift from idealism to realism coupled by a shift from broad proposals for *renovation* (of a valuable cultural asset) to specific ones for *rehabilitation* (of an irreplaceable housing stock), indeed a shift from the level of preliminary studies to that of immediate spot intervention.

The ASM owes much to its predecessors and it is just this superficial lack of novelty that could gain its proposals acceptance. The tie with the municipality is an old one and logical, especially since the dissolution of *habous** properties the city finds itself the proprietor of approximately 20 per cent of medina property and could, under laws applying to buildings risking collapse, take possession of much more. We should recall, too, that much of the responsibility of the Ministry of Culture for the restoration of historic monuments within the medina was assumed by the city. The municipality was the patron of a team headed by Jacques Revault (the leading architectural historian of the medina) that carried out a major restoration of the upper souks, thus far the only major campaign directed toward public areas accessible to tourists.

*Properties which had previously been used to provide income for pious purposes.

The current division of responsibility with the Ministry of Culture's Institutional National d'Art et d'Archéologie (INAA) is also based on precedent. The requirements imposed by the restoration of historic monuments are quite different than those posed by the rehabilitation of the average residential and commercial architecture of the quarter. While the ASM has made certain suggestions regarding zoning and the financing of restorations in the monumental area, they have decided to leave the responsibility for restoration and even reaffection of the monuments to the INAA. The ASM shift is *away* from "sauvegade du patrimoine monumental" toward "savegarde du patromoine immobilier". And this is nothing less than a philosophical re-evaluation of the medina in favor of its actual function.

The data leading to this philosophical shift are of course inherited from earlier ASM studies. The minute sectorial analysis of the medina, contents and containers alike, has been completed so that the data for any sort of intervention are available. While none of the older ASM/PTC documents is now available, nor are many of the original researchers still working in Tunis, data culled from the best of the documents have served as the basis for the series of recommendations issued by ASM early in 1974.[13]

The presentation is extremely factual, showing why something should be done and how it can be done. Certain key perceptions have been maintained while everything relating to refunctioning for tourists or others has been let go along with histories of, and eulogies to, the medina and polemics against whatever may have "ruined" this once perfect urban form. The medina and its two traditional *faubourgs* are still intimately associated. Intervention in this area must take place by sectors rather than by buildings because in preserving the medina one is preserving a traditional urban fabric from which it is impossible to separate discrete elements. So far this reads like older ASM recommendations. The difference comes with suggestions for the mode of intervention.

In fact around 1971 ASM did have a great deal of power in the medina. Granted the right to pass on all new construction, a right that was exercised by imposing a mode of traditionalizing decoration of old and new façades, ASM dreamed of pilot projects, of *quartiers témoins*. Actual interventions were merely cosmetic, while those proposed would have only superimposed new quarters made to appear old.

Now ASM opposes, with sound financial reasoning, any form of demolition and renovation. A *quartier témoin* would be one where the following specifications have been met:

Walls have been made safe to bear their loads. Surfaces are protected against humidity, the single worst enemy of the medina.

Buildings are remodeled so that each has electric outlets and a window in every room, and sanitary facilities, water, and access to a sewage system for at least every three families or for every floor.

Each family has two useable rooms, facilities, and access to a patio or terrace.

Rents have been adjusted to a rate compatible with the quality of the lodging. (Actually they vacillate from nothing to 7–9 dinars a month for a room. The average rent is now 0.450 m² compared to an average of 0.660 m² for the District as a whole.)

The legal status of the building has been regulated to allow for eventual purchase of the lodging by the renters.

The passage fronting the houses follows the traditional layout of the quarter.

Any empty spots have been filled with constructions serving the same social needs as the surrounding buildings.

There is a narrow but significant range in economic levels among neighbours.[14]

Translated into such norms for the rehabilitation of quarters as these, ASM intervention in the medina seems to be purely pragmatic, a quality unusual enough to be refreshing. The outlook that has led to such proposals is, in fact, entirely new. The ASM personnel stress above all that they are different from earlier planning groups in the workable and finite (*opérationel* and *ponctuel*) nature of their proposals. They do not stress at all that which is unprecedented in Tunisia in their planning. The earlier ASM and then the PTC were hailed as pilot projects because they approached problems from interdisciplinary directions. Each discipline, however, went its own way. Now ASM incorporates a variety of disciplines in the following manner.

The first concern is what can be done within the existing legal and administrative framework. Indeed, statutes on sanitation dating to the Protectorate have served as the wedge with which to enter the medina and put it in order. To begin with, the legal framework for intervention is laid, or if lacking is proposed, as a draft law.[15] The second concern is how much things cost and how they may be paid for within the range of normal expenditures since there should be no recourse to foreign or even to unusual state aid. Implied is the powerful economic logic of rehabilitation of existing housing stock which Nicholas Taylor argued so eloquently in *The Village in the City* and which the oil embargo made the best weapon of American preservationists from Boston to Seattle. The Fond National pour l'Amélioration de l'Habitat (FNAH), an obscure resource available since 1956, can serve for much of the financing solely by applying funds that accrue to it from taxes on medina properties.[16] The economist and the legal advisor are perhaps the most important members of the group in direct contact with earlier procedure. Next come the sociologists for the human content of the medina and only then the architects for the constructed content.

The intent of ASM is to show medina residents – of whom less than 30 per cent are owners – what they can do for themselves. This is the only large residential quarter of the city which has remained free of constant piecemeal remodelling. Typically, Tunisians do not merely inhabit; they live in and tinker with. Whether such unusual passivity is due to outmoded zoning regulations, to lack of clear legal status, to sheer poverty, or to fear of eviction and/or demolition, most of which are even more operative in the *gourbivilles*, the earlier aesthetic exigencies of ASM/PTC cannot have helped. The ASM has now to jolt medina residents into using available resources to help themselves according to their legal rights. Such advocacy planning – planning with or by rather than for the people – is certainly new in Tunisia.[17]

For advocacy planning is exactly what has been proposed. To the degree that it is feasible the ASM would provide only the preliminary studies and technical aid to encourage people to reconstruct their own environment with the help of traditional artisans. Equally new is the apparent official acceptance of auto-construction and evolutive housing. Neither of these has ever been officially agreed to in Tunisia although they are common practice in the "savage urbanism" of the *gourbivilles*.[18] Yet each new housing project has revealed again the fallacies of government-sponsored "low-cost" housing. Tunisia's modern construction industry has nearly priced itself out of the housing market in the past few years, making a return to traditional methods and innovative procedures mandatory if governmental responses are to answer to the demonstrated needs.[19]

End Notes

The Israeli Concept of
National Security   Dan Horowitz

1. See, for example, Ben Gurion, *Pigishot Im Manhigim* (1967, pp. 7–8) and Peres (1965, pp. 14, 42).
2. The rationale of this basic premise is spelled out by Yigal Allon (1968, pp. 35-82).
3. The most explicit expression of this view is General Dayan's speech at the funeral of Roy Rotberg in 1965. See *Davar*, 2 May 1965. See also Dayan's speech at the Israeli Army's Command and Staff College on 1 Aug 1968, quoted in Dayan (1968, pp. 19-29).
4. The term "self-emancipation" was coined by Dr Leon Pinsker, an early Zionist thinker who published a pamphlet on this subject in 1882. The idea of self-reliance in defence led to the establishment of an independent military organization of the Jewish community in Palestine, the Haganah. The impact of the idea of self-reliance in defence on the history of the Jewish community in Palestine is discussed in Professor B. Dinur (1954, Introduction).
5. See Ben Gurion's statement in *Davar*, 16 Oct 1957. See also Ben Gurion's account of his discussion with President Eisenhower's special envoy, Robert B. Anderson, on 9 March 1956, in *Ma'ariv*, 16 July 1971. Ben Gurion's account of these secret talks includes some of the most explicit presentations of various aspects of the Israeli concept of national security.
6. See Ben Gurion's introduction to the Israeli Army's official history of the War of Independence (1949).
7. See Prime Minister Moshe Sharett's speech in the Knesset, *Divrei Ha-Knesset*, 30 Aug 1954; Ben Gurion's speech, *Divrei Knesset*, 1 July 1959; Peres (1970 ch. I).
8. See Rabin's (1967).
9. See Ben Gurion's speech in the Knesset, *Divrei Ha-Knesset*, 2 Nov 1955.
10. "Military Operations in Peacetime" is the title of a Dayan lecture to Israeli officers published in *Ma'arachot*, 118–19. 1956.
11. See Ben Gurion's account of his talk with President Eisenhower's envoy on 24 Jan 1956, in *Ma'ariv*, 9 July 1971.
12. The need to take into consideration the international framework in deciding on an exercise of force was discussed by Israel's Foreign Minister, Abba Eban, on a radio

programme "Adoni Ha-Mahlit" over the Israeli Army's radio station Galei Zahal on 9 Dec 1969.

13. For example, Ben Gurion regarded the diminishing of Nasser's stature as one of the main achievements of the Sinai Campaign. See David Ben Gurion (1967, p.6).

14. The impact of this restriction on the conduct of the military operations is described in Yeruham Cohen (1969, pp. 186–7, 232–52, 267–8).

15. Fifty-one thousand cars and lorries of all kinds crossed the "open bridges" on the Jordan between June 1967 and Dec 1969. During the same period there were 3,425 incidents along the Jordanian border. See articles by Brigadier Shlomo Gazit and Brigadier Y. Raviv in *Ma'arachot*, 204. 1970.

16. The tacit understanding concerning the oil production in Ras Sudor in the Sinai involved not only the Israelis and the Egyptians, but also the Italian holders of the Egyptian oil-production concession, the Company of Petrolio Egiptio.

17. The increased exercise of violence culminated in the 1969–70 War of Attrition. Following the summer 1970 ceasefire the amount and scope of violent incidents along the borders of Israel were reduced markedly. For statistical data on military actions along the ceasefire line to 1 January 1970, see Brigadier Raviv's article in *Ma'arachot* 204. 1970.

18. Ben Gurion emphasised this feature of the 1948 war in his address to Israel's Provisional State Council on 27 Sep 1948. See Ben Gurion (1969, vol. I, pp. 291–4).

19. The main exponent of this approach was David Ben Gurion whose political strategy invariably reflected a clear distinction between ultimate goals and operational objectives. See Yigal Dunyetz on Ben Gurion's conception of politics and security in *Medina u Mimshal*, no. 1 (1971) pp. 60–76.

20. On "basic" and "current" security see Shimon Peres in *Niv Hakvutza*, June 1954; Ben Gurion in *Divrei Ha-Knesset*, 2 Jan 1956; Allon in *Divrei Ha-Knesset*, 3 Feb 1956.

21. See Ben Gurion on the Defence Service Law in *Divrei Ha-Knesset*, 15 Sep 1949.

22. The saying is attributed to Israel's second Chief of Staff, General Yigal Yadin.

23. See Dayan's comments on the memoirs of General Burns in *Ma'ariv*, 26 Oct 1962, and 2 Nov 1962.

24. See an interview with General Rabin over *Kol Israel* (Israel Broadcasting Service), 25 July 1970 (interviewer Y. Hameiri); Dayan on the memoirs of General Burns, *Ma'ariv*, 26 Oct 1962.

25. See General M. Peled's comments on the philosophy of the Israeli reprisals in *Ma'ariv*, 24 Sep 1971.

26. See S. Aronson and Dan Horowitz on the reprisals of the 1950s in *Ha'aretz*, 13 Aug 1971.

27. The theory of a skilful use of force is presented in Schelling's (1960) and Schelling and Halperin (1961). These authors were introduced to Israeli readers by General Harkabi (1963) in his book *Milhama Garinit ve Shalom*.

28. The degree to which Israeli decision-makers thought in terms of deterrence is reflected in an interview with Prime Minister Levi Eshkol in *Ma'ariv*, 4 Oct 1967.

29. See General M. Peled's article in *Ma'ariv*, 16 May 1959.

30. One of the consequences of this influence was the Israeli sensitivity about the credibility of their "power of deterrence". See interviews with General Peled in *Ma'ariv*, 16 May 1959; General Gavish in *Al Ha-Mishmar*, 7 June 1968.

31. See Ben Gurion on the accumulation of power in *Divrei Ha-Knesset*, 3 Nov 1955; 19 June 1956.

32. On the Israeli doctrine in this respect see General Rabin in *Academy in Memory of Yizhak Slade;* Colonel D. Wallach's article on Israeli security doctrine in *Yediot Ahronot*, 5 Oct 1958; General H. Laskov in *Ma'arachot*, 132. 1960 p. 7.

33. For Israeli references to this situation, see Allon, *Massach Shel Hol*, pp. 338–55; Peres, "Mimad Ha-Zman" in *Ma'arachot*, 146. 1962.

34. According to General Laskov the formula for an Israeli strategy agreed upon as early as 1949 was "A defensive strategy, carried out in an offensive way". See Laskov in *Hayom* 1 May 1968.

35. See Ben Gurion's account of his talks with Robert Anderson in *Ma'araiv*, 9 July 1971; see also Peres's account of the negotiations with the Johnson Administration on arms purchases in 1964 in *David's Sling* (1970, ch. 5).

36. See Dayan's article in *Davar*,. 31 Mar 1957. See also Ben Gurion's account of his talk with Anderson on 9 Mar 1967 in *Ma'ariv*, 16 Aug 1971.

37. See the Knesset debates in *Divrei Ha-Knesset*, 3 Nov 1955, 2–3 Jan 1956.

38. See Ben Gurion's Knesset speech in *Divrei Ha-Knesset*, 19 June 1956.

39. See Ben Gurion's account in *Ma'ariv*, 16 Aug 1971.

40. See Moshe Dayan's letter to Ben Gurion of 5 Dec 1955, quoted in the introduction to Dayan (1966).

41. See Peres (1970, ch. 9) (the book is based on the personal diaries of the then Director-General of Israel's Ministry of Defence, Shimon Peres). See also Yossef Evron (1968, pp. 120–55).

42. Colonel M. Bar-On in *Yediot Ahronot*, 19 Oct 1971 (Colonel Bar-On was Dayan's aide-de-camp in the period of the Sinai campaign).

43. See Shimon Peres on "The Time Dimension" in *Ma'arachot*, 146. 1962; *Ha-Shalav Ha-Ba*, pp. 11–12, 113–17.

44. See Allon (1968, pp. 400-2); Nevo (1968, pp. 22-32). The technological aspect of the problem is referred to in General Weizman's introduction to Shiff, (1970).
45. See Gilboa, (1969 pp. 29–30, 64–5); Allon (1968, pp. 400–2). Nevertheless the qualitative gap between Israel and Egypt demonstrated in the June 1967 war was wider than Israeli military planners expected. See interviews with General Rabin, *Ot*, 3 June 1971, and General Gavish, *Al Ha-Mishmar*, 7 June 1968.
46. For Allon's view, see (1968, pp. 171–80, 400–2).
47. It is characteristic of Israel's *status quo* approach that when she eventually went to war in 1967, she did so in response to the collapse of the *status quo* and without defining the political objective of the war. See references to this situation by General Rabin in *Ot*, 3 June 1971; General Matityahu Peled in *Ma'ariv*, 16 May 1969; General Weizman and General Y. Geva in *Yediot Ahronot*, 4 June 1971.
48. On the "orientations" debate, see an interview with Shimon Peres on Ben Gurion's policies in *Ot*, 3 Oct 1971. On Eshkol's inclination toward an "American orientation", see General Matityahu Peled's article in *Ma'ariv*, 15 May 1969, See also the Knesset debates on foreign policy in *Divrei Ha-Knesset*, 21 Oct 1963, 15 July 1964.
49. See Ben Gurion's private letter to President de Gaulle of 6 Dec 1967, quoted in Ben Gurion (1969, pp. 839–51).

The Arab Oil Economy   Y.A. Sayigh

1. Data for production for 1979 comes from *Petroleum Economist*, Jan 1980. Oil revenues have been calculated by the author on the basis of a weighted average price of $19 per barrel of oil produced, or some 21.8 million b/d for OPEC members and 1.2 million b/d for non-members. (Price information is taken from US Department of Energy, 'Energy Information Administration – Weekly Petroleum Statistical Report', 5 Sep 1980, p. 41.) GDP data for 1979 are taken from the Arab Fund for Economic and Social Development, *Country Tables of National Accounts*. Conversion of national currencies into US dollars has been made at rates quoted in the Arab Fund source.
2. According to calculations made in a study entitled 'The Development of Human Resources and Manpower", by the *Arab Fund for Economic and Social Development*, Mar 1978 (in Arabic).
3. See League of Arab States, Directorate-General of Economic Affairs, "Arab Reserves Abroad", 5 July 1980 (in Arabic).
4. Two important aspects of public consumption – the costliness

of the "welfare state" and the costliness of modern arms imports – will not be discussed here. They constitute a large portion of government spending.
5. Data calculated from *Country National Account Tables, 1969–79*, prepared by the Arab Fund for Economic and Social Development, Spring 1980.
6. League of Arab States, Directorate-General of Economic Affairs, "Economic Conditions of the Arab Countries and Relations Among them", 5 July 1980 (in Arabic). See also the Federation of Arab Chambers of Commerce, Industry and Agriculture, Arab Economic Report. Beirut, Jan 1980.
7. League of Arab States, Directorate-General of Economic Affairs, "Economic Conditions" (n.6).
8. Population and GDP data come from the Arab Fund for Economic and Social Development, "Study on Development Achievements for the 1970s and the Outlook for the 1980s in the Arab Homeland", Apr 1980 (in Arabic). For remaining information, see sources mentioned above in notes 1, 5, and 6.
9. Calculated from Country Tables in International Monetary Fund, *International Financial Statistics*, Aug 1980.

Arab Labour Migration   T. Farah *et al.*

1. State of Kuwait, Ministry of Planning, Central Statistical Office, *Annual Statistical Abstract, 1978*, pp. 110 and 124 (hereafter referred to as *ASA*).
2. *ASA*, p. 38.
3. *Financial Times* (London), 26 Feb 1979, p. 21.
4. Egyptian civil servants are bound by the government's contracts to return to Egypt after being "borrowed" by Kuwait after four years.
5. *ASA*, table 118, p. 130. There are a total of 29,982 illiterate civil servants in the government, 18,717 non-Kuwaiti and 11,265 Kuwaiti. In the authors' opinions the "illiterate" and "read and write" categories can be considered educationally unqualified for civil service posts. These comprise 25,907 or 55 per cent of the total number of Kuwaiti civil servants. The government has made primary education compulsory and no longer hires people without a high school degree, except for the army, police and national guard.
6. State of Kuwait, Ministry of Planning, Central Statistical Office, "Manpower in Government Administration" (July 1978) pp. 73–6 (Arabic).
7. *Al Kuwait Al Youm* (government official paper), Issue No. 1157, 19 Sep 1977, quoted in Al Eassa (1978, p. 77).
8. State of Kuwait, Ministry of Social Work and Labour,

"Qanun al Alel Fee Al Qata'eh el Ehli Qaqon No. 38 Issedin 1964" (Labour Law in the Private Sector, Law No. 38 for the Year 1964).

9. See Articles 2 and 17 of the 1964 Law in Hamed Al Essa (n.d.).
10. 26 Feb 1979, p. 21. The recent Rent Law stipulates that a landlord may increase the rent by no more than 100 per cent after five years.
11. Ibid., p. 22, states

Education is perhaps the area that provokes the most discord. To qualify for a government education grant a school must not contain more than 90 per cent of one nationality, and teaching must be in Arabic. This provision means that Indian schools, by necessity privately owned, are generally badly run and the cost of KD 80 per semester is almost prohibitive for an Indian servant couple who earn something in the region KD 50-80 per month.

In the government-aided schools everything is free for the child of a Kuwaiti. It is free for the child of any expatriate doctor and for those foreigners who work for the Ministries of Health or Education. For the others the cost is KD 40 a term. Salaries of staff vary enormously – anything up to KD 100 a month more is paid to a Kuwaiti teacher than to any expatriate Arab. The government tries to camouflage this obvious discrepancy by allotting a higher starting grade to a Kuwaiti and then promoting them faster than the other teachers.

12. Amiri Decree, Nationality Law, No. 15, 1959.
13. Izz Al Din Abdulla, "Taheah Al Jenseah Al Kuwateeah" (Kuwaiti Nationality Law), *L'Égypte contemporaine*, No. 361 (July 1975) Cairo, Egypt.

Economic and Cultural Dependence　G.A. Amin

1. This tendency of the affluent society to replace an "activity" by a "good" to satisfy the same need may explain the tendency, noted by Ivan Illich (1973), to use nouns to describe what used to be designated by a verb; thus "people have knowledge, mobility, even health. They have not only work or fun but even sex."
2. Adopted by the General Assembly, Sixth Special session, 2229th Plenary Meeting, 1 May 1974.
3. Quoted by Toynbee (1947).

Egyptian State Capitalism in Crisis   Mark Cooper

1. Hassan Abbas Zaki, in *Arab Political Encyclopedia, Documents and Notes*, July-Dec 1968, p. 100 (Arabic).
2. Ibid. p. 14.
3. *Al-Ahram, Al-Goumhouriya*, Aug 1968.
4. *Arab Political Encyclopedia*, July-Dec 1968, p. 54.
5. *Official Gazette, Legislative Section, Minutes of the National Assembly*, 12th session, 15 Feb 1971, p. 6 (Arabic).
6. Ibid. p. 7.
7. Aziz Sidqi, in *Conference on Administrative Leadership, Session on Administrative Problems in Industry*, 27 Sep 1968, p. 133 (Arabic).
8. Hilmy Al A'yid, in *Conference on Administrative Leadership, Session on Financial and Economic Reform*, p. 370.
9. Ali Sabri, *Speech to the National Assembly* (4 Apr 1964). Cairo: n.d.
10. Sidqi, in *Conference* (above), p. 121.
11. Hegazi, in *Arab Political Encyclopedia* (above), Jan–June 1969, pp. 122-3.
12. Sidqi, in *Conference* (above), p. 122.
13. *Arab Political Encyclopedia*, July–Dec 1968, p. 201.
14. Ibid. p. 98.
15. Ibid. p. 101.
16. Ibid. p. 51.
17. Ibid. p. 48.

Minority and Political Elites in Iraq and Syria   Nikolaos van Dam

1. Marr (1975, p. 138).
2. Batatu 1978, p. 43).
3. Radio Baghdad, 1600 GMT, 17 Oct 1979.
4. Batatu (1978, pp. 1078–9).
5. Batatu (1978, pp. 1088–9).
6. Batatu (1978, p. 1088).
7. van Dam (1979, pp. 31–50).
8. Radio Damascus, 0850 GMT, 19 Sep 1979.
9. *Hizb al-Ba'th al-'Arabi al-Ishtiraki al-Qtar al-Suri al-Qiyadah al-Taqrir al-Watha'iqi li-Azmat, al-Hizb wa al-Muqaddam lil-Mu'tamar al-Qutri al-Istithna'i al-Mun'aqid bayn*, 10–27 March 1966 the documentary report on the Party's crisis presented to the extraordinary Regional Congress held between 10 and 27 March 1966, Damascus), pp. 65-6.
10. Ibid.

11. Hirst (1979).
12. Hirst (1979).

Popular Movements and Primordial Loyalties in Beirut   Michael Johnson

1. One of the best analyses of the Lebanon economy in the modern period is Nasr (1978). For more details, see Dubar and Nasr (1976).
2. For the systemic problems of factionalism in Lebanon, see Johnson (1978). The best account of the 1958 Civil War is in Qubain (1961).
3. Published by MECICO, Beirut. I made extensive use of the sixth edition, published in 1969.
4. Dubar (1974). This should be used with care as there are a number of arithmetical errors, particularly in table 4 on p. 318.
5. This argument about the role of the Deuxième Bureau in relation to *qabadays* is based on interview material collected by the author in Beirut, 1972–3.
6. Information on *qabadays* collected by the author. For Qulaylat's trial, see *L'Orient* (local French language newspaper), 16 Mar 1968.
7. *Arab World* (news digest published in Beirut), 2 and 3 Sep 1974. It should be emphasized that I have no evidence to suggest that members of this clan were involved in criminal activities. Not all *qabadays* were racketeers or smugglers.
8. For information on the economy and strike action during 1972–5, see *MERIP Reports*, Nos. 19. 1973, 44. 1976, and 73. 1978; and Salibi (1976, pp. 72 ff. *passim.*)
9. Police had opened fire on pickets outside the Ghandur confectionary factory in Beirut, killing two people, and excessive violence and brutality had been meted out to university and high school students who had demonstrated in support of striking workers and teachers.
10. On the eve of Sulayman Frangieh's election as President in August 1970, Kamal Jumblat, who was then Minister of Interior, legalized a number of Marxist and leftist parties: the Lebanese Communist Party (CPL) and various splinter groups, the two factions of the Ba'th Socialist Party (Syrian and Iraqi), and the Parti Populair Syrien (PPS), which had changed its ideology in the late 1960s to become a socialist grouping. These parties, together with Jumblat's Progressive Socialist Party (PSP), formed the nucleus of the National Movement which had been founded in 1969. By the time of the Civil War the Movement, with Jumblat as its chief spokes-

man, had expanded to include a number of Nasserist, socialist and Marxist organizations.

11. For the radicalism of Shi'ites as compared with Sunnis, see Salibi (1976, p. 143). Also see A. al-Azmeh (1976, pp. 62–3). The latter should be read with care; see Agha (1976).

12. *As-Safir* (local Arabic newspaper), 5 Jan 1976. Translation from *Journal of Palestine Studies*, 19/20, 1976. 267.

13. Ibid.

Palestinians in Camps   Rosemary Sayigh

1. The bulk of the information in this chapter comes from interviews conducted by the author herself.

2. UNRWA divides all registered refugees into three categories: (R), the smallest number, who qualify for rations as well as services; (S), who qualify only for educational and medical services; and (N), who are not eligible for any UNRWA aid, or are only eligible for restricted aid. In Tel al-Za'ter, one of the poorest camps, out of a total population of around 12,000 in 1972, 3,540 were ration receivers, 1,000 got medical and educational services, and around 6,500 got only education.

3. The Arab Higher Committee continued to exist acting as a focus for Palestinian nationalism, and publishing the magazine *Falasteen*. The Mufti continued to receive a small subvention from the Arab League until his death in 1974.

4. Palestinians in Jordan and Syria were encouraged to enlist in the national armies, and in Syria were subject to military conscription.

5. For example, unless they have Lebanese nationality, Palestinians are not allowed to work in banks, large foreign companies, hotels or as taxi-drivers.

6. So pervasive was the image of refugee dependence on UNRWA, that it influenced even Arab political analysts. For example the Lebanese Marxist Samir Franjieh (1972) wrote, "the refugees, expelled in 1948 from the lands they tilled, have not since been integrated into any economic productive process and so know nothing of the economic exploitation to which a normal proletariat is subjected, and against which it ultimately rebels with the aim of establishing a new system of social relationships" (p. 53).

7. UNRWA schools do not take children before the age of six, nor beyond fourth secondary. Scholarships are given by UNRWA and other bodies to the brightest children to continue their education, but these benefit perhaps less than 8 per cent of camp children.

8. It should not be forgotten that Arabs made large donations to the refugees via governments, religious institutions and private charity. Sayigh (1952) notes a donation of LS. 8 million from the Syrian government, of which LS. 2 million were voluntary contributions from the population.

9. Because the Lebanese terminal exam, the Baccalaureat, is exceptionally hard, many Palestinian students sit the easier *towijihiyyah* in Syria or Egypt.

10. Out of an approximate total of 100,000 Palestinian workers in Lebanon in 1969, only 2,362 had work permits (Mundus, 1974).

Urbanization, Urbanism and the Medina of Tunis   Ellen C. Micaud

1. Association Sauvegarde de la Médina, "Rapport de synthèse". Tunis, Feb 1974, p. 28, mimeographed.

2. The 1975 figures are drawn from preparatory unreleased studies done by the district of Tunis. Those for 1966 are the ones used by the Association Sauvegarde de la Médina for the reports cited in note 13.

3. The annual growth of Tunis from 1956 to 1966 average 5-6 per cent versus a high of 3.5 per cent for any other important city. Provisional 1975 Census figures are showing a decreased rate of growth for the capital which can only be explained by increasing immigration directly to Europe. The former director of Aménagement du Territoire (the national regional planning board) estimates that at least 30 per cent of the population of Greater Tunis is housed extralegally. According to the District of Tunis at least that percentage of the city's housing stock is in very poor repair with some 22,000 lodgings in the medina alone needing major repairs and another 5,000 facing certain demolition within a decade.

4. El Kafi (1970) spells out the argument in full detail.

5. An *oukala* is a traditional rooming house. The term *oukalisé* is now used to describe residences that are rented out room by room to family units having no relationship to one another. This is true of the majority of medina properties.

6. Association Sauvegarde de la Médina, "Rapport de synthèse", p. 20.

7. Hédi Eckert (1970) Also Eckert and El Kafi (1974) pp. 211–35).

8. Eckert (1970). This study and El Kafi's (1970) were presented at a colloquium at Aix-en-Provence in May 1970.

9. *Mise en valeur du patrimoine monumental* (UNESCO, 1969).
10. This is best left untranslated. R. de Francesca's report on tourism in UNESCO (1969).
11. Eckert (1970, p. 8). Figures now available from the 1975 Census indicate no change for the better.
12. The new 'low-cost' apartments in Hafsia I require monthly payments from 80-92 dinars making purchase price, including interest, close to the cost of an American tract house in 1970. (A dinar's worth hovers around $2.00.) The architect attributes the cost overrun to chronic confusion on construction sites and to overly conservative building codes requiring in this case that all bearing walls be reinforced concrete.
13. These are: "Rapport de synthèse; "Note de synthèse et planning de travail"; "Protection du patrimoine monumental" (Dossier 1); "Mise en valeur des monuments historiques" (Dossier 2); "Patrimonine immobilier" (Dossier 3); "Hypothése de financement" (Dossier 4); "Activités opérationelles de l'ASM" (Dossier 5); "Rehabilitation de l'Ilot III E–50" (Dossier 6); "Artisanat: Propositions de développement" (Dossier 7); "Commerce: Principes d'une politique commerciale" (Dossier 7). Together these constitute a complete "plan de sauvegarde" for the quarter issued by ASM in June 1974. By mid-1976 this plan had not yet met the acceptance of the authorities. The nature of the difficulties can be discerned in a paper presented in Tunis at a seminar on the preservation and rehabilitation of historic cities by Daoulatli 1976.
14. ASM, Dossier 6, and "Rapport de synthèse". Figures for rents were furnished by the district of Tunis.
15. For example, a proposal to create an agency for the revalorization of historical monuments which is based on a nuanced rezoning of the whole medina (Dossier 2, Annexe).
16. Dossiers 5 and 6 make the method clear.
17. Hassan Fathy's (1970), originally published in English in 1969, has had considerable influence on recent planning theory as have the studies of John Turner on the squatter settlements of South America. While Fathy's book had an aesthetic impact, Turner's studies have led to a radical re-evaluation of savage urbanism (Turner, 1976; Turner with Robert Fichter, 1972).
18. This term seems to have been coined by Jacques Berque (1958).
19. Construction workers' pay doubled from January 1973 to January 1975, while in the same period most construction materials only went up about 50 per cent in price. Source, data furnished by the Sociéte nationale d'Investissement tunisienne.

Bibliography

Other Readers and Collections with Reference to the Sociology of Middle Easter Development

Antoun, R., and Harik, I., eds, 1972. *Rural Politics and Social Change in the Middle East.* Bloomington and London: Indiana UP.

Beck, L., and Keddie, N., eds, 1979. *Women in the Muslim World.* Cambridge, Mass.: Harvard.

Brown, L.C., ed., 1973. *From Medina to Metropolis: Heritage and Change in the Near Eastern City.* Princeton, NJ: Princeton.

Fisher, S.N., ed., 1955. *Social Forces in the Middle East.* Ithaca, NY: Cornell UP.

Gendzier, I.L., ed., 1969. *A Middle East Reader.* New York: Pegasus.

Ibrahim, S.E., and Hopkins, N.S., eds, 1977 *Arab Society in Transition: A Reader.* Cairo: American UP.

Karpat, K.H., ed., 1982. *Political and Social Thought in the Contemporary Middle East.* London: Pall Mall. 1968; 2nd revised and enlarged edn. New York: Praeger.

Kiray, M.B., ed., 1973. *Social Stratification and Development in the Mediteranean Basin.* The Hague, Paris: Mouton.

Landau, J.M., ed., 1972. *Man, State and Society in the Contemporary Middle East.* London: Pall Mall.

Laqueur, W.Z., ed., 1958. *The Middle East in Transition.* New York: Praeger.

Lutfiyya, A.M., and Churchill, C.W., eds, 1970. *Readings in Arab Middle Eastern Societies and Cultures.* The Hague, Paris: Mouton.

Milson, M., ed., 1973. *Society and Political Structure in the Arab World.* New York: Humanities Press.

Sweet, L.E., ed., 1970. *Peoples and Cultures in the Middle East: An Anthropological Reader,* vol. I: *Cultural Depth and Diversity.* Garden City, NY: The Natural History Press.

Thompson, J.H., and Reischaur, R.D., eds, 1966. *Modernization of the Arab World: New Perspectives in Political Science.* Princeton NJ, Toronto, New York, London: Van Nostrand.

Zartman, I.W., ed., 1972. *Man, State and Society in the Contemporary Maghrib.* London: Pall Mall.

Notes for Further Reading

Part I

Nationalism, Arab Nationalism and Arab Unity

Ajami, F., 1981. *The Arab Predicament: Arab Political Thought and Practice since 1967.* Cambridge, London, New York, New Rochelle, Melbourne, Sydney: Cambridge UP.

Amin, S., 1978. *The Arab Nation: Nationalism and Class Struggle.* London: Zed Press.

Antonius, G., 1938. *The Arab Awakening: The Story of the Arab National Movement.* London: Hamish Hamilton.

Buheiry, M.R., ed., 1981. *Intellectual Life in the Arab East, 1890-1939.* Beirut: American University of Beirut.

Dawn, C.E., 1973. *From Ottomanism to Arabism: Essays on the Origins of Arab Nationalism.* Urbana, Illinois: University of Illinois Press.

Devlin, J.F., 1976 *The Ba'th Party: A History from its Origins to 1966.* Stanford, California: Hoover Institute Press.

Gellner, E., 1982. *Nationalism.* Oxford: Blackwell.

Gomaa, A., 1977. *The Foundation of the League of Arab States: Wartime Diplomacy and Inter-Arab Politics 1941 to 1945.* London and New York: Longman.

Haim, S., ed., 1962. *Arab Nationalism: An Anthology.* Berkeley and Los Angeles: University of California Press.

Hobsbawm, E., 1977. "Some Reflections on the 'Break-up of Britain' ", *New Left Review*, 105. Sep-Oct.

Hourani, A.H., 1962. *Arabic Thought in the Liberal Age, 1798-1939.* London, New York, Toronto: Oxford UP.

Kazziha, W., 1975. *Revolutionary Transformation in the Arab World: Habbash and his Comrades from Nationalism to Marxism.* London and Tonbridge: Knight.

Kerr, M., 1967. *The Arab Cold War 1958-1967.* 2nd edn. London: Royal Institute of International Affairs.

Macdonald, R.W., 1965. *The League of Arab States: A Study in the Dynamics of Regional Organization.* Princeton, NJ: Princeton UP.

Nairn, T., 1977. *The Break-up of Britain.* London: New Left Books.

Seale, P., 1965. *The Struggle for Syria: A Study of Post-War Arab Politics, 1945-1958.* London, New York, Toronto: Oxford UP.

Smith, A.D., 1971. *Theories of Nationalism.* London: Duckworth.

—— ed., 1976. *National Movements.* London and Basingstoke: Macmillan.

Tibi, B., 1981. *Arab Nationalism: A Critical Enquiry.* London and Basinsgtoke: Macmillan.

Zeine, Z.N., 1973. *The Emergence of Arab Nationalism: With a Background Study of Arab-Turkish Relations in the Near East*, 3rd edn. Delmar, NY: Caravan Books.

Zubaida, S., 1978. "Theories of Nationalism", in G. Littlejohn *et al.*, eds, *Power and the State*. London: Croom Helm.

Israel, Palestine and the Middle East State System

Amos II, J.W., 1979. *Arab-Israeli Military/Political Relations: Arab Perceptions and the Policies of Escalation*. New York, Oxford, Toronto, Sydney, Frankfurt, Paris: Pergamon.
———1980. *Palestine Resistance. Organization of a Nationalist Movement*. New York, Oxford, Toronto, Sydney, Frankfurt, Paris: Pergamon.
Bar-Yaacov, N., 1967. *The Israeli-Syrian Armistice: Problems of Implementation, 1949-1966*. Jerusalem: Magnes Press.
Binder, L., 1958. "The Middle East as a Subordinate International System", *World Politics*, X, 3.
Brecher, M., 1972. *The Foreign Policy System of Israel*. London, Toronto, Melbourne: Oxford UP.
Bulloch, J., 1973. *The Making of a War: The Middle East from 1967 to 1973*. London: Longman.
Chaliand, G., 1972. *The Palestinian Resistance*. Harmondsworth, Baltimore, Ringwood: Penguin Books.
Cooley, J.K., 1973. *Green March, Black September: The Story of the Palestinian Arabs*. London: Cass.
Horowitz, D., and Lissak, M., 1978. *Origins of the Israeli Polity: Palestine under the Mandate*. Chicago and London: University of Chicago Press.
Kazziha, W., 1979. *Palestine in the Arab Dilemma*. London: Croom Helm; New York: Barnes & Noble.
Khalidi, W., 1979. *Conflict and Violence in Lebanon: Confrontation in the Middle East*. Cambridge Mass.: Center for International Affairs, Harvard University.
Peri, Y., and Lissak, M., 1976. "Retired Officers in Israel and the Emergence of a New Elite", in G. Harries-Jenkins and J. Van Doorn, eds, *The Military and the Problems of Legitimacy*. Beverly Hills, California: Sage.
Perlmutter, A., 1969. *Military and Politics in Israel: Nation-building and Role Expansion*. London: Cass.
Plascov, A., 1981. *Palestine Refugees in Jordan, 1948-57*. London: Cass.
Quandt, W.B. 1977. *Decade of Decisions: American Policy towards the Arab-Israeli Conflict 1967-76*. Berkeley, Los Angeles and London: University of California Press.
Rodinson, M., 1973. *Israel: A Colonial-Settler State*. New York: Monad Press.
Rubin, B., 1981. *The Arab States and the Palestine Conflict*. Syracuse, NY: Syracuse UP.

Safran, N., 1978. *Israel: The Embattled Ally*. Cambridge, Mass., and London: Harvard UP.

Schlaim, A., and Yaniv, A., 1980. "Domestic Politics and Foreign Policy in Israel", *International Affairs*, 56, 2. Apr.

Turner, B.S., 1976-7. "Avineri's View of Marx's Theory of Colonialism: Israel", *Science and Society*, XL, 4. Winter.

Whetton, L., 1974. *The Canal War: Four Power Conflict in the Middle East*. Cambridge, Mass.: MIT Press.

Arab Economic Relations, Oil and Middle Eastern Labour Migration

Abadan-Unat, N., ed., 1976. *Turkish Workers in Europe*. Leiden: E.J. Brill.

Abu-Lughod, J., 1982. "Causes and Consequences of Recent International Labour Migrations in the Arab World", in M. Hudson, ed., *Arab Resources: The Transformation of a Society*. London and Canberra: Croom Helm.

Adler, S., 1977. *International Migration and Dependence*. Farnborough, Hants: Saxon House.

Alnasrawi, A., 1979. "Arab Oil and the Industrial Economies: the Paradox of Oil Dependency", *Arab Studies Quarterly*, I, L. Winter.

Askari, H.K., and Cummings, J., 1977. "The Future of Economic Integration within the Arab World", *International Journal of Middle East Studies*, VIII, 3 July.

Attiga, A., 1980. "Oil and Regional Cooperation among the Arabs", in R. Mabro, ed., *World Energy: Issues and Policies*. Oxford and New York: Oxford University Press.

Bennoune, M., 1975. "Maghrebin Workers in France", *MERIP Reports*, 34. Jan.

Birks, J.S., and Sinclair, C.A., 1980. *Arab Manpower: The Crisis of Development*. New York: St. Martin's Press; London: Croom Helm.

Bonnefant, P., 1978/1979. "Utilisation des recettes petrolières et strategie des groupes sociaux en Peninsule arabe", 1 and 2, *Maghreb/Machrek*, 82 (Oct-Dec 1978) and 83 (Jan-Mar 1979).

Al-Chalabi, F.J., 1981. *OPEC and the International Oil Industry: A Changing Structure*. Oxford: Oxford UP.

Demir, S., 1976. *The Kuwait Fund and the Political Economy of Arab Regional Development*. New York: Praeger.

—— 1979. *Arab Development Funds in the Middle East*. Oxford: Pergamon.

Ghantus, E.T., 1982. *Arab Industrial Integration*. London and Canberra: Croom Helm. 1982.

Halliday, F., 1977. "Arab Labour Migration in the Middle East", *MERIP Reports*, 59. Aug.

Hallwood, P., and Sinclair, S., 1981. *Oil, Debt and Development: OPEC and the Third World.* London: Allen & Unwin.

Ibrahim, S.E., 1982. *The New Arab Social Order: A Study of the Social Impact of Oil Wealth.* London and Canberra: Croom Helm.

Katouzian, M.A., 1978. "Oil versus Agriculture: A Case of Dual Resource Depletion in Iran", *Journal of Peasant Studies*, April.

Kurbursi, A., 1980. *Arab Economic Prospects in the 1980s.* Beirut: Institute of Palestine Studies.

Lawless, R., Findlay, A.M., and Findlay, A., 1982. *Return Migration to the Maghreb: People and Policies*, Arab Papers, No. 10. London: Arab Research Centre.

Owen, R., 1981. "The Arab Economies in the 1970s", *MERIP Reports*, 100/101. Oct-Dec.

Paul, J.A., 1976. "Algeria's Oil Economy: Liberation or Neo-Colonialism?", in R.A. Stone, ed., *OPEC and the Middle East: The Impact of Oil on Societal Development.* New York: Praeger.

Payne, S., 1974. *Exporting Workers: The Turkish Case.* Cambridge: Cambridge UP.

Poulson, W.B., and Wallace, M., 1979. "Regional Integration in the Middle East: the Evidence of Trade and Capital Flows", *Middle East Journal*, XXXIII, 4. Autumn.

Quandt, W.B., 1976. "US Energy Policy and the Arab-Israeli Conflict", in N.A. Sherbiny and M.A. Tessler, eds., *Oil: Impact in the Arab Countries and Global Implications.* New York: Praeger.

Sayigh, Y.A., 1982. "New Framework for Complementarity among the Arab Economies", in M. Hudson, ed., *Arab Resources: The Transformation of a Society.* London and Canberra: Croom Helm.

Seymour, I., 1980. *OPEC: Instrument of Change.* London and Basingstoke: Macmillan.

Shihata, I.F.I., 1982. *The Other Face of OPEC: Financial Assistance to the Third World.* London and New York: Longman.

Stork, J., 1976. *Middle East Oil and the Energy Crisis.* New York and London: Monthly Review Press.

Swanson, J.W., 1979. *Emigration and Economic Development: The Case of the Yemen Arabic Republic.* Boulder, Colorado: Westview.

Tsakok, I., 1982. "The Export of Manpower from Pakistan to the Middle East, 1975-85", *World Development*, X, 4. Apr.

Völker, G.E., 1976. "Turkish Labour Migration to Germany: Impact on both Economies", *Middle Eastern Studies*, XII, 1. Jan.

Dependencies: Economic, Military and Cultural

Abshire, D.M., 1976. *International Broadcasting: A New Dimension of Western Diplomacy.* Beverly Hills, California: Sage.

Amin, G.A., 1980. *The Modernization of Poverty: A Study of the Political Economy of Growth in Nine Arab Countries.* 2nd edn. Leiden: E.J. Brill.

——"Armed Forces and Society" 1981, *Current Sociology*, XXIX, 3 Winter.

al-Azm, S., 1980. "Orientalism and Orientalism in Reverse", *Khamsin*, 8. Fall.

Bouza, H., 1978. *Décoloniser l'information*. Paris: Éditions Cana.

Bourdieu, P., 1969. "Systems of Education and Systems of Thought", *International Social Studies Journal*, XIX.

Boyd, D.A. 1977. *Egyptian Radio: Tool of Political and National Development*. Lexington, Kentucky: Association of Educators in Journalism.

Clawson, P., 1978. "Egypt's Industrialization: A Critique of Dependency Theory", *MERIP Reports*, 72. Nov.

Colonna, F., 1974. "Cultural Resistance and Religious Legitimacy in Algeria", *Economy and Society*, III.

Dessouki, A.E.H., and El-Lanhan, A., 1981. "Arms Race, Defence Expenditures and Development: the Egyptian Case 1952-1973", *Journal of South Asian and Middle Eastern Studies*, IV, 3. Spring.

Glassman, J.D., 1975. *Arms for the Arabs: The Soviet Union and War in the Middle East*. Baltimore and London: Johns Hopkins UP.

Gundar-Frank, A., 1980. "Arms Economy and Warfare in the Third World", *Third World Quarterly*, II, 2. Apr.

Heggoy, A., and Zingg, P., 1976. "French Education in Revolutionary North Africa", *International Journal of Middle East Studies*, VII, 4. Oct.

Kaldor, M., and Eide, A., eds, 1979. *The World Military Order: The Impact of Military Technology on the Third World*. London and Basingstoke: Macmillan.

Katouzian, H., 1981. *The Political Economy of Modern Iran, 1926–1979*. London and Basingstoke: Macmillan.

Katz, E., and Wedell, G., 1981. *Broadcasting in the Third World: Promise and Performance*. London and Basingstoke: Macmillan.

Keydar, C., 1979. "The Political Economy of Turkish Democracy", *New Left Review*, 115. May-June.

Naur, M., 1980. "Industrialisation and Transfer of Civilian and Military Technology to the Arab Countries", *Current Research on Peace and Violence*. Copenhagen.

Rachty, G., 1978. "Broadcasting Systems in the Arab World", *Arab States Broadcasting Union Review*. Jan.

Said, E., 1978. *Orientalism*. London and Henley: Routledge & Kegan Paul.

Schiller, H.I., 1969. *Mass Communications and the American Empire*. New York: Kelley.

—— 1978. *Communications and Cultural Domination*. New York: Pantheon.

Smith, A., 1980. *The Geopolitics of Information: How Western Culture Dominates the World*. London and Boston: Faber & Faber.

Stork, J., 1982. "Israel as a Strategic Asset", *MERIP Reports*, 105. May.

Van Dorn, J., ed., 1968. *The Armed Forces and Society*. The Hague, Paris: Mouton.

Part II

Class, State and Development

Abdel-Fadil, M., 1975. *Development, Income Distribution and Social Change in Rural Egypt*. Cambridge: Cambridge UP.
——1980. *The Political Economy of Nasserism*. Cambridge: Cambridge UP.
Abdel-Malek, A., 1968. *Egypt: Military Society*. New York: Random House.
Alexander, N., 1981. "Libya: the Continuous Revolution", *Middle Eastern Studies*, XVII, 2. Apr.
Amin, G.A., 1980. *The Modernization of Poverty: A Study in the Political Economy of Growth in Nine Arab Countries 1945–1970*. Leiden: E.J. Brill.
Batatu, J., 1978. *The Old Social Classes and the Revolutionary Movements of Iraq*. Princeton, NJ: Princeton UP.
Cooper, M.N., 1982. *The Transformation of Egypt*. London: Croom Helm.
First, R., 1974. *Libya*. Harmondsworth: Penguin Books.
Hagnebi, H., Machover, M., and Orr, A., 1971. "The Class Nature of Israeli Society", *New Left Review*, 65. Jan-Feb.
Halliday, F., 1979. *Dictatorship and Development in Iran*. Harmondsworth: Penguin Books.
Keydar, C., 1979. "The Political Economy of Turkish Democracy", *New Left Review*, 115. May/June.
Lackner, H., 1978. *A House Built on Sand: A Political Economy of Saudi Arabia*. London: Ithaca Press.
Ozbudun, E., 1977. *Social Change and Political Participation in Turkey*. Princeton, NJ: Princeton UP.
Schmeil, Y., 1976. "Le Système politique irakien enfin stabilisé", *Maghreb/Machrek*, 74. Oct-Dec.

Class, Bureaucracy and State Power

Ayubi, N., 1980. *Bureaucracy and Society in Contemporary Egypt*. London: Ithaca Press.
——1982. "Bureaucratic Inflation and Administrative Inefficiency: the Deadlock in Egyptian Administration", *Middle Eastern Studies*, XVIII, 3 July.

Berger, M., 1957. *Bureaucracy and Society in Modern Egypt*. Princeton: Princeton UP.

Binder, L., 1978. *In a Moment of Enthusiasm: Political Power and the Second Stratum in Egypt*. Chicago: Chicago UP.

Burgat, F. 1982. "Les nouveaux paysans algériens et l'État", Maghreb/Machrek, 95. Jan-Mar.

Clegg, I., 1971. *Workers' Self-Management in Algeria*. London: Allen Lane.

Entelis, J., 1981. "Élite Political Culture and Socialization in Algeria: Tensions and Discontinuities", *Middle East Journal*, XXXV, 2. Spring.

El-Fathaly, O.I., Palmer, M., and Chackerian, R., 1977. *Political Development and Bureaucracy in Libya*. Lexington, Mass.: Lexington Books.

Heper, M., 1976. "The Recalcitrance of the Turkish Public Bureaucracy to 'Bourgeois Politics' ", *Middle East Journal*, XXX-4, Autumn.

Hussein, M., 1973. *Class Conflict in Egypt: 1945-1971*. New York: Monthly Review Press.

Lazrag, M., 1976. "Bureaucracy and Class in Algeria", *Dialectical Anthropology*, I.

Springborg, R., 1979. "Patrimonialism and Policy Making in Egypt: Nasser and Sadat and the Tenure Policy for Reclaimed Lands", *Middle Eastern Studies*, XV, 1. Jan.

Tibi, B., 1979. "Trade Unions as an Organizational Form of Political Opposition in Afro-Arab States: the Case of Tunisia", *Orient*, XX.

Trimberger, E.K., 1977. *Revolution from Above: Military Bureaucrats and Development in Japan, Turkey, Egypt and Peru*. New Brunswick: Transaction Books.

State and Tribe

Antoun, R., and Harik, I., eds., 1972. *Rural Politics and Social Change in the Middle East*. Bloomington: Indiana UP.

Asad, T., 1970. *The Kababish Arabs*. London: Hurst.

——1979. "Equality in Nomadic Social Systems?" in *Pastoral Production and Society*. Cambridge: Cambridge UP.

Helfgott, L., 1977. "Tribalism as a Socio-Economic Formation in Iranian History", *Iranian Studies*, X, 1-2.

Khoury, F.I., 1980. *Tribe and State in Bahrain*. Chicago: Chicago UP.

Nelson, C., ed., 1973. *The Desert and the Sown: Nomads in the Wider Society*. Berkeley: California UP.

Peterson, J.E., 1977. "Tribes and Politics in Eastern Arabia", *Middle East Journal*, XXXI. Summer.

Seddon, D., 1981. *Moroccan Peasants*. Folkestone: Dawson.

Ethnic Groups and State Power

Batatu, H., 1981. "Some Observations on the Social Roots of Syria's Ruling Military Group and the Causes for its Dominance", *Middle East Journal*, XXXV, 3. Summer.

Dam, N. van, 1979. *The Struggle for Power in Syria: Sectarianism, Regionalism, and Tribalism in Politics, 1961-1978*. London: Croom Helm.

Entelis, J., 1979. "Ethnic Conflict and the Re-emergence of Radical Christian Nationalism in Lebanon", *Journal of South Asian and Middle Eastern Studies*, II, 3.

Gellner, E., and Micaud, C., eds., 1973. *Arabs and Berbers*. London: Duckworth.

Owen, R., ed., 1976. *Essays on the Crisis in Lebanon*. London: Ithaca Press.

Salibi, K.S., 1976. *Crossroads to Civil War: Lebanon 1958-1976*. London: Ithaca Press.

Race and Citizenship in Israel

Davis, U., and Mezvinsky, N., eds, 1975. *Documents from Israel 1967-1973*. London: Ithaca Press.

Jiryis, S. 1976. *The Arabs in Israel*. New York: Monthly Review Press.

Nakhleh, K., and Zureik, E., eds, 1980. *The Sociology of the Palestinians*. London: Croom Helm.

Schwarz, W., 1959. *The Arabs in Israel*. London: Faber & Faber.

Selzer, M. 1967. *The Aryanization of the Jewish State*. New York: Black Star Books.

——ed., 1975. *The Non-Jew in the Jewish State: A Collection of Documents*. Jerusalem: Professor Israel Shahak, 2 Bartenuru Street, Jerusalem, Israel.

Shahak, I. 1981. "The Jewish Religion and its Attitude to Non-Jews", Parts I and II in *Khamsin*, 8 (1981); Part III in *Khamsin*, 9.

Tamarin, G.R. 1973. *The Israeli Dilemma: Essays in a Warfare State*. Rotterdam: Rotterdam UP.

Part III

Rural Transformation: the Household, the Village and the National Economy

Barnett, T. 1975. "The Gezira Scheme: Production of Cotton and Reproduction of Underdevelopment", in I. Oxaal, T. Barnett and D. Booth, eds, *Beyond the Sociology of Development*. London and Boston: Routledge & Kegan Paul.

Chayanov, A.V. 1966. *the Theory of the Peasant Economy*. Trans. and ed. by D. Thorner, R.E.F. Smith and B. Kerblay. Homewood, Illinois: Irwin.

Daoud, Z. 1981. "Agrarian Capitalism and Moroccan Crisis", *MERIP Reports*, 99. Sep.

Griffin, K.B. 1976. *Land Concentration and Rural Poverty*. London and Basingstoke: Macmillan.

Hinderink, J. and Kiray, M.B. 1970. *Social Stratification as an Obstacle to Development: A Study of Four Turkish Villages*. New York: Praeger.

Karpat, K.H. 1960. "The Social Effects of Farm Mechanisation in Turkish Villages", *Social Research*, XXVII.

Loeffler, R.L. 1976. "Recent Economic Changes in Boir Ahmad: Regional Growth without Development", *Iranian Studies*, IX, 4. Autumn.

Pfiefer, K. 1981. "Algeria's Agricultural Transformation", *MERIP Reports*, 99. Sep.

Radwan, S., and Lee, E. 1979. "The State and Agrarian Change: A Case Study of Egypt, 1952-1977", in D. Ghai, A.R. Khan, E. Lee and S. Radwan, eds, *Agrarian Systems and Rural Development*. London and Basingstoke: Macmillan.

Richards, A. 1982. *Egypt's Agricultural Development, 1800-1980: Technical and Social Change*. Boulder, Colorado: Westview.

Robinson, R. 1952. "Tractors in the Village: A Case Study in Turkey", *Journal of Farm Economics*, XXXIV, 4.

Wharton jr, C.R., ed., 1970. *Subsistence Agriculture and Economic Development*. London: Cass.

Cities, Patterns of Political Control, Urban Violence

Abrahamian, E. 1968. "The Crowd in Iranian Politics, 1905-1953", *Past and Present*, 41.

Abu-Laban, B. 1970. "Social Change and Local Politics in Sidon", *Journal of Developing Areas*, V.

Abu-Lughod, J. 1969. "Varieties of Urban Experience: Contrast, Coexistence and Coalescence", in I.M. Lapidus, ed., *Middle Eastern Cities. Ancient, Islamic and Contemporary Middle Eastern Urbanism: A Symposium*. Berkeley and Los Ángeles: University of California Press.

—— 1971. *Cairo: 1001 Years of "the City Victorious"*. Princeton, NJ: Princeton UP.

—— and Hay Jr, R., eds, 1977. *Third World Urbanization*. New York and London: Methuen.

Antoun, R. 1979. *Low-Key Politics: Local-Level Leadership and Change in the Middle East*. Albany: State University of New York Press.

Batatu, J. 1978. *The Old Social Classes and the Revolutionary Movements of Iraq: A Study of Iraq's Old Landed and Commercial Classes and of its Communists, Ba'thists, and Free Officers*. Princeton, NJ: Princeton UP.

—— 1981. "Iraq's Underground Shi'a Movement: Characteristics, Causes and Prospects", *Middle East Journal*, XXXV, 4. Autumn.

Blake, G.H., and Lawless, R.I. 1980. *The Changing Middle Eastern City*. London: Croom Helm.

Gilsenen, M. 1977. "Against Patron-Client Relations", in E. Gellner and J. Waterbury, eds, *Patrons and Clients in Mediterranean Societies*. London: Duckworth.

Gubser, P. 1973. *Politics and Change in Al-Karak, Jordan: A Study of a Small Arab Town and its District*. London and New York: Oxford UP.

—— 1975. "The Politics of an Economic Interest Group in a Lebanese Town", *Middle Eastern Studies*, XI, 3. Oct.

Ibrahim, S.E. 1980. "Anatomy of Egypt's Militant Islamic Groups: Methodological Note and Preliminary Findings", *International Journal of Middle East Studies*, XII, 4. Dec.

Johnson, M. 1977. "Political Bosses and their Gangs: *Zu'ama* and *Qabadayat* in the Sunni Muslim Quarters of Beirut", in E. Gellner and J. Waterbury, eds, *Patrons and Clients in Mediterranean Societies*. London: Duckworth.

Karpat, K.H. 1976. *The Gecekondu: Rural Migration and Urbanization in Turkey*. New York: Cambridge UP.

Khalaf, S., and Konstas, P. 1973. *Hamra of Beirut: A Case of Rapid Urbanisation*. Leiden: E.J. Brill.

Khuri, F.I. 1974. *From Village to Suburb: Order and Change in Greater Beirut*. Chicago: Chicago UP.

Mitchell, R.P. 1969. *The Society of the Muslim Brothers*. London: Oxford UP.

Rondot, P. 1976. "Ibrahim Koleilat", *Maghreb/Machrek*, 71.

Samin, A. 1981. "The Ordeal of the Turkish Left", *New Left Review*, 126. Mar-Apr.

Stoakes, F. 1975. "The Supervigilantes: The Lebanese Kataeb Party as Builder, Surrogate and Defender of the State", *Middle Eastern Studies*, XI, 3. Oct.

The Old Quarters of Middle Eastern Cities, Tourism and Attitudes to the Urban Past

Abu-Lughod, J. 1980. *Rabat: Urban Apartheid in Morocco*. Princeton, NJ: Princeton UP.

Brown, K.L. 1976. *People of Sale: Tradition and Change in a Moroccan City, 1830-1930*. Manchester: Manchester UP.

Dwyer, D.J., ed., 1974. *The City in the Third World*. London and Basingstoke: Macmillan.

Eikelman, D.F. 1974. "Is there an Islamic City? The Making of a Quarter in a Moroccan Town", *International Journal of Middle East Studies*, V.

Fathy, H. 1973. "Constancy, Transposition and Change in the Arab City", in L.C. Brown, ed., *From Medina to Metropolis*. Princeton, NJ: Princeton UP.

Graburn, N.H.H., 1980. "Teaching the Anthropology of Tourism", *International Social Science Journal*, XXXII.

Gulick, J. 1967. *Tripoli: A Modern Arab City*. Cambridge, Mass.: Harvard UP.

Kadt, E. De, ed., 1979. *Tourism: Passport to Development?* Oxford: Oxford UP for UNESCO and IBRD.

Lawless, R.I. 1981. "Social and Economic Change in the Medina of North Africa: the Case of Tunis", in J.I. Clarke and H. Bowen-Jones, eds, *Change and Development in the Middle East*. London and New York: Methuen.

MacCannell, D. 1976. *The Tourist: A New Theory of the Leisure Class*. New York: Schocken.

Roberts, M.H.P. 1979. *An Urban Profile of the Middle East*. New York: St. Martin's Press.

Sethom, H. 1976. "Agriculture et tourisme dans la region Nabeul-Hammamet: Coexistance feconde ou deséquilibre croissant?", *Cahiers de Tunisie*, XXIV, 93/4.

Palestinian Refugees, Palestinian Society Inside and Outside Israel/Palestine

Amun, H., Davis, U., San'Allah, N.D., Elrazik, A.A., and Amin, R., 1977. *Palestine Arabs in Israel: Two Case Studies*. London: Ithaca Press.

Asad, T. 1975. "Anthropological Texts and Ideological Problems: An Analysis of Cohen on Arab Villages in Israel", *Review of Middle East Studies*, I.

Dodd, P., and Barakat, H. 1968. *Rivers without Bridges: A Study of the Exodus of the 1967 Palestinian Arab Refugees*. Beirut: Institute for Palestine Studies.

Escribano, M., and El-Joubeh, N. 1981. "Migration and Change in a West Bank Village: the Case of Deir Dibwan", *Journal of Palestine Studies*, XI, 1. Fall.

Fluerh-Lobban, P. 1980. "The Political Mobilisation of Women in the Arab World", in J. Smith, ed., *Women in Contemporary Muslim Societies*. Cranbury, NJ: Bucknell UP.

Franjieh, S. 1971. "How Revolutionary is the Palestine Resistance?", *Journal of Palestine Studies*, I, 2. Winter.

Jiryis, S. 1969. *The Arabs in Israel*. Beirut: Institute for Palestine Studies.

Lustick, I. 1980. *Arabs in the Jewish State*. Austin: University of Texas Press.

Nakhleh, K., and Zureik, E.T. 1979. *The Sociology of the Palestinians*. New York: St. Martin's Press. 1979.

Plascov, A. 1982. "The Palestinians of Jordan's Border", in R. Owen, ed., *Studies in the Economic and Social History of Palestine in the Nineteenth and Twentieth Centuries*. London and Basingstoke: Macmillan.

Rosenfeld, R. 1978. "The Class Situation of the Arab National Minority in Israel", *Comparative Studies in Society and History*, XX, 3. July.

Rudkin-Jones, J. 1982. "The Palestine Refugee Camps", 1 and 2, *Middle East International*, 170 (12 Mar 1982) and 171 (26 Mar 1982).

Sayigh, R. 1979. "The Palestinian Experience: Integration and Non-Integration in the Arab Ghourba", *Arab Studies Quarterly*, I, 2. Spring.

Shaath, N. 1972. "Palestinian High Level Manpower", *Journal of Palestine Studies*, I, 2. Winter

Shamir, S. 1980. "West Bank Refugees: between Camp and Society", in J.S. Migdal, ed., *Palestinian Society and Politics*. Princeton, NY: Princeton UP.

Sirhan, B. 1974. "The Palestine Camps: a Sociological View", *Palestine Affairs*, 36. Aug.

—— 1975. "Palestine Refugee Life in Lebanon", *Journal of Palestine Studies*, IV, 2. Winter.

Tamari, S. 1981. "Building Other People's Homes: the Palestine Peasant Household and Work in Israel", *Journal of Palestine Studies*, XI, 1. Fall.

Zureik, E.T. 1977. "Towards a Sociology of the Palestinians", *Journal of Palestine Studies*, VI. Summer.

—— 1979. *The Palestinians in Israel: A Study in Internal Colonialism*. London and Boston, Mass.: Routledge & Kegan Paul.

Useful Journals, Reports and Bibliographies

Journals, Reviews and Reports

Arab States Broadcasting Union. *Review*. Cairo, ASBU; then Tunis, ASBU.

Khamsin. Journal of Revolutionary Socialists of the Middle East, 8 Honiton Road, London NW6.

MERIP. Reports. PO Box 1247, New York, NY 10025, USA.

Middle East Contemporary Survey. Homes & Meier Publishers, Inc., IUB Building, 30 Irving Place, New York, NY 10003, USA.

Middle East Review. World of Information, 21 Gold Street, Saffron Walden, Essex.

United Nations Economic Commission for Western Asia. *Population Bulletin of ECWA.* Population Division, ECWA, PO Box 4656. Beirut, Lebanon.

Bibliographies

Clements, F., ed., 1976. *The Emergence of Arab Nationalism from the 19th Century to 1921: A Bibliography.* London: Diploma Press.

Current Bibliography on African Affairs. African Bibliography Center, PO Box 13096, Washington, D.C., 20009.

Khalidi, W. and J. 1974. *Palestine and the Arab-Israeli Conflict: An Annotated Bibliography.* Beirut: Institute for Palestine Studies.

Pearson, J.D. *et al.*, 1958. *Index Islamicus: A Catalogue of Articles on Subjects in Periodicals and Other Collective Publications*, Cambridge: Heffer; then London: Scholar Mansell.

Reeva, S. 1978. *The Modern Middle East: A Guide to Research Tools in the Social Sciences.* Boulder, Colorado: Westview Press.

United Nations Economic Commission for Western Asia, 1980. *Bibliography of Population Literature in the Arab World.* Pt 1, *Non-Arabic Literature.* Beirut: ECWA.

World Bibliographical Series, including *Algeria*, ed. R.I. Lawless; *Lebanon*, ed. S. Khairallah; *Oman*, ed. F.A. Clements; *Qatar*, ed. P.T.H. Unwin; *Sudan*, ed. M.W. Daly; *Tunisia*, ed. A.M. Findlay, and R.A. Lawless, and *Turkey*, ed. M. Guclu. Oxford: Clio Press. 1979-83.

List of Works cited in Texts

Abadan-Unat, N., ed., 1976. *Turkish Workers in Europe.* Leiden: E.J. Brill.

Agha, H. 1976. "The Conflict in Lebanon", *Gazelle Review*, 1. London.

al-Azmeh, A. 1976. "The Progressive Forces", in R. Owen, ed., *Essays on the Crisis in Lebanon.* London: Ithaca UP.

Al Eassa, H. 1978. "Towards Manpower Planning in Kuwait". Ph.D. Thesis, Fletcher Law of Law and Diplomacy.
—— n.d. *Al Majmua'h Addaeeman Lel Agwneen el Kuwateeah*, The Permanent Collection of Kuwaiti Law, vol. 5. Kuwait: Al Resala.
Allon, Y. 1968. *Massach Shel Hol*, 3rd edn. Tel Aviv: Hakibbutz Hameuchad.
Allum, P.A. 1973. *Politics and Society in Post-War Naples*. Cambridge: Cambridge UP.
Amin, G.A. 1974. *The Modernization of Poverty*. Leiden: E.J. Brill (2nd edn. 1980).
Ammour, K., Leucate, C. and Moulin, J.-J., 1971. *La Voie algérienne*. Paris: Maspero.
Aronson, S. and Horowitz, D. 1971. In *Medina u Minshal*, I.
Ayoub, S. 1977. "Class Structure of the Palestinians" (in Arabic), M.A., Arab University, Beirut.
Batatu, H. 1978. *The Old Social Classes and the Revolutionary Movements of Iraq*. Princeton, N.J.: Princeton UP.
Beling, W.A. 1960. *Panarabism and Labor*. Cambridge, Mass: Harvard UP.
Ben Gurion, D. 1949. *Toldot Milhemet Ha - Komemiut*. Tel Aviv: Ma'arachot.
—— 1967a. *Pegishot Im Manhigim Aravim*. Tel Aviv: Am Oved.
—— 1967b. *Al Ma Lahamnu, Madua Pinina Ma Hissagnu*. Tel Aviv: Meraz Mapai, March.
—— 1969. *Medinat Israel Ham Mechudeshet*. Tel Aviv: Am Oved.
Berque, J. 1958. "Medinas, villeneuves et gourbivilles", *Cahiers de Tunisie*, 40.
—— 1978. *Cultural Expression in Arab Society Today*. Austin: University of Texas Press.
Bettelheim, C. 1970. *Calcul économique et formes de propriété*. Paris: Maspero.
Binder, L., ed. 1976. *The Study of the Middle East: Research and Scholarship in the Humanities and Social Sciences*. New York, London, Sydney, Toronto: John Wiley.
Birks, J.S., and Sinclair, C.A. 1980. *Arab Manpower*. New York: St. Martin's Press; London: Croom Helm.
—— 1982. "Employment and Development in Six Poor Arab States: Syria, Jordan, Sudan, South Yemen, Egypt and North Yemen", *International Journal of Middle Eastern Studies*, XIV, 1. Feb.
Chaliand, G. and Minces, J. 1972. *L'Algerie indépendante*. Paris: Maspero.
Clegg, I. 1971. *Workers' Self-Management in Algeria*. London: Allen Lane, The Penguin Press.
Cliff, T. 1970. *Russia - a Marxist Analysis*. London: Pluto Press.
Cohen, Y. 1969. *LeOr Ha-Yom U-Baachshach*. Tel Aviv: Amikam.
Colonna, F. 1974. "Cultural Resistance and Religious Legitimacy in Colonial Algeria", *Economy and Society*, vol. 3, no. 2.

Dam, N. van. 1979. *The Struggle for Power in Syria: Sectarianism, Regionalism and Tribalism in Politics, 1961-1980*. London: Croom Helm.

Daoulatli, M. 1976. "Principles pour une politique opérationelle". Tunis: ASM, April.

Dayan, M. 1959. "Military Operations in Peacetime", *Ma'arachot*, 118-19.

—— 1966. *Diary of the Sinai Campaign*. London: Weidenfeld & Nicholson.

—— 1968. *Mapa Hadasha Yehasim Aherim*. Haifa: Shikmona.

Dinur, B. 1954. Introduction to *Sefer Toldot Ha-Haganah*. Tel Aviv: Ma'arachot, vol. 1.

Djilas, M. 1957. *The New Class*. London: Thames & Hudson.

Dubar, C. 1974. "Structure confessionelle et classes sociales au Liban", *Revue Française de Sociologie*, 15, 3.

—— and Nasr, S. 1976. *Les Classes sociales au Liban*. Paris: Foundation nationale des sciences politiques.

Eckert, H. 1970a. "Les Populations du Grand Tunis". Tunis: ASM/PTC.

—— 1970b. "La Medina de Tunis: faubourg ou gourbiville?". Tunis: ASM, May.

—— and El Kafi. 1974. "L'Espace traditionnel de la ville de Tunis: La Médina et les deux rbat: faubourg ou gourbiville?", in *Les Influences orientales dans les villes Maghrebines a' l'epoque contemporaine*. Etudes mediterranéenes. 2. Aix-en-Provence, Centre de Recherche et al'Etudes sur les sociétiés Mediterráneenes.

El Kafi, J. 1970. "Croissance urbaine et modeles de croissance: la ville de Tunis, 1881-1970", mimeo. Tunis: ASM, May.

Entelis, J. 1974. *Pluralism and Party Transformation in Lebanon: al-Kataib, 1936-1970*. Leiden, E.J. Brill.

Etienne, B. 1977. *L'Algerie, Cultures et Revolution*. Paris: Editions du Seuil.

Evron, Y. 1968. *Be Yom Sagrir*. Tel Aviv: Ot-paz.

Fathy, H. 1970. *Construire avec le peuple*. Paris: Bibliothèque Arabe, Editions Jérome Martueau. (originally published in English 1969: *Gourna: A Tale of Two Villages*).

Floy, M. 1962. *Consultation et représentation dans le Maghreb contemporaine* (in *Annuaire de Afrique du Nord*, Aix-en-Provence: CNRS.

Franjieh, S. 1972. "How Revolutionary is the Palestinian Resistance?", *Journal of Palestine Studies*, Winter.

Gilboa, M.A. 1969. *Shesh Shanim-Shisha Yamim*, 2nd edn. Tel Aviv: Am Oved.

Grimwood-Jones, D., ed. 1979. *Middle East and Islam: A Bibliographical Introduction*. Zug, Switzerland: Inter Documentation Company.

Hagopian, E., and Zahlan, A.B. 1974. "Palestine's Arab Population: the Demography of the Palestinians", *Journal of Palestine Studies*, IV, 4.

Halliday, F. 1977. "Labour Migration in the Middle East", *MERIP Reports*, 59. Aug.

Harkabi, G. 1963. *Milhama Garinit ve Shalom Garini*. Tel Aviv.

Hirst, D. 1979. "Divisive Rulers Threaten to Send Syria along the Road to Civil War", *The Guardian*, 26 June.

—— and Beeson I. 1981. *Sadat*. London: Faber & Faber.

Hobsbawm, E. 1971. *Primitive Rebels: Studies in Archaic Forms of Social Movements in the 19th and 20th Centuries*. Manchester: Manchester UP.

Hopkins, T.K., and Wallerstein, I. 1981. "Structural Transformation of the World Economy", in R. Rubinson, ed., *Dynamics of World Development*. Beverly Hills, California: Sage.

—— *et al.*, 1982. *World Systems Analysis: Theory and Methodology*. Beverly Hills, California, and London: Sage.

Horowitz, D. 1982. "The Israel Defence Forces: A Civilianized Military in a Partially Militarized Society", in R. Kolkowicz and A. Korbanski, eds, *Soldiers, Peasants and Bureaucrats*. London: Allen & Unwin.

Illich, I. 1973. *Tools of Conviviality*. London: Calder & Boyars.

IRFED Mission. 1961. *Besoins et possibilitiés de développement du Liban*. Beirut: Republique Libanaise, Ministère du Plan, 1960-1.

Johnson, M. 1977. "Political Bosses and their Gangs: Zu'ama and Qabadayat in the Sunni Muslim Quarters of Beirut", in E. Gellner and J. Waterbury, eds, *Patrons and Clients in Mediterranean Societies*. London: Duckworth.

Johnson, M. 1978. "Factional Politics in Lebanon: The Case of the 'Islamic Society of Benevolent Intentions' (al-Maqasid) in Beirut", *Middle Eastern Studies*, 14, 1.

Kahn, H. 1965. On Escalation: Metaphors and Scenarios. New York: Praeger.

Kaldor, M., and Eide, A., eds, 1979. *The World Military Order: The Impact of Military Technology on the Third World*. London and Basingstoke: Macmillan.

Katouzian, M.A. 1978. "Oil versus Agriculture: a Case of Dual Resource Depletion in Iran", *Journal of Peasant Studies*, V, 3.

Kazziha, W. 1975. *Revolutionary Transformation in the Arab World: Habbash and his Comrades from Nationalism to Marxism*. London and Tonbridge: Knight.

Khalaf, N.G. 1971. "Size and Growth of the Lebanese Economy", *Princeton Near East Paper*, 14.

Khouja, M.W., and Sadler, P.G. 1979. *The Economy of Kuwait. Development and Role in International Finance*. London and Basingstoke: Macmillan.

Klich, I. 1980. "L'Amerique latine, principal client de l'industrie d'armament israelienne", *Le Monde diplomatique*. Sep.

Laroui, A. 1976. *The Crisis of the Arab Intellectual*. Berkeley: University of California Press.

Lascov, General. 1968. In *Hayom*, 1 May.

Lebanon Ministry of Planning. 1971. *Recueil de Statistiques Liban-*

aises. Année 1971. Beirut Ministry of Planning.

—— 1972. *L'Enquête par Sondage sur la population active au Liban, Novembre 1970.* Beirut: Ministry of Planning.

Luckham, R. 1976. "The Military, Militarism and Dependence in the Third World: a Theoretical Sketch" in C. H. Enloe and U. Semin-Panzer, eds, *The Military, the Police and Domestic Order: British and Third World Experiences.* London: Richardson Institute for Conflict and Peace Research. Ap.

Luttwak, E., and Horowitz, D. 1975. *The Israeli Army.* London: Allen Lane.

Mahbub Ul Haq. 1973. "Developing Countries' Alternatives", in Hughes, H. ed., *Prospects for Partnership: Industrialization and Trade Policies in the 1970s.* Baltimore: Johns Hopkins UP.

Mallakh, E. El, and Atta, J.J. 1981. *The Absorptive Capacity of Kuwait: Domestic and International Perspectives.* Lexington, Mass., and Toronto: Lexington Books.

Mandel, E. 1968. *Marxist Economic Theory.* London: Merlin Press.

Marr, P.A. 1975. "The Political Elite in Iraq", in G. Lenczowski, ed., *Political Elites in the Middle East.* Washington, DC: American Enterprise Institute for Public Policy Research.

Marx, K. 1970. *Introduction to a Critique of Hegel's Philosophy of Right, Introduction to a Critique of Hegel's Philosophy of Right; Critique of the Gotha Programme;* all in *Selected Works.* London: Lawrence & Wishart.

—— and Engels, F. 1957. *On Religion.* Moscow: Progress Publishers.

Micaud, E.C. 1974. "Belated Urban Planning in Tunis: Problems and Prospects". *Human Organization,* vol. 33, Summer.

Mishan, E. 1974. "Growth and Anti-Growth: What are the Issues?", in Weintraub, A. *et al.* eds., *The Economic Growth Controversy.* London: Macmillan.

Moubarak, W. 1979. "Kuwait's Quest for Security: 1961–1975". Ph.D. thesis, Indiana University.

Mundus, H. 1974. *Al-'Amal wa al-'Umal fi al-Mukhayam al-Falastini.* Beirut: Palestine Research Centre.

Mustafa, M. El-M., 1980. "Development Planning and International Migration in the Sudan", *Labour and Society,* V, 1. Jan.

Nasr, S. 1978. "Backdrop to Civil War: The Crisis of Lebanese Capitalism", *MERIP Reports,* 73. Dec.

Nevo, Y. 1968. *Bitachon Lelo Shalom, Shalom Lelo Bitachon.* Israeli Government Publications Service.

Owen, R. 1981a. "The Arab Economies in the 1970s", *MERIP Reports,* 100/101. Oct-Dec.

—— 1981b. "Income Distribution and Social Welfare in the Arab World", *Journal of the Institute for Socioeconomic Studies,* VI, 4. Winter 1981-2.

Palma, G. 1978. "Dependency: A Formal Theory of Underdevelopment or a Methodology for the Examination of Concrete Situations of Underdevelopment?", *World Development,* VI, 7/8. July.

Payne, S. 1974. *Exporting Workers: The Turkish Case.* Cambridge: Cambridge UP.

Peres, S. 1965. *Ha-Shalav Ha-Ba.* Tel Aviv. Am Hasefer.

—— 1970. *David's Sling.* Jerusalem: Weidenfeld & Nicolson.

Plascov, A. 1982. "The Palestinians of Jordan's Border", in R. Owen, ed., *Studies in the Economic and Social History of Palestine in the Nineteenth and Twentieth Centuries.* London and Basingstoke: Macmillan.

Qubain, F.I. 1961. *Crisis in Lebanon.* Washington.

Rabin, I. 1967. In "Academy in Memory of Yitzhak Sade", typescript, Tel Aviv.

Rachty, G. 1978. "Broadcasting Systems in the Arab World", *Arab States Broadcasting Union Review.* Cairo. Jan.

Raffinot, M., and Jacquemot, P. 1977. *Le Capitalisme d'Etat algérien.* Paris: Maspero.

Rolbant, S. 1970. *The Israeli Soldier: Profile of an Army.* Cranbury, N.J.: A.S. Barnes.

Ruppin, A. 1916. "Syrian als Wirtschaftsgebeit", *Beihefte zum Tropenpflanzen,* XVI, 3/5 (Berlin), trans. as *Syria: An Economic Survey.* New York: The Provisional Zionist Committee, 1918.

Said, E. 1978. *Orientalism.* London: Routledge & Kegan Paul.

Salibi, K.S. 1976. *Crossroads to Civil War: Lebanon 1958-1976.* London: Ithaca UP.

Sayigh, Y. 1952. *Implications of UNWRA Operations in Host Countries.* Beirut.

—— 1962. *Entrepreneurs of Lebanon: The Role of the Business Leader in a Developing Economy.* Cambridge, Mass.: Harvard UP.

Schelling, T.C. 1960. *Strategy of Conflict.* Cambridge, Mass.: Harvard UP.

—— 1966. *Arms and Influence* New Haven, Conn.: Yale UP.

—— and Halperin, M.H. 1961. *Strategy and Arms Control.* New York: Twentieth Century Fund.

Schiff, Z. 1968. "Retaliation and Reprisals in Arab-Israeli Relations", *Ha'aretz,* 29 Sep.

Seers, D., ed., 1981. *Dependency Theory: A Critical Reassessment.* London: Francis Pinter.

Shaath, N. 1971. "Palestinian High Level Manpower", *Journal of Palestine Studies,* I, 2. Winter.

Slutzki, Y. 1972. *Seffer Toldot HaHaganah.* vol. III. Tel Aviv: Am Oved.

Teveth, S. 1971. *Moshe Dayan.* Tel Aviv: Schocken.

Toynbee, A. 1947. *A Study of History.* New York: Oxford UP.

Trotsky, L. 1972. *The Revolution Betrayed.* New York: Pathfinder Press Inc.

Turner, B.S. 1978. *Marx and the End of Orientalism.* London, Boston, Sydney: Allen & Unwin..

Turner, John F.C. 1976. *Housing by People: Toward Autonomy in Building Environments.* London: Calder & Boyars.

—— and Fichter, Robert, eds, 1972. *Freedom to Build*. New York: Macmillan.

UNESCO. 1969. *Mises en valeur — du Patrimoine Monumental de la region Tunis-Carthage en vue du développement economique*. Paris.

Vatikiotis, P.J. 1967. *Politics and the Military in Jordan: A Study of the Arab Legion 1921-1957*. London: Cass.

Wallach, D. 1970. *Bitachun*. Jerusalem: Government of Israel.

Veblen, T. 1959. *The Theory of the Leisure Class*. New York and Scarborough: Mentor Books.

Wallerstein, I., Martin, W.G., and Dickson, T.O. 1982. "Household Structures and Production Processes: Preliminary Theses and Findings", *Review*, V, 3. Winter.

Weizman, E. 1970. Introduction to Z. Schiff, *Knaifaim Me-Al Le-Suez*. Haifa: Shikmona.

Index